# MODEL
# BUSINESS PLANS
# FOR
# SERVICE BUSINESSES

## OTHER BOOKS BY DR. WILLIAM A. COHEN

Model Business Plans for Product Businesses (John Wiley & Sons)

Building a Mail Order Business (John Wiley & Sons)

The Entrepreneur and Small Business Problem Solver (John Wiley & Sons)

Developing a Winning Marketing Plan (John Wiley & Sons)

The Entrepreneur and Small Business Marketing Problem Solver (John Wiley & Sons)

The Entrepreneur and Small Business Financial Problem Solver (John Wiley & Sons)

How To Make It Big as a Consultant (AMACOM)

The Paranoid Corporation and 8 Other Ways Your Company May Be Crazy (AMACOM) (with Dr. Nurit Cohen)

Making It! (Prentice-Hall) (with E. Joseph Cossman)

The Art of the Leader (Prentice-Hall)

# MODEL
# BUSINESS PLANS
# FOR
# SERVICE BUSINESSES

**William A. Cohen, PhD**

**John Wiley & Sons, Inc.**
New York • Chichester • Brisbane • Toronto • Singapore

*This book is dedicated to my clients and students from workshops, seminars, and the university. Through their initiative, inquisitiveness, and creativity, they have taught me as much as I have taught them.*

This text is printed on acid-free paper.

Copyright © 1995 by William A. Cohen.
Published by John Wiley & Sons, Inc.

This publication is designed to provide accurate and authoritative information in regard to the subject matter covered. It is sold with the understanding that the publisher is not engaged in rendering professional services. If legal, accounting, medical, psychological, or any other expert assistance is required, the services of a competent professional person should be sought.

*Library of Congress Cataloging-in-Publication Data:*

Cohen, William A., 1937–
    Model business plans for service businesses / William A. Cohen.
        p.    cm.
    Includes index.
    ISBN 0-471-03037-6 (cloth). — ISBN 0-471-03034-1 (pbk.)
    1. Service industries—Planning.   2. New business enterprises—
Planning.   I. Title.
HD9980.5.C64   1995
658.4′012—dc20                                                     94-41827

Printed in the United States of America

10  9  8  7  6  5  4  3  2  1

# Preface

Companies that develop business plans professionally charge up to $50,000 for each plan. I know, because that's the price quoted a few months ago to a friend of mine.

If you want to start your own business, you can save a bundle if you develop your own business plan. And many times, your plan will be a lot better than if someone else developed it. That's because no one knows you, your capabilities, limitations, strengths, weaknesses, desires, interests, and ultimate goals better than you.

However, to create a really outstanding plan, you must first see what a business plan looks like. In fact, you should study several plans before you start composing one. Anything short of outstanding won't do when potential lenders review 1,000 plans or more a month and fund maybe one or two. You have to thoroughly examine more than a few plans to know what is really expected and how to sell your concept to investors.

Some books on entrepreneurial endeavors contain a few business plans. Most contain none. This book contains 9 outstanding business plans for new businesses that provide services. A companion book, *Model Business Plans for Product Businesses*, features 9 plans that are suitable for businesses selling a product. With this book and its companion, you should be able to find a plan that fits your needs, no matter what your field.

All the plans contain complete financial information for the time and geographic location for which the plan was prepared. Many of these plans aim at millions in sales. No wonder a professional firm would charge so much to develop even one of them!

Let's face facts. You can't go into a serious business today without a business plan. The competition is too tough, and banks and other lenders won't lend you the money.

If you are going into business, you need a business plan:

- To borrow money.
- As a road map to reach your business objectives and goals.
- To make the most efficient use of money and other resources.
- To measure progress and make corrections on your way to success.
- To assist in management control and implementation of your strategy.
- To inform new people you hire of their role and function.
- To assign responsibilities, tasks, and timing to your employees and others.

- To forecast your costs and cash flow on a monthly basis.
- To become aware of problems and opportunities inherent in your business situation.

Why aren't more business plans published? Frankly, the effort to put a single business plan together is considerable. The research required can be difficult if you don't know how to do it. That's one of the reasons that professionally prepared plans are so expensive. When people put that much work into a plan, they don't want to give it away.

There are companies that sell generic business plans for as much as $100 apiece although such plans can't be as complete as if they were for a specific business. Yet, in this book, you will find 9 model business plans for a variety of businesses.

How did I get so involved in business planning? My early training came as an officer in the military. We were taught how to plan because it was the basis of securing any military objective. The process started with something called "The Estimation of the Situation." In business, we call this a "situation analysis" or "environmental scanning." It serves the same purpose.

At any rate, when I got into business, I found that organizing for the development of new products and business investments was easy because of my early training. It wasn't a case of so-called marketing warfare. I just had to translate terms and concepts from the battlefield to the boardroom.

Later, when I became a business professor, I was amazed at the inability of business students to produce quality business plans. I vowed to change all that. I started in the classroom. Then, as Director of the Small Business Institute at California State University, Los Angeles, I supervised students and other professors consulting for more than 500 small businesses. Between this work and my work in the classroom, I supervised the preparation of more than 1,000 business plans. I spent 15 years refining my methods of teaching the development of business and marketing plans.

Over the years, my methods proved themselves again and again. In competitions involving many of the best business schools in the country, some of my students won national awards offered by a number of private and governmental organizations.

But, it is even more significant that the students who implemented their own plans frequently got terrific results. One student, Robert Schwartz, put together a plan for a fast-food pizza restaurant. Within a year, he had three outlets and was written up in *Entrepreneur* magazine. He was managing a $48,000 monthly cash flow while still a student. Leon Ashjian, a student from Egypt, made several thousand dollars implementing his plan during my course. Then, he sold it to someone else for another $5,000.

Some time ago, I spoke at the University of Missouri, Kansas City, on how to teach students to develop these plans. Both professors and business leaders were in my audience. During my presentation, I showed some sample plans and described how Leon had sold his plan for $5,000.

A businessman from a firm developing business plans for clients examined my sample plans very carefully. He told me they were the equal of the professional plans his firm produced. "However," he said, "they aren't worth $5,000 each . . . they're worth $25,000 each. I know because that's what we charge."

Since that time, several of my students have elected to become independent consultants after graduation. They make their living developing business plans for others.

My wife and I are continually running into results from my business plan instruction. A few weeks ago, a new restaurant opened in my hometown of Pasadena, California. The restaurant is called "Little Rickey's," and the menu is Cuban and Mexican. We tried it, and the food was delicious. I was surprised to learn that one on my former students, Mary Needham, started Little Rickey's in partnership with her friend, Rachel Perez. And yes, the business plan from my class was the basis for this enterprise that offered such delightful meals.

I especially selected the plans in this book for their variety. The were developed by my students and are used with their permission. You may not find the particular business you are interested in among them, but you are very likely to find one that is close. You will also find somewhat different styles and methods for organizing the plans.

You have in your hands everything you need to develop your own successful business plan. Start off by reviewing the Introduction, which tells you how to go about developing your plan. Then, all you need to do is look through the book for one or more plans for businesses that resemble the one you have in mind. Adapt these plans and the financial and other information to your situation and you are all set. Good luck—I'll be happy to hear about your success!

WILLIAM A. COHEN

*Pasadena, California*
*April 1995*

# Acknowledgments

Though the responsibility for this book is mine alone, I would like to make the following acknowledgments.

First, the work by those whose plans are contained in this volume. Through their efforts, many can benefit in developing business plans which lead to successful enterprises.

Excel Aire: Rose Simon, John Iezza, Carlton Skerrett, Angel Camargo, and Danielle Benson

El Flaco Mexican Restaurant: Emilio C. Ledesma

The Chu Tutoring Service: Tom Urbanski

Alternative Pool Hall: Bernadette Gines, Bryan Sue, Frances Vien, Joshua Que, and Shant Koumriqian

Professional Fitness: Iain Mozoomdar

Call Home for Lunch: Carole A. Lane

East-Bound Traders: Lydia Bilynsky

Cartridge Recycling Services, Inc.: Luanne Tadian

Canevari & Canevari, An Accountancy Corporation: Mark L. Canevari

Next, the important contributions in review and editing made by my research assistant, Danielle Benson, as well as those made by Nancy Marcus Land at Publications Development Company of Texas, under the supervision of Mary Daniello at John Wiley & Sons, Inc. Finally, the superb overall development work by my editor at John Wiley & Sons, Ruth Mills.

W.A.C.

# Contents

Luncheon food delivery service is usually limited to pizza or executive catering. This plan is for a food service company that offers quality food at affordable prices.

Every country wants to export to promote a favorable balance of trade. The United States is no different, and the Department of Commerce will do anything it can to help you out. This company provides services unavailable from the Department of Commerce to help companies that want to export to Eastern Europe and former Soviet bloc countries.

Increased use of laser printers and copiers has created the growth of a new market for recycled toner cartridges. At 28.45 million new cartridges in 1993, it's quite a market.

All types of small businesses need business plans, including accounting practices. Here's one for a partnership specializing in tax planning and small business. First-year revenues are $146,808, growing to $353,627 by the fourth year.

# Save $50,000 and Succeed Where Others Fail

Developing your own business plan is not difficult . . . once you know how. After you have decided on the business, your task is to learn all you can about it as well as the business climate you will enter. This is what I call doing a situation analysis. As a result of this analysis, you will be able to decided on initial goals and objectives, designate your target market, and obtain other essential information. You will be in a position to develop strategy and tactics to reach your goals and objectives successfully. Flesh this out with tasks to implement your strategy and monitor it with financial data that you assume or calculate, and you're set. That's all there is to it.

In this chapter, I will cover every important element of the business plan. Along the way, I'll tell you where to get the information you'll need. Important elements of the business plan are shown in Exhibit 1. Let's look at each of these in detail.

---

### Exhibit 1   A Business Plan Structure

---

**Executive Summary** (Overview of entire plan, including a description of the product or service, the differential advantage, the required investment, and anticipated sales and profits.)

**Table of Contents**

I. **Introduction** (What is the product or service and why will you be successful with it at this time?)

II. **Situation Analysis**

1. The General Situation

   A. Demand and demand trends. (What is the forecast demand for the product? Is it growing or declining? Who is the decision maker, the purchase agent? How, when, where, what, and why do they buy?)

   B. Social and cultural factors that may bear on your business.

   C. Demographics in your area of operation.

   D. Economic and business conditions for this product at this time in the geographic area selected.

   E. State of technology for this class of product. Is it high-tech state of the art? Are newer products succeeding older ones frequently (very short life cycle)? How will technology affect this product or service?

(continued)

Exhibit 1  (*Continued*)

      F.  Politics. Will politics (current or otherwise) in any way affect the situation for marketing this product?

      G.  Laws and regulations. (What laws or regulations are applicable here?)

  2.  The Situation of Neutral Organizations

      A.  Financial. (How does the availability or nonavailability of funds affect the situation?)

      B.  Government. (Will legislative action or anything else currently going on in federal, state, or local government be likely to affect marketing of this product or service?)

      C.  Media. (What's happening in the media? Does current publicity favor or disfavor this project?)

      D.  Special interests. (Aside from direct competitors, are any influential groups likely to affect your plans?)

  3.  Your Competition's Situation

      A.  Describe your main competitors and their products, plans, experience, know-how, suppliers, strategy, and financial, human, and capital resources. (Do they enjoy any favor or disfavor with the customer? If so, why? What marketing channels do competitors use? What are your competitors' strengths and weaknesses?)

  4.  Your Situation

      A.  Describe your product, experience, know-how, suppliers, strategy, and financial, human, and capital resources. (Do you enjoy any favor or disfavor with the customer? If so, why? What are your strengths and weaknesses?)

III.  **The Target Market**  Describe your target market in detail. (Why is this your target market and not some other?)

IV.  **Problems, Threats, and Opportunities**  State or restate every problem and every opportunity. Indicate how you will handle each problem and take advantage of each opportunity.

V.  **Objectives and Goals**  Precisely state your objectives and goals in terms of sales volume, market share, return on investment, or other objectives of your plan.

VI.  **Competitive Advantage**  State the advantages you have over your competition.

VII.  **Marketing Strategy**  Consider alternatives for overall strategy. Fully describe the strategy you are going to adopt and why you are going to adopt it. Note what your main competitors are likely to do when you implement this strategy and what you will do to take advantage of the opportunities created and avoid the threats.

VIII.  **Marketing Tactics**  State how you will implement the marketing strategies you chose in terms of product, price, promotion, selling, publicity, distribution, and other actions you will take.

IX.  **Schedule and Budget Marketing Actions**  What are the actual actions you must take to set your business plan in motion?

X.  **Implementation and Control**  Calculate the break-even point for your project. Compute sales projections on a monthly basis for a three-year period. Compute cash flows on a monthly basis for a three-year period. Indicate start-up costs and monthly budget for this period.

XI.  **Summary**  Summarize advantages, costs, and profits, and clearly restate the competitive advantage that your plan for this product or service offers over the competition and why your plan will succeed.

XII.  **Appendixes**  Include all relevant supporting information in your biography and background that support your ultimate success in achieving your goals and objectives in this business.

# THE EXECUTIVE SUMMARY

As the name implies, the executive summary is an overview or abstract of your entire business plan, and it is written for an executive audience. The summary is a brief statement describing your business and its potential. It includes what you want to do, how much money and what other resources you will need. The executive summary is extremely important.

Sure, you write the business plan for your own guidance. However, the executive audience reading it may be almost as important. The executives I'm talking about are venture capitalists, decision makers at banks, the Small Business Administration, or others from whom you may want a loan. As these individuals study your business plan, they will frequently skip around to parts that are of most interest to them. In fact, few business plans will be read by others word for word. Rather, certain sections will be read in detail and other sections, only scanned. Almost everyone, however, will read your executive summary.

So, that section should capture the essence of your plan in a few concise paragraphs. Say what your business is about—your objectives and goals—and provide a bird's-eye view of the strategy you will use to accomplish those objectives and goals. The executive summary shouldn't be longer than two or three pages at most. Many very effective summaries are only one to two paragraphs.

After reading your executive summary, the executives should understand what you want to do, how much it will cost, and what the chances are of success. Of course, you should make clear that your chances are very good. Otherwise, you shouldn't be entering this business in the first place. Readers should also understand the unique advantages you have that will ensure your success.

Although the executive summary comes first, you should write it last. This is because it must capture all the essential points in your business plan and emphasize how you approach starting and building your business. If you write your executive summary first and don't go back to rework it after you complete your plan, you are very likely to miss something important.

# TABLE OF CONTENTS

You may wonder why I am discussing something so ordinary as a table of contents. Yet, it is also an important part of your plan. As I said before, most lenders will not read your entire plan in detail. They will look for the executive summary and certain areas they find of particular interest.

Here's what I mean. Financial experts will be very interested in the financial part of your plan. They will want to know how much money you will need and when it will be needed. Others will be more interested in the technical aspects and performance characteristics of your product or service. These technically oriented executives may even skip items that you know are crucial, such as your location or selling methods.

So, not only should every subject area critical to the project be covered in your business plan, you must make it as easy as possible for anyone to find a specific area of interest quickly. The table of contents serves this purpose. If you do not have a table of contents, searching decision makers—after a brief attempt to locate the information—may assume that it is not there. Many borrowers don't get the money they need because someone couldn't find some piece of information the lender considered important. So, don't omit this "mundane" element of your business plan. It can turn out to be more important than you thought.

# THE SITUATION ANALYSIS

The situation analysis is a detailed description of the environment for your entry into business and for the time period covered by your plan. You should include a detailed discussion of the overall situation, the situation of neutral organizations as well as those with which you will compete, and your own. Don't omit anything you consider relevant. Discuss business conditions, technological trends, distribution factors, the law, and all other major situational issues that impact your planned business.

I recommend that you divide this section into four subareas. The first is the general situation. This includes economic and business conditions, cultural or social factors and their impact on what you want to do, the state of technology, and so on. The second section concerns "neutral" organizations whose actions can help you or hurt you. Examples would be consumer advocacy groups and federal regulatory agencies.

In the third subarea, you discuss your competition. Don't tell me you "don't have any competition." This is never true because even though you may not have any direct competitors, there are always alternative ways your prospective customers can spend their money. So there are, at the very least, indirect competitors. For example, you may have the only dry-cleaning establishment in town. But a steam iron used in the home is still indirect competition. You may have developed some breakthrough computer software far in advance of any older program. Well, guess what? Those old obsolete programs are still in competition with you even though the performance of your new program is light years ahead.

You want to find out all you can about the strengths and weaknesses of the competition vying with you for the same market. With only so much business out there in a mature or even declining market, your competition will be a major factor affecting your success.

You can find out all you need to know about the competition by looking at annual reports if they are public companies, talking to suppliers and customers, reading their advertisements and literature, and actually buying from them or using their service.

Finally, you want to analyze your own strengths and weaknesses, just as you did the competition. More than two thousand years ago, the Chinese strategist Sun Tzu noted that he never suffered defeat because he not only knew the strengths and weaknesses of his enemies, but also knew his own.

## Where to Get Information for This and Other Sections of Your Business Plan

There are numerous sources for the information you need for your business plan. Most won't cost you a cent. Besides using the following primary sources, you'll want to look at the suggestions for additional research in Appendix A.

### Magazine and Newspaper Articles

General magazines have business sections. Many general business magazines such as *Business Week, Entrepreneur, Fortune,* and *INC,* are available at your public library. You will also find *The Wall Street Journal* and other pertinent newspapers. In addition, the library has directories of specialized periodicals. Every industry has publications devoted to its particular products and services. These periodicals may have articles containing information important to your business. These specialized sources can be helpful in other ways. If you are searching for certain information, the editorial staff of an industry magazine, journal, or newsletter may be able to tell you where to get it. Sometimes, the staff may have done studies or surveys of their readership on the very topic you are interested in.

### Specialized Books about Your Business

With more than 40,000 books published every year, books are found on every topic imaginable. I have seen books on mail order, consulting, and the restaurant businesses, multilevel marketing, silk screen printing, and hundreds of others. In fact, I wrote books on the first two topics (*Building a Mail Order Business,* New York: John Wiley & Sons, 1983, 1985, 1991; and *How to Make It Big as a Consultant,* New York: AMACOM, 1985, 1991). You can also find booklets on a variety of businesses and business topics published by the U.S. Small Business Administration (SBA). Check with your local office of the SBA and ask for a complete list. Some of these may also be available at a U.S. government bookstore if one is in your area. Check in your telephone white pages under "U.S. Government."

### Professional and Trade Associations

Just as there are books and magazines for every type of business, there are also professional and trade associations. Frequently these associations have done studies or surveys themselves or can direct you to another source for the information you need. Check your library for directories of national associations. The reference desk librarian will help you. You can also check the phone book under associations to see if it lists one related to your business interests.

### Databases

If you have a computer, or maybe even if you don't, you probably already know about databases. There are databases containing information on every topic. Some libraries will do a search for you. If you have a modem and belong to one of the computer services such as CompuServe™ or Prodigy™, you can do your own search.

### The Department of Commerce

If you are planning a product or service for export, look under U.S. Government in the white pages of your telephone book and contact the Department of Commerce. You will be amazed by the wealth of information and services available for those who want to export. A "trade specialist" may be willing to come out to see you and provide help as a consultant right away. This won't cost you anything. The department also offers a seminar on the basics of exporting at a nominal cost and can point you in the right direction to get any information about potential markets in various countries, and how to reach them. But to really understand the full ranges of the services currently being offered, check and see if there is an office in your area and visit it in person.

### Chambers of Commerce

Almost every city or town has a chamber of commerce with data on the people living, working, and conducting business in that area. If you want to set up shop, it makes sense to investigate who your target market is likely to be, what competitors you may have, and so on.

### Embassies and Consulates

If you are fortunate enough to live in or near a large city, chances are there will be foreign consulates nearby. And if you live in or near Washington, DC, you'll be able to reach the embassies themselves. Access to embassies and consulates can be a great help if you want to import products. Every country wants exports to help out its balance of trade. That's why U.S. Department of Commerce is so eager to help you if you want to export American goods. If you are interested in imports, contact a foreign consulate or embassy and ask for the commercial or trade attaché. If you have a particular product in mind, the attaché will probably invite you to the consulate or embassy where you can look at catalogs and prospectuses relevant to your area of interest.

### Government Books on Statistics, Industry, and the Economy

One of the best publications I've seen along these lines is the *Statistical Abstract of the United States,* which is published every year. Two other books published annually that will provide background information are *U.S. Industrial Outlook* and *Economic Report of the President.* These books can be obtained at a U.S. government bookstore if you have one in your city. Otherwise, write to the Superintendent of Documents, U.S. Government Printing Office, Washington, DC 20402, and ask for a catalog.

### Primary Marketing Research

You are already doing market research by using the sources I've given you. But primary marketing research means you gather the data yourself, instead of looking it up in a book or magazine where someone else has already put it together for you.

There are three main means of marketing research: mail, telephone, and face-to-face. Just as with the business plans, companies exist that will do this for you, and they will charge you a bundle. But there is much you can do for yourself fairly easily. For example, if you wanted to determine the best location for a service station, one factor would be the motor vehicle traffic. You could get this information by simply counting cars going by at similar hours at each potential location. Or, if you wanted to discover whether you could wholesale a particular product, you could obtain one and meet with the appropriate buyer for the type of store that would carry this merchandise. Similarly, if you have a particular service, do a limited mailing to prospective customers and see how many takers you get.

You won't get perfect results by asking people if they would buy a product or service if it were on the market. You should still do this, but keep in mind that many respondents who say yes may still not buy when the product is actually introduced. So, even if the results of interviews and surveys indicate that you have a spectacular winner, be a little conservative in your estimate of potential sales.

## THE TARGET MARKET

In this section, you include a complete description of the target market or market segments you are going to service. This should include market characteristics, growth trends, buyer attitudes and habits, geographic location of the market segments, industry pricing, and size of the various market segments in dollars and units.

These decisions and the information for them come from the information sources listed previously. What you must do is study the data to see where the best opportunity is. You can rarely be everything to everybody. You will have a much greater chance of success if you pick a particular niche or market segment to sell to instead of trying to sell your product or service to everybody.

## PROBLEMS, THREATS, AND OPPORTUNITIES

Here, you restate some of the results of the situation analysis in a summary of problems, opportunities, and threats. However, it is insufficient simply to state these factors. You must also describe alternative courses of action for overcoming the problems, taking advantage of the opportunities, and avoiding the threats.

Some think that their plan will be more attractive if they omit the problems and threats. Not true. Would-be lenders, such as venture capitalists, may review thousands of business plans every month. They are very knowledgeable about business start-ups and growing businesses. If you omit negative elements, they won't be fooled. They will think you are stupid, dishonest, or both.

It's OK to anticipate problems, threats, or challenges. Every new business idea has such possibilities. What is important is that you think through what you will do about them. How will you avoid the threats? How will you solve the problems? How will you exploit the opportunities? That's what should go in this section. All you need to do is to review what you learned from your situation analysis, and exercise your ingenuity in spotting critical areas, and figuring out what to do about them.

## OBJECTIVES AND GOALS

Clearly write out your objectives and goals. An objective might be to become the leading supplier of a certain product or service. That's good. But what exactly will it mean to be "the leading supplier?" To define this means establishing specific goals.

One goal might be attainment of 30 per cent market share within the next three years. Goals could pertain to volume of sales, return on investment, or other measurable aims. Be careful that objectives or goals are not mutually exclusive. For example, attaining a very high sales volume could require sacrifice of some profit over the short term. So you might not be able to achieve certain very high levels of sales and profits simultaneously.

Establishing your goals and objectives will probably do more than anything else to make you successful. First, you can't get "there" until you know where "there" is. If you don't describe what success is for you, you won't even know whether your business plan has reached success or not. Your goals and objectives give you a target to shoot at. If you aren't hitting the target, you can make adjustments or midcourse corrections. The nature of business is that you will make mistakes, and since there is no such thing as a "perfect" plan, some of your ideas and concepts will prove faulty and your plans won't work. That's OK as long as you have a clear target that you are heading for. But if you don't know exactly where you are going, you won't know what action to take to get back on course, because there won't be any course to get back on.

# COMPETITIVE ADVANTAGE

Now I want to tell you something that you probably already know. You can't succeed unless you have one or more advantages over others in the same business. You can gain competitive advantages through having exclusive rights to sell a product or service, by being faster, by offering higher quality, better value, or lower price, by providing better service, by having a unique means of distributing your products and so forth. Almost anything can be a competitive advantage if it offers a significant benefit to your customers.

Reread the review of yourself and your competitors in the situation analysis. This may help you find a competitive advantage that you overlooked. You should have a clear handle on your competitive advantages, and of course, potential lenders will want to know what they are as well.

# MARKETING STRATEGY

Strategies are the actions that you must take to reach your goals and objectives. Mass marketing, which involves selling the same product to everyone, is a marketing strategy (although I seldom recommend it). The opposite strategy is niching, where you dominate a very specific segment of the market and sell your product or provide your services only to that group. Your timing in introducing a new product or service into the market is a strategy. How you differentiate your product or service from those of your competitors is also a strategy. If you position your offering a certain way relative to similar offerings in the market, then that is a strategy, too.

If you decide to sell worldwide, you have a choice of two major strategies. You can sell the same product in the same way in every country. That's called a global marketing strategy. Or you can modify your product so that it's different in every country. You optimize it for the specific country depending on local customs, needs, and buyer behavior.

Whatever you decide, describe your strategies in detail and remind your readers of the competitive advantages and other variables in your situation that make this strategy advisable. Just remember one thing, which is the basis of every strategy: Always strive to concentrate superior resources at the decisive point. Be stronger where it counts. Don't try to be strong everywhere. Concentrating your strength where it counts is the key to success.

# MARKETING TACTICS

Tactics are the marketing actions you take to carry out your strategy. A strategy of product differentiation may require product tactics that alter the packaging; pricing tactics that raise or lower the price from standard; promotional tactics that emphasize and promote a previously ignored difference; or distribution tactics that use a faster means of getting the product to the consumer or buyer. If you think about it, you will see how all of these tactics differentiate your product from that of your competitors.

# SCHEDULES, BUDGET, AND MARKETING ACTIONS

Marketing actions cost effort, time, and money. Money is the most important. You want to know when and how much is required. Sometimes having money when you don't need it is almost as bad as not having it when you do need it. For example, if you borrow $100,000 and don't need it for several months, your timing error could cost you several thousand dollars in interest that you are paying to the lender unnecessarily.

The solution is to use a planning schedule as shown in Exhibit 2. Each task is listed along with its projected time frame and cost. This is usually prepared on a monthly basis. In this way, not only do you know the resources required to implement your plan, but once you have implemented it, you can use the schedule to monitor what you are doing and to make changes as needed to keep within planned budget, on time and headed toward your objectives and goals.

# IMPLEMENTATION AND CONTROL

Once your plan is underway, you'll want to know how you are doing in order to keep on schedule. Your business plan schedule will help you, but you also need other financial information. Because the implementation of your plan requires money, finances and financial data are closely integrated with business planning. Resources are never unlimited and insufficient funds may make an ideal strategy impossible. You need to adopt a strategy and tactics consistent with your available money, time, and other resources.

Include sales estimates on a monthly basis through the life of the plan, usually about three years. Also include cash flow requirements based on the sales or revenue

Exhibit 2   Project Development Schedule

Months after Project Initiation

| Task | 1 | 2 | 3 | 4 | 5 | 6 | 7 | 8 | 9 | 10 | 11 | 12 |
|---|---|---|---|---|---|---|---|---|---|---|---|---|
| Manufacture of units for test manufacturing | $5000 | | | | | | | | | | | |
| Initial advertisement in test area | $10,000 | $10,000 | $10,000 | | | | | | | | | |
| Shipment of units in test market area | $300 | $200 | | | | | | | | | | |
| Analysis of test | | $500 | $700 | $200 | | | | | | | | |
| Manufacture of units—1st year | | | | $5,000 | $10,000 | $10,000 | $10,000 | $10,000 | | | | |
| Phase I advertising and publicity | | | | $10,000 | $30,000 | $30,000 | $15,000 | | | | | |
| Shipment of units | | | | | $1,000 | $1,000 | $1,000 | $1,000 | $500 | | | |
| Phase II advertising | | | | | | | | $10,000 | $10,000 | $5,000 | $5,000 | $5,000 |

coming in less your costs. You may have already calculated that you should make a huge profit at the end of the year. But, if you have a similarly huge negative cash flow at the halfway point, you may never get to the end of the year to realize that profit.

Certain other calculations and ratios may also be important. One of the easiest to calculate, and most useful, is called "break-even." This is simply the point at which your business has no profits and no losses.

## How to Calculate Your Break-Even Point

Here's how to calculate your break-even point. First, what is profit? Profit will be equal to the quantity of your sales less your costs. Now costs are of two basic types. The first type is *fixed costs*. That means you pay the same amount no matter how many units you sell. If you buy a computer for your business, what you pay for that machine won't vary no matter how many or few products you sell.

We refer to the second type of costs as *variable costs*. These costs are directly connected to the sales of your product and vary with each unit. If you have manufacturing costs of $1.00 a unit, your costs vary depending on how many units you sell.

So, profit equals quantity sold times selling price less quantity sold times variable cost and less fixed cost. The break-even point occurs when profits and losses both equal zero. To learn the quantity we must sell to break even, we can move all this information around algebraically and come up with a simple foolproof formula to calculate this required amount:

$$\text{Break-even quantity} = \text{Fixed cost} \div \text{Price} - \text{Variable cost}$$

It's that simple. Let's say you add up all your variable costs and come up with $4.50 per unit. You add up all your fixed costs and come up with $7,700. We'll say your price is $10.

Our equation says that break-even quantity will be $7,700 divided by $10 minus $4.50. That's $7,700 divided by $5.50 or 1,400 units. That means you must sell 1,400 units before you start making any money.

There is a way of calculating all of this graphically without using the formulas. A *break-even chart* has a major advantage over the break-even and profit formulas: It shows pictorially the relationship of fixed variable and total expenses to sales at all volumes of sales. That means that you can calculate profits at any level of sales without using an equation. Here is how to construct a break-even chart.

**Step 1.**  Get some graph paper and label the horizontal line on the bottom *Units Sold*. Label the vertical line at the left of the graph *Dollars (Sales and Expenses)*. Divide each line into equal parts of dollars and units and label it appropriately.

**Step 2.**  Analyze all of your costs for the project and decide whether each is fixed or variable. Decide on the period of sales for your project. Total up your fixed and variable costs.

**Step 3.**  Draw a horizontal line to intersect the proper point on the vertical line to represent fixed costs, as at A in Exhibit 3.

Exhibit 3   A Break-Even Chart

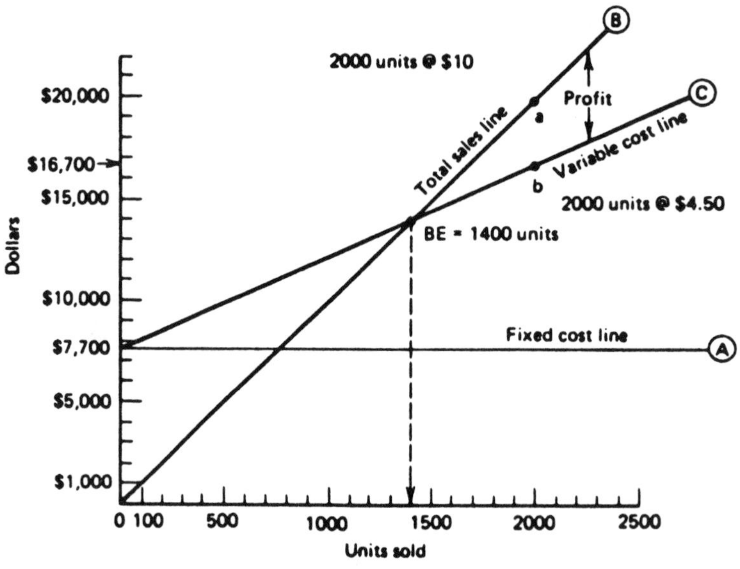

**Step 4.** Calculate the dollar value of sales for any unit number. For example, if we sell 2,000 units, how much is this in sales dollars? For red widgets, total sales volume could be 2,000 × $10, or $20,000. Plot this point at 2,000 units and $20,000 on the chart as point a. Put one end of a ruler at the 0 point in the lower left corner of the chart and the other end at the point you just plotted. This is the total sales line B in Exhibit 3.

**Step 5.** Calculate the dollar value for variable cost for any unit number. For example, for red widgets, variable cost is $4.50 per unit. At, say, 2,000 units, total variable cost is 2,000 × $4.50, or $9,000. Add $9,000 to the fixed cost (in this case, $7,700) to come up with $16,700. Plot this on the chart (b in Exhibit 3). Lay one end of the ruler at the point where the fixed cost line B intersects the vertical dollar scale and the other at the point you just plotted. Draw a line to form the variable cost line C in Exhibit 3.

Now your break-even chart is complete. The point at which the total sales line and variable cost line intersect is the break-even point, which you read on the horizontal unit scale at the bottom of the chart. In Exhibit 3, break-even is 1,400 units, as we calculated before using our formula.

To calculate profit for any number of units you want, simply subtract the dollar value read at opposite the proper point on the variable cost line C from the dollar value read opposite the proper point on the total sales line B. For example, to calculate the profit if you sell 2,000 red widgets, read right up from 2,000 units on the unit scale to point b on the variable cost line. Read straight across from point b to $16,700 on the vertical dollar scale. Now read straight up from 2,000 units on the unit scale to point a on the total sales line. Read straight across from point a to $20,000 on the vertical dollar scale: $20,000 minus $16,700 equals $3,300 if you sell 2,000 units. Do the same thing for any number of units to calculate profit.

While there are many ways that break-even might be calculated, and you will see several in these business plans, this method, using either the formula or the chart is recommended.

## Monitor and Adjust for the Environment . . . It Changes

Simply initiating the plan and hoping for the best isn't enough to ensure success. Because the environment is constantly changing, such a procedure is almost certain to result in failure. Therefore, it is important to specify a means of evaluation and control even before implementing the plan as well as including this process in the plan itself.

What will you do if sales are not at the level you forecast? Will you drop the plan? Modify it? How will you modify it? What if certain tactics in your plan are profitable and others not? What if certain geographic areas are profitable and others not? What will you do about new competitors entering the market or a change in an old competitor's strategy? How will these facts alter your plan? How will you find out these results and determine their effects?

Failing to prepare for evaluation and control is like pointing an automobile at a destination, closing your eyes, pushing the gas pedal, and crossing your fingers. You need feedback to measure the changes in the environment as you proceed. If the road curves, you surely want to know about it. Then, you can and must take action to get back on course to your destination. How you will do this is what I mean by implementation and control.

Now you know everything you need to get started. Start your research into your business, and begin. Refer to the many examples of real business plans that I have provided to see how you can make your business plan the best it can be. In Appendix B, you will find some forms that will help you to think through and complete various sections of the plan.

# 1

# BUSINESS PLAN FOR EXCEL AIRE

*Developed by*
**Rose Simon,
John Iezza,
Carlton Skerrett,
Angel Camargo, and
Danielle Benson**

# Table of Contents

## EXECUTIVE SUMMARY

Excel Aire is about providing nonscheduled convenient, fast, safe, efficient, professional, and comfortable air flight services to the top executives of the Greater Western Region of the United States.

We will be the "new kids on the block" starting January 1994 when we launch our new charter services stationed at the Santa Monica Airport, 3100 Donald Douglas Loop North, Santa Monica CA 90405.

We chose this location because of the convenience and accessibility it provides our target customers. Located at the Santa Monica Airport, in the heart of the Los Angeles area, Excel Aire will be within 15 minutes of all main business and entertainment areas of Los Angeles. Just where we want to be.

In launching this new charter service, we are in need of at least $3,890,916 capital for the first year just to run the operation. We will be providing you with the financial analysis to give you a fuller picture of this charter operation.

We at Excel Aire are excited about this new venture, as we are confident that the service that we are about to offer is one that is nonexistent in the market today. Excel Aire offers service—personalized service. We fully stand by our motto when we say "Your need is our service."

## INTRODUCTION

There are several important reasons why one would choose a charter service. First, chartering saves time, otherwise lost by inflexible schedules. Second, it compresses time so that an hour-long transaction out of town does not require an overnight stay. Third, it expands time so that overall productivity is greater. Excel Aire will offer this and more, not to mention the intangible benefits to executives such as comfort, convenience, and prestige.

Ground service is another reason why Excel Aire should be your first choice in air charter. We will offer the finest in service and safety at a price that is highly competitive within the business jet community. Our personalized service extends from the moment you call our office, to the air and back down to the ground because "Your need is our service" at Excel Aire. We provide hotel reservations, taxi/car/limo service, personal services (laundry, dry cleaning, etc.) because we want to make life easier for you.

Our top priority at Excel Aire is customer satisfaction, and our only means of achieving it is through employee commitment, reliability, speed of service, and excellent customer service. We will attempt to accomplish this specifically through our personalized, custom-tailored ground service.

## SITUATION ANALYSIS

There are several areas of concern in the situation analysis process—the technological environment, the neutral environment, the company environment, and the competitor environment. The following is an analysis of each of these areas.

### Company Environment

Company environment analysis is composed of three areas: (1) financial resources, (2) human resources, and (3) experience and expertise. Research is extremely important as this information becomes the backbone of the company's operation.

### Financial Resources

In trying to assess the financial resources aspect of this project, our company has in hand a capital of $500,000 to assure a solid start-up of the business. This figure is based on a $100,000 outlay of each of the five owners. We are additionally seeking a loan for the additional funds needed (see *Financial Summary Sheets*). This total capital pool will encompass all anticipated expenses; both fixed and variable.

### Human Resources

Human resources is another aspect of the company environment that needs research. This area of the business encompasses not only the who but also the what. The who of the human resources is the personnel who will make up the corporation. This is where the different functions of the organization are drawn out. The what of human resource has to do with the kind of training and any continuing education necessary to carry out the proposed functions or responsibilities each personnel will hold.

Human resources is also the area where a company determines its objectives, formulates policies, and plans programs and procedures to attain these objectives. This is also where a budget that will serve as a short-range plan of operations to meet the objectives is developed.

Excel Aire's personnel will consist of a president, a vice-president/director of marketing, director of flight operations/chief pilot, and a director of maintenance (provided by FBO, thus no cost to Excel Aire). We will be contracting our captains and flight crews.

The President will be responsible for the entire operations of the corporation and for coordination of all departmental activities to ensure a smooth functioning operation.

The Vice-President will be the Chief Financial Officer, responsible for accounting to ensure a smooth financial operation. This person will also be the Marketing Director for sales and customer service to ensure that our service is at the best possible standard we can offer.

The Director of Flight Operations will be responsible for the entire flight operations and for coordinating all flight activities. This person will also be the Chief Pilot and will be responsible for the management of the corporation's policies and compliance with all laws, rates, requirements, and regulations governing air taxi (135) operations as applicable to the corporation under its charter and certificate. He will also be responsible for the supervision and scheduling of pilot personnel and aircraft as well as act as liaison between the FAA and the corporation all matters pertaining to air taxi operations.

The Director of Maintenance is provided by the FBO (Flight Based Operation) and is responsible for the planning, organizing, and scheduling of maintenance and inspections. He is responsible for the maintenance records and the proper distribution of same. He will also act as liaison between the corporation and the FAA on maintenance matters. As mentioned earlier, he is paid by the FBO.

Our financial statements in the Appendix will show how the salaries of these employees fit in with our operational costs.

### Experience and Expertise

All officers of the corporation must have at least a bachelor's degree in business administration. All flight officers must have a high school diploma and have completed aviation school plus proper FAA certification. A captain must have a commercial license, an instructor rating, a multiengine rating, and an airline transport pilot certificate. A copilot must possess all of the above requirements except the airline transport pilot certificate. In addition, a captain needs 1,500 hours of total flight hours in order to be eligible and a copilot must meet a minimum of 50 to 100 total flight hours in type to be considered to fly any of Excel Aire's airplanes.

Continuing education is required annually to renew certificates. FAA-approved doctors administer medical certification biannually.

## Competitive Environment

Our company's competition is based on price and promotion. Though competition is very strong, chartering services are promoting lower rates rather than quality service. The price range for charting a plane is very tight, within a couple of hundred dollars of each other. Most chartering services fly worldwide giving them a broader market to deal with. With a broader market, they have to provide a wider range of services to capture market share.

Very few chartering services have a one-line fleet of planes to provide their services. For example, one chartering service has 54 planes ranging from turbo props to jet airplanes. A high number of planes has very high costs that will cut into profits. The average number of planes that our competitors have to provide for their services has a mean of 13 with a standard deviation of 2 that range in variety. Our company is focusing on capturing a niche with a one-line fleet that will provide safety, quality, and service that none of our competitors are stressing.

Through extensive studies on our competitors' environment, chartering services are shooting for the same idea. They are providing a wide range of service upon request. Through a telephone survey, when we asked about a specific service that they provide, such as full entertainment systems on the plane, that causes the chartering price to increase. This study concluded that the more a client requests, the more that client pays. Very few chartering services provide quality service as a standard policy. Our company standards are focusing on safety, quality, price, and service.

A weak area of our competition is the lack of services being provided on the ground. Although most chartering services provide ground transportation and hotel reservation services, they are not being stressed as a standard service. No personal services are being provided to help ease the pressure from traveling due to rushed time. In addition, incentives are not being offered to clients to encourage them to use the chartering services. Our company plans to use a flying incentive to capture market share.

Most of our competition is based out of Santa Monica Airport, Van Nuy Airport, Burbank Airport, and Los Angeles Airport. The reasons for this is due to the FAA requirements. The noises that the older planes create limit the flights in and out of Long Beach Airport. Our company chose Santa Monica Airport because of the location and its accessibility to the Greater Los Angeles Airport. Our choice of fleet is the new Citations, which utilize modern technology to produce less noise to meet FAA requirements.

All of our competitors promote their business through several sources. The number one way is through direct mail. In addition, companies advertise through magazines, newspapers, and phone books.

## Neutral Environment

### Legal Aspects of Regulations

The impact of regulations and CONTLOS upon the aviation business must be taken into consideration when conducting business operations. Recognizing this impact or influence and taking any required action is an important aspect of successful management.

Regulations are frequently associated with change that threatens the psychological, social, and economic aspects of the manager's world. To cope with regulations and change, there are some guidelines which might help establish a favorable viewpoint. Successful handling of regulations is facilitated by the creation and maintenance of an effective reports system that fits the needs of the individual business.

There are two broad categories of regulations which influence an aviation business: (1) regulations which deal with aviation operations and (2) regulations dealing with the business aspects of the organization. Aviation operations are regulated by the FAA, NTSB, and other federal, state, and local agencies. They cover flight regulations, personnel, support activities, safety, and security programs. The normal business activities are influenced by the regulatory aspects of federal and state taxes and the myriad controls and guidelines contained in the statutes, legislation, and guidelines covering unemployment compensation, Social Security, wage and hour administration, lessees, legal field, OSHA, insurance, licenses and permits, price, regulation, competition safeguards, consumer credit, advertising, and equipment regulations.

### Rules and Regulations

In charter operations, the company is selling air transportation to meet a customer's specific need. The aircraft, with our crew members, is provided to the customer according to agreement for exclusive use. In complying with Part 135 and other pertinent regulations, the company must ensure the following:

1. The receipt of an air taxi/commercial operator (ATCO) operating certificate.
2. A current manual for the use and guidance of flight, ground operations, and maintenance personnel in conducting operations.
3. Procedures for locating each flight for which an FAA flight plan is not filed.
4. Exclusive use of at least one aircraft that meets the requirements of the operations specifications.
5. Qualified air crew personnel with appropriate and current certificates and the necessary recency experience.
6. Maintenance of required records and submission of mechanical reliability reports.
7. Compliance with the operating rules prescribed in FAR Parts 91 and 135, including:

   Airworthiness check

   Area limitations on operations

   Available operating information for pilots

   Passenger briefing

   Oxygen requirements

   Night operations

   Fuel requirements, VFR and IFR

   VFR operations (Visual Flight Rules)

   IFR operations (Instrument Flight Rules)

These requirements reflect only a summary of the pertinent sections of Part 135. Refer to Federal Aviation Regulations for complete details of the requirements.

### Insurance

The typical aviation business is faced with many problems, but of special importance is the concern of insurance. The four general categories of insurance have been classified as (1) loss or damage to property, (2) bodily injury and property damage liability, (3) business interruptions and losses resulting from fire and other damages to the premises, and (4) death or disability of key executives. Insurance protection should be considered for those areas found in any business as well as in those areas which are unique to the aviation field. It is important to consider active risk reduction as a key element of risk management.

The actual quotes for our insurance needs can be found in the Appendix.

## Technological Environment

### *Aircraft Acquisition Analysis*

A major decision that needed to be made was how we were going to acquire our aircraft fleet. Some of the objectives that were really of concern were cost, tax advantage, and profitability. Our options were owning the aircraft or leasing them. In order to aid us in our decision, we compiled a comparison analysis and it follows.

### Company-Owned Aircraft

*Advantages:* Optimum utility, convenience and safety, tax benefits.

*Disadvantages:* Can be inflexible if the company is not getting the hourly utilization expected, or purchased the wrong aircraft and must dispose of it.

### Leasing

#### *Advantages*

1. *Conservation of working capital.* A big advantage of leasing is that it conserves working capital while allowing all the benefits of aircraft ownership. In a lease agreement, the leasing company acquires the aircraft at a specific request of the lessee with the lessee making the decision regarding the options, modifications, and price. At that point, the lessee signs a contract to lease a plane over a period of time for a specified monthly payment. With the exception of a possible advance payment of between one and five months, there is no other down payment. The down payment customary in other methods is saved, and that amount of working capital is available for other purposes.

2. *Tax Saving.* In financing an aircraft, only the interest portion of the monthly payment is a deductible expense. In addition, the company would depreciate that asset. In a lease situation, the entire lease payment is a deductible expense, effectively a straight line write-off of the asset over the term of the lease.

3. *Preservation of Credit Line.* A lease is generally not considered debt on the balance sheet. Keeping the additional debt off the balance sheets allow a higher availability of debt through normal banking transactions for other needs.

4. *Flexibility.* No assets are required to refinance or liquidate before upgrading equipment. Leasing makes it easier to upgrade and time acquisitions with market and company growth.

#### *Disadvantages*

1. *No Equity, No Asset.* A leased aircraft cannot be shown on the balance sheets as an asset since it is not considered a debt. During the term of the lease, the lessee usually cannot own the airplane or have equity in it.

2. *Extra Cost.* The main disadvantage of leasing is the extra cost over an outright purchase, including the interest rate and the profit to the lessor.

3. *Limited Flight Time.* In a leased aircraft, the lessor usually has the right to the use of the aircraft. This could somehow lessen the effectiveness of the charter business cutting into the availability of the aircraft and into profitability.

In view of the preceding findings, Excel Aire has opted to lease its aircraft as it is the most sensible option at this point in time. We will, however, evaluate the circumstances again in the future since we do plan to expand both our line of business and our target market. We will also continuously analyze our hourly plane usage to determine the affinity of each plane to the enduser.

## TARGET MARKET

We will be utilizing a concentration strategy to determine our segmentation. We are aware that cost will prohibit many people from utilizing our services, and know that we must target our promotion with that in mind.

### Geographic Segmentation

Based on Fortune 500 April 1992 listing of the location of the top 500 sales-producing companies in America, 44 corporations are based in California. Over half of these are located in Southern California. Likewise, the Southern California Business Directory's listing of the state's top 100 companies in California boasts over a 50% concentration in Southern California. Santa Monica Airport is a midway point accessible to both San Diego or the Greater Los Angeles Area. Los Angeles is the second largest metropolitan area in the country and is ranked as having the fourth busiest airport in the country. This leaves many business travelers wasting additional time in preparation which could easily be eliminated with charter service.

### Demographic Segmentation

We will be targeting the high-level executives within the top sales-producing companies, who have the authority to charter aircraft services. Our demographic research is based on a study by G.R. Bassiry and R. Hrair Dekmejian for *Business Horizons* magazine (May–June 1990). The average profile of a CEO is a 59-year-old male having a bachelor's degree, coming from middle/lower middle class socioeconomic background. He has served in the military and receives an average annual compensation package of $1,599,000. Although we will be targeting executives other than just CEOs, we find this information to be crucial in establishing our promotion and distribution tactics.

### Psychographic Segmentation

Through the initiation of primary research interviewing 25 executive managers who have traveled at least three times in the last year on business, certain demands became apparent. Every person interviewed stated service to be in the top four most important categories when it comes to air travel. When asked to be more specific, frequently required services included limousine service, quality food service, secretarial services, laundering and dry-cleaning services, and business equipment availability.

## BUSINESS OBJECTIVES AND GOALS

Excel Aire is an exciting venture. Our primary business objective is to provide outstanding jet transportation with the finest of service and safety. We feel our clientele would be willing to make a commitment to our company if they felt they were truly getting something they could not get elsewhere without additional expense.

Our projected financial objectives are to increase revenue at a 10% annual rate over the next three years. We are looking to gain a 10% market share. We are also concerned with keeping a low debt-equity ratio. Our control over costs and marketing objectives can be more consistent with what the five owners want when there are not shareholders to satisfy.

In terms of business expansion, we are looking to expand not only our product, but also our geographic target market. Within the next year, we plan to add a Citation 10 to the fleet to handle long-distance charters, and ideally double the existing fleet over the next three years. Our geographic expansion attainments will be a longer process depending on the growth of the company. However, we are looking at San Francisco, Dallas, and Orlando as sights for future Excel Aire locations.

## MARKETING TACTICS

### Promotion

Through extensive research of the competition's promotional tactics as well as consideration of financial control, the following is a promotional plan designed to establish Excel Aire as a company with an outstanding reputation and profit margin.

#### *Distribution Materials*

Our appendix includes samples of the competitors' distribution materials. We are looking to use the same quality in printing and graphics except we will be utilizing our five key owners' skills in desktop publishing to do our own layouts. This allows for at least a 28% reduction of cost in printing. The following are rates quoted by an independent printing company based on the assumption that the materials are already laid out.

Brochures–8 ½ by 11 trifold color cardstock brochures:

```
      1–100   = $0.99 each
    100–500   = $0.78 each
    501–1000= $0.57 each
   1001 & up = $0.36 each
```

Using the assumption of printing 2,000 to start, our cost would be $720 for the brochures. Our primary use of these brochures is to provide an introduction to the business community in a mass mailing, utilizing mailing lists, and data collected on the top 100 companies in sales in Southern California, and Fortune 500's issue of the top 500 companies each year. In-depth booklets—9 by 12 notebook with a pocket containing 8 ½ by 11 stationery with our company logo and an in-depth description of our company and the services available:

Stationery costs—8 ½ by 11 with company logo:

```
      1–100   = $0.06 each
    101–250   = $0.05 each
    251–500   = $0.04 each
    501 & up  = $0.035 each
```

Booklet style color folder with a pocket to hold stationery:

```
      1–100   = $4.99 each
    101–200   = $4.62 each
    201–300   = $4.25 each
    301–400   = $3.83 each
    401–500   = $3.46 each
    501–750   = $3.09 each
    750 & up  = $2.72 each
```

Using the assumption of printing 1,000 booklets to start, our costs would be $2,720 for the booklets and $3,500 for 10 pieces of stationery in each booklet, for a total cost of $5,720.

We would also print up an additional 5,000 pieces of stationery for business correspondence at a cost of $1,750. Business cards are also a cost factor at $50 per 1,000.

We would start with this level of business supplies and monitor closely the flow to determine our future needs. Thus, our overall start-up costs for printing will be $8,240.

### Distribution Methods

As previously stated in our competition environment, most companies utilize a direct mail approach. Our target market allows us to be quite specific in our approach. We will utilize direct mail as follows:
We will compile lists from the following sources:

1. Listing of the top 100 companies in sales in Southern California Business Directory.
2. Listing of the top 500 companies in America from Fortune 500's annual listing. We will not only send information to the companies based in Southern California (44), but also any company that has a sizable office in the area.
3. Listing of all executives working for the major motion picture and television studios based in California.
4. Listing of all CEOs for all companies based in Southern California from the D&B (Dun and Bradstreet).

Our postage cost will be approximately $580 for an initial mailing of 2,000 brochures. It is our intention to utilize our owners to compile these lists, thus saving the recurring fee of renting lists repeatedly each time we want to do a mailing.

### Advertising

Our advertising strategy is to establish that Excel Aire is responsible in providing solutions for the customers' needs without charging a premium for them. We are looking to appeal directly to business travelers whose time is so valuable, they don't have enough flexibility with a commercial carrier. The following is our logo and will be used in association with any promotional materials:

# ◆ Excel Aire ◆

**Your need is our service!**

The following are rates for advertising in the kind of magazines we would be able to reach our target market with:

| | |
|---|---|
| **Forbes Magazine-** | Full Page 1 × rate= $33,840 |
| Black and White | ⅔ Page 1 × rate = $24,360 |
| Non Bleed | ½ Page 1 × rate = $19,970 |
| | ⅓ Page 1 × rate = $12,860 |
| | |
| **Fortune Magazine-** | Full Page 1 × rate= $37,130 |
| Black and White | ½ Page 1 × rate = $21,910 |
| | ⅓ Page 1 × rate = $14,110 |

**Business Week-**
Black and White
Non Bleed

Full Page 1 × rate = $40,700
$2/3$ Page 1 × rate = $30,520
$1/2$ Page 1 × rate = $25,440
$1/3$ Page 1 × rate = $16,280

**Wall Street Journal (Western Region)**
Black and White

$1/2$ Page 1 × rate = $14,003.76
$1/3$ Page 1 × rate = $ 9,335.84
$1/4$ Page 1 × rate = $ 7,001.88
$1/8$ Page 1 × rate = $ 3,500.94

**Delta Sky Magazine (using a destination rate)**
Black and White

Full Page 1 × rate = $19,343
$2/3$ Page 1 × rate = $14,355
$1/2$ Page 1 × rate = $11,468
$1/3$ Page 1 × rate = $ 8,618

All costs quoted are based on a 1-time rate. Each magazine has different levels of multirating, and this definitely factors into our decision as to where we will advertise.

Based on the preceding quotes, we have decided on a concentration in the Western Region *Wall Street Journal.* By running our advertisement at least 10 times, we will discount our rates by 5%. We will take $1/8$ of a page for a price of $3,325.89 per ad with a total cost of $33,258.93. We are also going to advertise in the *Delta Sky Magazine.* During our primary research of business travelers, Delta Airlines was mentioned in approximately 84% of our surveys. We will take a $1/3$ page ad using a 3-time discount rate of $10,920 for a total cost of $32,760.

Our intention is to begin advertising with these sources, but with revenue coming in, we will expand into the other quoted magazines in a conservative, but deliberate manner.

## Product

We have decided to use the Citation Jets for our charter service for several reasons which are highlighted in our Comparison Chart of Optional Planes. Since the beginning of the jet era, Citations have had a tradition of producing the most efficient and cost-effective light jets. At a time when the industry is seeing a decrease in manufacturers, Citation has been producing a new line of jets. They provide more options in price, size, and category; and they represent the most impressive combination of efficiency, performance, and reliability in light jets.

From the new lineup, we have chosen the Citation Jet, Citation V, and the Citation VII. These airplanes meet many of today's tough regulations, and have very low acquisition costs in comparison to others in their class.

Each jet has outstanding fuel efficiency that is a high priority in the time of rising costs. Each provides the lowest cost of operation of any comparable new aircraft available. Every Citation is backed by a large dedicated support organization, with service centers around the country.

Through much deliberation over which kinds of aircraft would best suit our marketing and business needs, we decided to use the Citation Series of aircraft for these additional reasons.

1. Fleet unification allows for our flight operators to interchange much more effectively between planes.

2. The Citations are using some of the most current technology available, thus concurring with the FAA's newest regulations including those on noise.
3. The planes can be leased directly from Citation, Inc., allowing us to be in control of our specification needs.

The Comparison Chart shows the features of our particular choice of Citations at this point. We based our selection on trying to create a good mix of size, speed, distance capability, number of seats, and cost-effectiveness.

### Services Available

Aside from the regular flight services most charter companies provide, we at Excel Aire strive to be different. We are building our company on the motto "Your need is our service," and we fully intend to deliver. The following list is a sample of some of the services our primary research indicated people would be interested in using if there was no additional premium:

1. Limousine service.
2. *Quality* food service.
3. Secretarial services.
4. Laundry services.
5. Dry-cleaning services.
6. Business equipment on airplane.
7. Hotel reservations services.

We will specify the equipment needed for the Citation in our lease agreement, and utilize our staff to provide any of the other services mentioned.

## Price

Please refer to the appendix for an outline of charges for each aircraft. We based our decisions on establishing a price on competitive information as well as our break-even needs.

## Distribution

Excel Aire chose Santa Monica Airport to house its air charter business simply because of the accessibility of the location to our target clientele.

We have contracted a 15,000-square-foot facility with Gunnell Aviation. They are a step beyond the classic definition of an FBO (Fixed Base Operator). As Excel Aire's FBO, Gunnell Aviation will greet, fuel, store, and care for our fleet of aircraft where, for over 30 years, highly individualized service to demanding clientele has stood above all else.

Gunnell Aviation has fine-tuned an approach to FBO service that matches professionalism with instinct, detail with thoroughness, not to mention complete service with individual need. The following amenities lured us to Gunnell Aviation:

- Full-service FBO with 30 years of service.
- Corporate and executive hangars.
- World-class museum and art gallery.
- Premier gourmet restaurant, The DC3.

## Comparison Chart of Optional Planes

| | Citation Jet | King Air | Citation V | Lear Jet | Citation VII | Challenger |
|---|---|---|---|---|---|---|
| Seats | 5–6 | 6–7 | 9–13 | 10 | 8–13 | 10–19 |
| Price | 3.2 million | 2.1 million | 4.4 million | 4.6 million | 7.6 million | 10 million |
| Power plant | 2 William | 2 p & w | 2 p & w | 2 Gorrett | 2 Gorrett | 2 GE CF-34-319 |
| Fuel capacity | 3,070 | 2,573 | 5,771 | 6,198 | 7,384 | 17,900 |
| Gross weight | 10,100 | 10,100 | 16,100 | 18,500 | 22,650 | 44,750 |
| Empty weight | 5,730 | 6,634 | 8,827 | 10,119 | 11,686 | 25,760 |
| Useful load | 4,370 | 3,526 | 7,273 | 8,381 | 10,964 | 18,990 |
| Cruise speed | 322 @ 41,000 | 247 @ 16,000 | 370 @ 45,000 | 424 @ 43,000 | 424 @ 45,000 | 424 @ 41,000 |
| Fuel flow | 489/72 | 592/88 | 860/127 | 990/148 | 1,145/170 | 1,737/255 |
| Max endurance | 5.6 @ 41,000 | 7.1 @ 29,000 | 5.7 @ 45,000 | 5.5 @ 43,000 | 5.8 @ 47,000 | 3.8 @ 41,000 |
| Take off | 3,080' | 2,710' | 3,160' | 4,972' | 4,690' | 5,875' |
| Landing | 3,080' | 2,710' | 3,160' | 4,972' | 4,690' | 5,875' |
| Distance | 2,800' | 2,290' | 2,870' | 3,075' | 3,000' | 3,300' |
| Rate of climb | 3,450' | 2,005' | 3,684' | 4,340' | 4,000' | 4,259' |
| Engine out roc | 1,070 | 494 | 1,180 | 1,280 | 990 | 1,207 |
| Max optg. | 41,000 | 29,000 | 45,000 | 45,000 | 51,000 | 41,000 |
| Suc. ceiling | 26,500 | 13,100 | 31,100 | 25,000 | 23,000 | 26,500 |
| Stall speed | 78 | 78 | 85 | 96 | 98 | 103 |
| Landing config. | 77 | 80 | 85 | 110 | 98 | 116 |

- Commonwealth limousine.
- Avis rental car site.
- Complete line of aviation services.

At Excel Aire, we feel that the more sophisticated our distributor, the better our clients will be served. For Excel Aire's clients, Gunnell Aviation also boasts such conveniences as:

- Luxurious lobby area.
- Fully appointed conference room.
- 24-hour ground support services.
- Private offices and meeting rooms.
- Full telecommunication (telephone, fax, pager, portable phones).
- Complimentary message services.

These additional amenities, however, will mean nothing if not fully supported by the commitment that our clients' flight safety is our first priority. This is more reason that Excel Aire has chosen to be a part of the Gunnell Aviation family, because from minor maintenance services to major inspections, from aircraft parts sales to a fully equipped avionics department, Gunnell Aviation guarantees that each aircraft performs at its peak—on demand and at a moment's notice—because our clients' safety is our primary concern.

Furthermore, we chose Gunnell Aviation because of their high profile, their commitment to their clients. Gunnell Aviation gives Excel Aire the edge needed to operate the finest air charter service in Southern California due to a common goal we share, and that is "Customer Satisfaction."

We selected Santa Monica Airport because of its dedication to first-class general aviation. We selected Santa Monica because of its proximity to the important business and entertainment centers of Los Angeles. What this means to our clients is complete convenience without sacrifice.

## PROBLEMS/SOLUTIONS

Aviation managers are faced with many problems, some of which are more critical than others to the continued longevity and success of the business. Among the more critical problem areas are insurance, leases, and legal matters.

The manager's recognizing these problem areas, possessing the capability to deal with them, and initiating positive action for achievement in each area will be necessary to the success of our aviation business.

### Insurance

Risk is a part of doing business. Risk management is a part of the manager's job of directing the business. In running Excel Aire, few risks can be eliminated completely, although some can be reduced by safe operating procedures, thorough personnel training, and good equipment. Some risks can be transferred through the purchase of insurance. Some risks will be assumed by the business. Knowing what kind of insurance to carry and how much to purchase are important aspects of good risk management.

The average aviation business has considerable investment in buildings, furnishings, and inventory. These investments should be protected against fire and other perils such as smoke, windstorm, hail, civil commotion, explosion, and damage by aircraft or motor vehicles.

## Liability Exposure

There are four types of liability exposure:

1. Employer's liability and worker's compensation.
2. Liability to nonemployees.
3. Automobile liability.
4. Professional liability.

**1.** Under common law as well as workers' compensation laws, an employer is liable for injury to employees at work caused by his failure to provide safe tools and working conditions, hire competent fellow workers, or warn employees of an existing danger.

**2.** Nonemployee liability, general liability, or third-party liability is insurance for any kind of bodily injury to nonemployees except that caused by automobiles and professional malpractice. This includes customers, pedestrians, delivery people, the public at large, and may extend to trespassers or other outsiders even when the manager exercised "reasonable care."

**3.** Cars and trucks are a serious source of liability. This is encountered primarily in vehicles owned by the business, but can be experienced under the doctrine of agency when the employee is operating his own or someone else's car in the course of employment. In this instance, the business could be held vicariously liable for injuries and property damage caused by the employee. If customary or convenient for an employee to operate his own car while on company business, the business is well advised to acquire nonownership automobile liability insurance.

**4.** Our hiring policies will assure a minimization of professional risk pursuant to professional malpractice as well as proper certification. We are also establishing a check system for all procedures required in proper flight operation.

## Legal Affairs

Eventually, the company will be faced with legal problems. In view of this possibility, it is highly desirable that the organization have a sound legal foundation and that the services of a competent lawyer be available for assistance when needed. Although legal services are myriad, the following represent possibilities:

1. Establishing, maintaining, or changing the correct legal form of organization.
2. Preparing contracts, deeds, and other legal documents.
3. Determining legal liability in accident cases involving company personnel, vehicles, or premises.
4. Interpreting the regulations of governmental agencies such as the Internal Revenue Service, the FAA, and the Wage and Hour Law.
5. Conducting all necessary litigation such as those associated with damage suits and contractual problems.
6. Legal assistance necessary in obtaining and executing specific technical or exacting contracts.
7. Maintaining the correct legal position when dealing with employees or unions on labor relations problems.

## SUMMARY

Based on the findings of this research, we are confident that Excel Aire will be a successful operation and will find its way to the top of the industry given what we have to offer and our deep commitment to the needs of our clients.

We fully stand behind our product, that is our "personalized service" both in the air and on the ground. Our commitment to providing the finest jet transportation which focuses on a convenient, fast, safe, efficient, professional, and comfortable air flight service is the essence of our business and that is our promise to our customers. We mean it when we say "Your need is our service!"

## REFERENCES

**Magazines**

Popkin, J.: "Charters Are Cheaper, Most of the Time"; *U.S. News and World Report*; February 26, 1990

Collins, R.: "The Citation Turns 20"; *AOPA Pilot,* September 1992

Lacagnina, M.: "Golden Eagle"; *AOPA Pilot,* August 1993

General: "Fortune 500 Listing for 1992"; *Fortune Magazine,* April 1992

Bassiry, G. & Dekmejian, R.: "Corporate Elite, A CEO's Profile"; *Business Horizons Magazine,* January, 1991

**Business Publications**

Southern California Business Directory, 1992

Dun and Bradstreet CEO's Listings, 1992

ADPA's Aviation USA, 1992

**Books**

Pride/Ferrell: *Marketing,* 8th Edition

Richardson, J.D. and Rodwell, J.F.: *Essentials of Aviation Management,* 3rd Edition

Wells, A. and Chadbourne, B.: *General Aviation Marketing,* 1987

**Interviews**

Barton, Gault S.: President of Premiere Air.

Buell, Brian: Property Manager, Gunnell Aviation.

Caridi, Penny: Underwriter, Aviation West Brokers.

Duggan, James: Charter Dispatcher, Zephyr Aviation.

Goode, Ken: Credit Representative, Cessna Finance Corporation.

Griffith, Shawn: Chief Pilot, Argosy Airlines.

Higares, Chris: Service Scheduler, Cessna Aircraft Company.

Hiney, Richard C.: Underwriter, USAIG.

Krebs, Tisha: Office Manager, Civic Helicopters.

Lefezar, Mark: Vice President, AvJet Aviation.

Shoody, Jonathon: Service Person, KINKO'S Desktop Publishing.

Rizzi, Wayne J.: Director of Marketing, Premier Air.

Simon, Michael: Flight Officer, Premier Air.

# APPENDIX

# Insurance Information

UNITED STATES AVIATION UNDERWRITERS
Incorporated

| Code | Description | Exposure | Rate | Est. Premium |
|------|-------------|----------|------|--------------|
| 8810 | Clerical | $59,800.00 | .98 | $ 586.00 |
|      | President Payroll Max | | | |
| 8742 | Outside Sales (V.P.) | 50,000.00 | 1.40 | 700.00 |
| 7424 | Flight Crew | 88,060.00 | 7.23 | 6,367.00 |

| | |
|---|---|
| Employers Liability Increased Limits—Minimum Fee (1,000,000.00/1,000,000.00/1,000,000.00) | 150.00 |
| CA User Fund Assessment 7,803.00 @ .00126 | 10.00 |
| CA Fraud Investigation Surcharge 7,803.00 @ .000548 | 4.00 |
| ESTIMATED ANNUAL PREMIUM | $7,817.00 |

Rates are subject to change without prior notice.

Rose, with the above figures projected for your project (which are only estimates) the total premium would be $92,537.00.

We would also require all pilots to attend formal simulator based recurrent training every six months. For an idea on this price, you can call Flight Safety International in Long Beach. Explain your project and I am sure they would be glad to help (213-420-7660).

I hope this is of help to your project. Remember that these estimates are only an idea. We are in a hardening market and expect the rates to continually go up.

Please, call if I can help anymore.

Best Regards,

Richard C. Hiney

RCH/mad

# Sample Job Order

**♦ Excel Aire ♦**

**Your need is our service!**

Trip Planning Form
24 Hour Reservation Line
(818) 752-2009

Today's Date: _____          Confirmation #: _____

Hotel code: _____

Itinerary: (Please include any requested stop-overs, drop-offs, or overnights)

_____

_____

Date of Travel: _____

Time of Travel: _____

Number of Passengers: _____

Departure Location: (If other than Santa Monica Airport)

_____

Amount and Type of Luggage (i.e., Golf Clubs, Skiing Equipment, etc.)

_____

Passenger Name: _____

Contact Name and Phone #: _____

Form of Payment: _____

Special Catering Requests: _____

_____

Notes: _____

_____

_____

_____

(*Note:* Copies of this form may serve as original)

# Interview Questionnaire

Name of Interviewer: _____    Date: _____

Name of Interviewee: _____    Company: _____

Number of times you travel for business in 1 year: _____

Typical service used (commercial or charter): _____

Which companies? _____

Please rate the following factors you consider when choosing an air travel service on a scale from 1 (most important) to 10 (least important):

Cost: _____

Location of airport: _____

Pilot: _____

Competition incentives: _____

Flexibility of schedule: _____

Services available: _____

Plane type: _____

Staff: _____

Ground handling: _____

Safety records: _____

What specific services do you ever require when traveling?

_____

_____

_____

What rules does your company enforce when it comes to chartering an airplane?

_____

_____

_____

Other comments:

_____

_____

_____

## Citation Jet

*$1250/hr*

| Leg Num | From Apt | To Apts | Tru Crs | Dist nmi | Fuel Stop | ETE Hrs + Min | Allow Load Pounds | Fuel Burn |
|---|---|---|---|---|---|---|---|---|
| 1 | SMO | DAL | 8 | 1,082 | 0 | 3 + 12 | 1,306 | 2,744 |
| 2 | DAL | SMO | 280 | 1,082 | 1 | 4.33 | 843 | 3,960 |
| Subtotals | | | | 2,164 | | 7.8 Hrs | | 6,704 |
| Flight time charges | | | | | | | | $ 9,750 |
| 0.0 Individual standby hour(s) | | | | | | | | 0 |
| 1 Overnight(s) (Include 1 day's standby each) | | | | | | | | 300 |
| Extra items | | | | | | | | 0 |
| 10% tax | | | | | | | | 1,005 |
| Totals | | | | 2,164 | | 7.8 Hrs | | $11,055 |

DAL  Love Field—Dallas TX
SMO  Excel Aire—310-222-1325

## Monthly Breakeven Point

Breakeven point computed as average for all three planes:

|  | *Price per hour* |
|---|---|
| Citation Jet | 1,250 |
| Citation V | 2,700 |
| Citation VII | 3,300 |
| Total divided by 3 = avg. price/hr | 2,417 |

Average breakeven point for all three planes in hours:

$$\text{Breakeven} = \frac{FC}{S} - VC = \frac{213,021}{1,710} = 125$$

FC = 213,021
Sale (avg.) = 2,417
VC = 95507/135 = 707

Average breakeven point in sales:

$$\text{Breakeven} = \frac{FC}{1} - \frac{VC}{S} = \frac{213,021}{.70} = \$304,316$$

*Note:* 45 hours were used as a base for variable cost expenses; 135 hours were divided into the variable cost to get a unit cost of $707.

### Expense Breakdown per Month Basis

**Expenses**

Fixed costs:

Leases:

| | | |
|---|---|---|
| Citation Jet | $37,333 | |
| Citation V | 51,333 | |
| Citation VII | 88,666 | $177,332 |
| Office rental | | 6,000 |
| Insurance | | 7,753 |
| Hanger rental | | 6,000 |
| Other expenses | | 1,500 |
| Advertising (printing costs) | | 687 |
| Officers salaries (3) | | 13,749 |
| Total Fixed Costs | | $213,021 |
| Variable costs: | | |
| Crew salaries (3) | | 5,355 |
| Fuel | | 54,000 |
| Maintenance reserves | | 27,000 |
| Routine maintenance | | 900 |
| Other variable expenses | | 1,500 |
| Transportation expenses | | 1,250 |
| Advertising expenses | | 5,502 |
| Total Variable Costs | | 95,507 |
| Total Fixed and Variable Costs | | $308,528 |

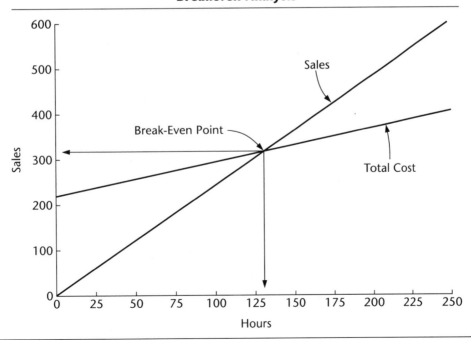

### Breakeven Analysis

## A Four-Year Projection of Earnings before Interest and Taxes
### on a 10% Growth Rate per Year

|  | Year 0 | Year 1 | Year 2 | Year 3 | Year 4 |
|---|---|---|---|---|---|
| Sales | $3,651,792.00 | $4,016,971.00 | $4,418,669.00 | $4,860,535.00 | $5,346,589.00 |
| Variable costs | (1,095,540.00) | (1,205,094.00) | (1,325,603.00) | (1,458,164.00) | (1,603,980.00) |
| Contribution margin | 2,556,252.00 | 2,811,877.00 | 3,093,066.00 | 3,402,371.00 | 3,742,609.00 |
| Fixed costs | (2,556,252.00) | (2,556,252.00) | (2,556,252.00) | (2,556,252.00) | (2,556,252.00) |
| Earnings before interest and taxes | $         0.00 | $ 255,625.00 | $ 536,814.00 | $ 846,119.00 | $1,186,357.00 |

## Graph Showing a 10% Growth Rate per Year

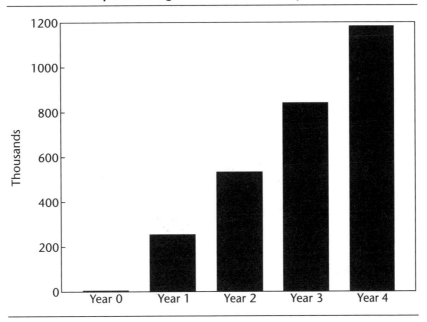

## Ranking of Busiest Metropolitan Areas

| | | 1980 Census | 1985 Projection | Percent Change 1980–85 |
|---|---|---|---|---|
| 1 | Dallas-Fort Worth, TX | 3,885 | 4,334 | 11.0% |
| 2 | Los Angeles-Anaheim-Riverdale, CA | 14,532 | 16,090 | 10.5 |
| 3 | Seattle-Tacoma, WA | 2,559 | 2,811 | 9.8 |
| 4 | Portland-Vancouver, OR-WA | 1,478 | 1,586 | 7.3 |
| 5 | San Francisco-Oakland-San Jose, CA | 6,253 | 6,679 | 6.8 |
| 6 | Philadelphia-Wilmington-Trenton, PA-NJ-DE-MD | 5,899 | 6,254 | 6.0 |
| 7 | Hartford-New Britain-Middletown, CT | 1,086 | 1,151 | 6.0 |
| 8 | Chicago-Gary-Lake County, IL-IN-WI | 8,066 | 8,417 | 4.4 |
| 9 | Denver-Boulder, CO | 1,848 | 1,928 | 4.3 |
| 10 | Cincinnati-Hamilton, OH-KY-IN | 1,744 | 1,817 | 4.2 |
| 11 | Miami-Fort Lauderdale, FL | 3,193 | 3,301 | 3.4 |
| 12 | New York-Northern New Jersey-Long Island, NY-NJ-CT | 18,067 | 18,272 | 1.0 |
| 13 | Houston-Galveston-Brazoria, TX | 3,711 | 3,715 | 0.1 |
| 14 | Cleveland-Akron-Lorain, OH | 2,760 | 2,747 | −0.5 |
| 15 | Detroit-Ann Arbor, MI | 4,665 | 4,626 | −0.8 |
| 16 | Milwaukee-Racine, WI | 1,097 | 1,586 | −1.3 |
| 17 | Pittsburgh-Beaver Valley, PA | 2,243 | 2,153 | −4.0 |
| 18 | Buffalo-Niagara Falls, NY | 1,189 | 1,139 | −4.2 |
| 19 | Boston-Lawrence-Salem, MA-NH | 4,172 | 3,779 | −0.4 |
| 20 | Providence-Pawtucket-Fall River, RI-MA | 1,142 | 944 | −17.3 |

*Note:* Consolidated Metropolitan Statistical Areas, ranked by percent change 1980–85, population in thousands.

*Source:* Census Bureau, Equifax Marketing Decision Systems.

## The Busiest Airports

*Chicago is the third most populous metropolitan area, but it has the country's busiest airport. Almost one-quarter of all airline passengers board in one of the top five airports.*

| Rank | Airport | Passengers | Percent |
|------|---------|------------|---------|
| 1 | Chicago (O'Hare), IL | 25,664,266 | 6.0% |
| 2 | Dallas/Ft. Worth (Regional), TX | 22,623,065 | 5.3 |
| 3 | Atlanta, GA | 20,397,697 | 4.8 |
| 4 | Los Angeles, CA | 18,583,292 | 4.3 |
| 5 | San Francisco, CA | 13,326,085 | 3.1 |
| 6 | Denver (Stapleton), CO | 12,320,246 | 2.9 |
| 7 | New York (La Guardia), NY | 10,839,833 | 2.5 |
| 8 | Phoenix, AZ | 10,166,095 | 2.4 |
| 9 | New York (John F. Kennedy), NY | 10,081,490 | 2.3 |
| 10 | Newark, NJ | 9,822,491 | 2.3 |
| 11 | Detroit (Wayne County), MI | 9,739,265 | 2.3 |
| 12 | Boston (Logan), MA | 9,661,258 | 2.2 |
| 13 | St. Louis, MO | 9,396,335 | 2.2 |
| 14 | Honolulu, Oahu, HI | 8,943,521 | 2.1 |
| 15 | Miami, FL | 8,591,936 | 2.0 |
| 16 | Minneapolis/St. Paul, MN | 8,469,115 | 2.0 |
| 17 | Pittsburgh, PA | 7,940,962 | 1.8 |
| 18 | Orlando, FL | 7,373,449 | 1.7 |
| 19 | Seattle-Tacoma, WA | 7,059,777 | 1.6 |
| 20 | Houston (Intercontinental), TX | 7,039,001 | 1.6 |
| 21 | Las Vegas (McCarran), NV | 7,026,900 | 1.6 |
| 22 | Charlotte, NC | 6,903,482 | 1.6 |
| 23 | Washington (National), DC | 6,895,563 | 1.6 |
| 24 | Philadelphia, PA | 6,247,289 | 1.5 |
| 25 | San Diego, CA | 5,317,177 | 1.2 |
|  | Total U.S. | 429,654,602 | 100.0% |

*Note:* Total revenue passengers enplaned annually for the 25 busiest airports and the United States, and percent of passengers enplaned in the United States, 1989.

*Source:* Airport Activity Statistics of Certificated Route Air Carriers, FAA, 1989.

**Excel Aire Salary Breakdown 1994**

| Title | Annual Salary |
|---|---|
| President | $ 75,000.00 |
| Vice president/marketing | 50,000.00 |
| Chief pilot | 40,000.00 |
| Total Officers' Salaries | $165,000.00 |
| | |
| *Contract Employees* | |
| 2 Captains | |
| ($20 p/hr @ 45 hrs p/mth × 2) | $ 21,600.00 |
| 3 Co-pilots | |
| ($13 p/hr @ 45 hrs p/mth × 3) | 21,060.00 |
| 1 Attendant | |
| ($10 p/hr @ 45 hrs p/mth) | 5,400.00 |
| Total Contract Salaries | $ 48,060.00 |
| Total Annual Salaries | $213,060.00 |

# 2

# BUSINESS PLAN FOR EL FLACO MEXICAN RESTAURANT

*Developed by*

**Emilio C. Ledesma**

# EXECUTIVE SUMMARY

## PRODUCT

El Flaco is a sit-down family restaurant specializing in a variety of Spanish and Aztec dishes. The menu will also include a limited number of seafood entrees prepared in the Spanish tradition. Also, El Flaco will feature both domestic and imported beers, soft drinks, and juices. The average price for a meal is $10.00. The restaurant will be open seven days a week for breakfast, lunch, and dinner.

## DIFFERENTIAL ADVANTAGE

El Flaco's competitive advantages lie in its convenient accessible location, high quality food items, and its emphasis on customer service. Furthermore, the restaurant offers pleasant sit-down dining service including meals at affordable prices. Also, El Flaco's location is in a new shopping mall which has ample parking.

## REQUIRED INVESTMENT

The anticipated start-up costs are $35,000 for restaurant furnishings and kitchen equipment plus $20,000 to launch El Flaco's opening advertising and promotional costs.

## ANTICIPATED SALES AND PROFITS

El Flaco's first-year sales are projected at $550,000 with a three-year sales peak of $650,000. Profits are projected at $14,080 the first year with a $16,640 peak at the end of three years. The break-even point is $525,000.

# LIST OF TABLES

# TABLE OF CONTENTS

# I. INTRODUCTION

In the years 1985 through 1989, 11,441 restaurants ended in financial ruin in this country and many others are losing money. Although the reasons are varied, one of the main causes for failure is a lack of pertinent knowledge about setting up, operating, and managing a financially successful restaurant. The following is a business plan for opening up a new restaurant that documents the major planning issues.

## A. The Product

El Flaco is a sit-down family restaurant that specializes in a variety of authentic Mexican dishes. The restaurant's menu will feature Spanish and Aztec dishes that originated in Mexico's central area. The menu will include several seafood entrees prepared in the Spanish tradition. In addition, El Flaco will feature a number of domestic and imported beverages such as soft drinks, juices, and beer.

In keeping with the times, El Flaco's menu items will be prepared in line with health consciousness. For example, pinto beans are traditionally refried with lard and heavy doses of salt. However, El Flaco's cooks will rely more on the tastes of roasted chillies instead of salt, and olive oil instead of lard to prepare the various food items.

The restaurant's target market will be the middle-income households who are employed as professionals in the service industry. El Flaco will rely on low prices and excellent service as strategies over competitors. Furthermore, the restaurant is committed to using only high quality ingredients in each of its menu entrees.

Low prices, high service, and quality appear to be redundant goals that are stated by every new entrepreneur. However, in a city such as Redondo, with a high population density, many businesses seem to adopt the notion that they have a "captured" clientele and begin to "cut corners" to increase their profit margins. These "corners" are in the form of low quality products and services. Therefore, as elementary as they may seem, the emphasis of this business plan is on pricing, service, and quality as the cornerstones to achieve a competitive advantage.

## B. Mexican Restaurant Industry

Mexican dinner chains are enjoying an average 15 to 20 percent annual growth at a time when the restaurant industry is flat. Mexican restaurants bring in an average of four times the revenues of a steakhouse of comparable size.[1]

Besides good food and service, a key ingredient to success is low prices. Since tacos and tortillas are less expensive than beef, the Mexican restaurant can afford to charge less per meal than the steakhouse and still enjoy high profit margins. With the current troubled economic climate, this becomes an important competitive advantage.

## C. Restaurant Industry Background

Food service continues to lead other industries in total sales such as housing, automaking, and electronics. The food industry continues to gain a greater share of all food dollars spent in America, moving up to 45 percent versus 55 percent for retail food which represents a gain of 20 share points since 1960.[2] As these figures show, there is room for entry into the restaurant marketplace.

In spite of the bright picture for the restaurant industry, careful planning is a prerequisite for success. Many restaurants are being shaken out of the industry due to heavy debt, an excess of outlets, and stiff competition. This is because recessions tend to keep Americans from dining out. The successful restaurants are those who have midprices and are perceived by the customer as offering price value entrees.

Many larger restaurant chains are embarking on a strategy of offering "meal deals" and giveaways to lure customers. Moreover, these large chains are quick to either open new outlets as their weaker competitors fold or acquire their financially distressed competitors.[3]

Industry followers are projecting modest sales growth for restaurants. These industry watchers stress that the companies that are loaded with debt are in for tough times.

Also, demographics will continue to favor the midprice chains as baby boomers with kids seek out such eateries. Much competition will come from large fast-food chains who are launching price wars which threaten to cut everyone's profit margins.[4]

The big bright spot for everyone is that labor and commodity costs will go down as the economic recession continues. This should be a big break for restaurants, whose other key operating costs, particularly promotions, seem to be heading up.


## II. SITUATION ANALYSIS

### A. The Situational Environs

#### 1. Demand and Demand Trends

Despite the current recessionary times, the restaurant business remains strong. According to Rukeyser, Americans eat out 3.7 times a week for a total of $45 billion spent in meals in restaurants. About 42 percent of American's food dollar goes to restaurants which is an increase over 1952 when it was 25.4 percent. An analysis of Copely readers of the Los Angeles market reports that the average annual expenditure in restaurants per capita is $660.63. Mexican restaurants represent $2.4 billion of the total $156.4 billion Americans spend in restaurants.[5]

Moreover, commercial eating places, or restaurants open to the public, are the fastest growing segment of the food-service industry. Studies show that changes in how we live and work are having a profound effect on the industry. Specifically, our shorter work week, two careers, and single-person households are causing us to eat out more frequently.

According to the Small Business Administration, 90 percent of a given restaurant's customers live within a one-mile radius of the restaurant's location. This is good news in Redondo Beach due to the city's high population density.

Table I lists the annual per capita sales for restaurants and various retail stores within the South Bay. The table highlights the sales potential of restaurants in the area.

#### 2. Economics and Business Conditions

Redondo Beach was incorporated in April 29, 1892. The city is located 18 miles southwest of Los Angeles and 424 miles south of San Francisco. Redondo Beach lies within the South Bay beach area. This area is characterized by an affluent mix of young professionals who reside in the beach cities of Hermosa, Manhattan, Redondo, and Palos Verdes. Due to the harbor and LAX, many high-tech corporations have been drawn to the area and have established their headquarters in the South Bay. This has resulted in a highly educated and productive market area.

**Table I   Annual per Capita Sales
of South Bay Retail Businesses**

| Business | Per Capita | Annual Sales |
|---|---|---|
| Department stores | $   713.01 | $278,356,252 |
| Variety stores | 47.76 | 18,645,313 |
| Grocery stores | 1,245.47 | 486,226,506 |
| Convenience stores | 79.58 | 31,067,714 |
| Apparel stores | 325.02 | 126,886,508 |
| Shoe stores | 54.44 | 21,253,158 |
| Jewelry stores | 65.75 | 25,668,537 |
| Furniture stores | 126.77 | 49,490,501 |
| Appliance stores | 41.97 | 16,384,920 |
| Restaurants | 660.63 | 257,907,309 |
| Drug stores | 227.43 | 88,787,762 |
| Liquor stores | 141.48 | 55,233,226 |
| Garden stores | 18.25 | 7,124,727 |
| Paint stores | 21.48 | 8,385,706 |
| Hardware stores | 49.75 | 19,422,201 |
| Flooring stores | 44.86 | 17,513,165 |

*Source:* Urban Decision Systems, 1989 Estimates, *Retail Potential Report.*

### 3. Demographics[6]

The *County and City Data Book for 1988* lists a total population for Redondo Beach of 63,830 with a density per square mile of 10,295. During the years between 1980 and 1986, the city's population has increased 11.8 percent. The city has 6.2 square miles and has a coastal border along the Pacific Ocean.

The city's population is evenly divided between males and females. The racial mix is 51,260 white and 6,542 Spanish. The balance of the population consists of 630 Blacks, 2,070 Asians, 451 American Indians, and 2,682 other.

Per capita income has grown from $10,569 in 1980 to $17,313 in 1985. This is considerably higher than the county averages. Los Angeles County's per capita income was $8,303 in 1980 and $11,842 for 1985. The median household income is $21,828, while the median family income is $21,786. In Los Angeles County, the median household income is $17,551 and the median family income is $21,125.

The number of persons at the poverty level in Redondo is 4,405 which represents 6.9 percent of the city's population. In Los Angeles County, the total poverty level is 984,816 or 13.1 percent of the county's population.

There are 13,778 households in Redondo Beach which make up a civilian labor force of 35,590. The majority of these individuals are employed as managers, professionals, and in service-related occupations. The totals for the three groups are 10,189, 12,056, and 3,612 respectively. The balance of the labor force are employed in manufacturing, as laborers, or are self employed.

The educational attainment levels in Redondo are quite high compared to the county. The number of high school graduates is 21,643 or 37.9 percent of the total population, whereas the county has 2,275,804 high school graduates, which is 30 percent of the population. Also, the number of college graduates for Redondo is 8,764 which is 15.3 percent of the city's population. This compares to 818,658 or 10.9 percent for the county.[7]

## B. The Neutral Environs

### 1. Financial Environment

Presently, the outlook to obtain low-cost funding is quite promising. In its efforts to spur the economy, the Federal Reserve Board has embarked on a policy of "easy funding" supported by low interest rates. The financial section of *The Wall Street Journal* for February 7, 1992 reports bank lending interest rates hovering between 8 and 8 ½ percent. This is due to the board's reduction of the discount rate to 3 ½ percent which drove down the prime rate to 6 ½ percent. Truly, this is an ideal time to obtain low-cost funding.

Another source of funds is through the Small Business Administration (SBA). The SBA makes loans through private lenders (banks) which are guaranteed up to 90 percent for amounts up to $750,000. Also, the SBA has a number of lending incentive programs for small businesses for amounts under $50,000. However, before applying for an SBA loan, applicants are legally required to first seek financing from a bank or another lending institution.[8]

### 2. Government Environment

Research did not uncover any particular federal legislation that was either detrimental or advantageous to the restaurant industry. However, a review of Redondo Beach's city zoning ordinances for businesses shows they are oriented towards concerns relating to land use and parking standards. This is understandable in view of the city's limited space coupled with its high population density.

Redondo's municipal ordinance No. 2643, Section 8, establishes parking rules for restaurants that it feels are necessary to protect the health, safety, and general welfare of the public. The ordinance stipulates that there shall be one space for every four seats but not less than one space for each 50 square feet of gross floor seating area plus aisles. This same rule applies to both bar and cocktail lounges. The ordinance was adopted and approved by the city's officials on November 5, 1991.

## C. The Competitor Environs

The *1987 Census of Retail Trade* indicates that the city of Redondo Beach is host to 117 eating places. These businesses produce an annual sales volume of $63.2 million, which averages to $540,200 per business establishment. Of the 117 businesses, 31 are single proprietorships and 21 are in the form of partnerships.

Redondo Beach's restaurants range from small "hole in the wall" types to large upscale diners. For example, there is "Little Joe's" along Pacific Coast Highway that provides take-out food such as hamburgers and the like. Although this small food place has very limited seating, it is very popular with the people in the area. On weekends, it not uncommon to see long lines of people waiting for seating. Little Joe's popularity is primarily due to its great quality food and low prices.

### 1. Redondo Beach Pier

Most of the "fancier" restaurants are located within Redondo's pier area. The beach pier area attracts numerous tourists year round which makes it ideal for the restaurants. One of the older restaurants along the pier is "Tony's." The founder of Tony's began his entrepreneurship by selling fresh fist off a cart. The restaurant features a number of standard and exotic seafood entrees at upscale prices.

Across from Tony's is El Torrito's Mexican restaurant. This restaurant is part of a chain that is located throughout the Southwest and includes a number of well-known restaurant names such as the Red Onion. The restaurant features quality Mexican food dishes at prices that are higher than average for Mexican food.

### 2. Restaurant Row

Another area of restaurant concentration is along Redondo's Harbor Drive which is the road that leads into the pier. This area is referred to as "restaurant row" by the locals. The "row" has a number of upscale restaurants such as the Cheesecake Factory, Beachbum Berts, and the Red Onion. Most of these restaurants are expensive and cater to the upscale market in the beach area.

Although these restaurants have large parking facilities, parking is a problem for patrons. The parking has to be paid for and many restaurants do not validate parking. In addition, the lots are usually full on weekends and patrons can spend a considerable amount of time looking for a space.

Another major problem for these restaurants has to do with crime. A number of local youth gangs frequent the pier which has adversely affected the local restaurant business. There have been a number of crime incidents including auto theft and rape. A few years back, a patron of Tony's was stabbed to death while waiting in line for seating in the restaurant. Crime has been so rampant that the Redondo Beach police have an outpost at the pier's entrance.

## D. The Company Environs

### 1. Experience

Although this will be my first business venture, I have considerable experience dealing with the public. I have eighteen years' experience in retail sales with Sears Roebuck and Company. I have managed a number of retail departments and was responsible for profit, inventory, and payroll control. Although operating a retail business differs from that of a restaurant, I consider my experience in business operations and working with the public as an important business asset.

Also, I have a business degree with an emphasis in marketing. My attendance in business college has been in recent times which means that my business education is current and timely. I have completed business courses dealing with current business practices, strategies, and theories.

### 2. Financial

In the financial area, I have very little debt and a spotless credit history. My liquidity and credit history should enable me to obtain the necessary financing to operate my new business. I have a sizable amount of cash in my savings account which I have accumulated in anticipation of starting my new business.

Start-up costs are estimated at $35,000 for supplies and equipment plus an additional $50,000 for promotional advertising, beginning working capital, and other miscellaneous cash expenses. The source for starting costs was obtained from Mr. Rick Bernstein who owns Denny's Fixture Co, Inc., which is a company that specializes in restaurant equipment sales. The firm, located in Gardena, California, also offers consultation services that include planning and designing layouts for new restaurants.

These funds will be obtained through a commercial bank on an asset form basis. Although most commercial banks shy away from first stage working capital loans, they will be willing to approve such a loan if the borrower has enough collateral to use as security.[9] In the case of El Flaco, I shall use my home and personal assets as collateral to secure my loan.

## III. TARGET MARKET

The selected target market is individuals employed as managers, professionals, and those in service occupations. These groups comprise the single and family median income group, with incomes over \$20,000. Moreover, they make up the majority of the city's household families with an average size of 2.82. The target market includes all age groups, male and female, and does not take into account any race distinction.

The following two points were made earlier in this report: (1) Redondo Beach has a population density of over 10,000 per square mile and (2) research reveals that most of a given restaurant's patronage reside within one square mile of the establishment's location. Therefore, marketing efforts, such as promotion, will be focused on the group of residents localized near the restaurant.

However, the balance of the city's population will also need to be considered in all of El Flaco's marketing plans. This is because the bay cities' residents are very mobile and will commute across town to patronize their favorite restaurant. Moreover, the beach cities that border Redondo are within close proximity and also have a high population density. Therefore, although promotional efforts will focus on the restaurant's immediate area, this plan also includes promotional efforts to tap the broader beach area market.

# IV. PROBLEMS AND OPPORTUNITIES

## A. Problems

One of the major problems (or challenges) relates to competition due to the large number of restaurants in the beach area. There exist just a few locations in the South Bay where large famous name restaurants, including Mexican, are concentrated. El Flaco's location is less than one mile from these dining centers—the previously discussed restaurant row and Redondo Beach's pier. These are the restaurants that are patronized by the residents when they want to go out for a "nice dinner."

## B. Opportunities

In spite of the nearby competition, a number of favorable factors increase El Flaco's opportunities for success. El Flaco's location is off the Pacific Coast Highway which means easy access to the restaurant's location. Also, the location's shopping complex has very large parking capacity that patrons do not have to pay for. Moreover, El Flaco's location does not have the stigma of being located in a crime area. As mentioned, the pier location has a reputation of not being a safe place late at night.

These are positive factors that will enhance El Flaco's opportunity for success, which will be exploited through its marketing campaign. All this, of course, assumes that El Flaco will feature quality meals and service at reasonable prices.

# V. BUSINESS OBJECTIVE AND GOALS

## A. Market Share

The market share objective is to capture 1.03 percent of Redondo Beach's restaurant market. The total dining sales in Redondo is \$63.2 million; therefore, a market penetration of 1.03 percent would yield a targeted sales goal of \$650,000.

### B. Sales Objectives

The sales objective is to attain an annual sales volume of $650,000. Since El Flaco will be a brand-new entity, it is projected that the ultimate sales objective will be attained at the end of a three-year period. The sales goal for the first year is $550,000 with annual growth increments of 10 percent.

### C. Profit Objectives

The profit goals are to achieve a 3.2 percent gross profit percent of sales before taxes. As with sales, these profit goals will take three years to attain. However, it is estimated that the first year's profits will be in the 3 percent range. Profits will continue to improve over the three-year period as the restaurant approaches its full operating potential by developing a regular clientele, economies of scale, and historical cost control standards.

## VI. MARKETING STRATEGIES

The strategies to achieve the restaurant's marketing goals and objectives will focus on providing customers with a pleasant dining atmosphere, high quality food products, and excellent service. This strategy calls for close screening and selection of all restaurant personnel to ensure they have the necessary training and experience in dealing with the public.

### A. Customer Service

Only individuals with experience will be hired as waitresses and waiters. Although El Flaco is a Mexican restaurant, the practice employed by many other Mexican eating places of hiring only Hispanic help will not be followed. The only prerequisite is that the applicants have prior restaurant experience, a positive disposition, and have good customer service skills.

To locate help, the restaurant will feature advertisements in the local newspapers announcing the availability of positions as cooks, cashiers, busboys, waiters, and waitresses. The advertisements will list the job qualifications, company benefits, and starting pay. To attract high quality people, the restaurant will offer a higher than average starting pay.

### B. Quality Meals

El Flaco is committed to serving high quality meal products. Quality and freshness will be the guiding principles when selecting vendors for the restaurant's food stock.

### C. Competitive Prices

A preliminary survey of the few Mexican restaurants in the area reveals that their entrees are priced higher than average for Mexican dishes. For instance, El Torrito's dinner menu prices average at $8.95. Add to this amount the cost of a beverage and an appetizer, the price can easily exceed $15.00 per individual. El Flaco's price strategy is to be priced below competition.

## VII. MARKETING TACTICS

### A. Promotional Format

A sustained and concentrated promotional advertising effort is planned in the entertainment sections of the local beach newspapers. This will be especially crucial when El Flaco first opens. The beginning format of advertisements will be to announce the restaurant's opening date and location. The copy will also include general information about the restaurant's menu and price structure.

Each advertisement will feature a "special" price reduction on one of the main entrees. This will consist of coupon specials such as "two meals for the price of one" and coupons for a certain amount off the price of a meal. The coupon specials will contain expiration dates which will be valid on a specific day of the week. At first, the coupon specials will be designed to introduce the restaurant in order to develop a clientele. After the restaurant has been established, the coupon specials will continue but with the purpose of bringing in business during slack periods.

### B. Promotional Vehicle

The selected promotional media is *The Daily Breeze* which has the widest distribution in Redondo Beach. The bay area has three major community newspapers: *The Daily Breeze, The Beach Reporter,* and *The Easy Reader.* Table II lists the readership of these publications.

Table II illustrates the dominance of *The Daily Breeze* in the target area. The figures indicate that 35.5 percent of Manhattan, Hermosa, and Redondo Beach read or looked at an issue of the *The Daily Breeze* "yesterday." Over 17 percent read or looked into The Beach Reporter in the past week, and 15.5 percent read or looked into *The Easy Reader* in the past week. In other words, one issue of *The Daily Breeze* has more than doubled the weekly readership of the competitors.

In addition, the circulation for *The Daily Breeze* includes the cities of El Segundo, Gardena, Harbor City, Hawthorne, Hermosa, Lawndale, Lomita, Manhattan Beach, Palos Verdes Estates, Rolling Hills Estates, and Torrance. The paper has grown 64.5 percent since 1969 compared to a growth rate of 8.9 percent for the *Los Angeles Times.* Much of this growth is related to the city's population growth over the past 10 years.

*The Daily Breeze* is part of Copley Los Angeles Newspapers, which publishes three daily afternoon papers in the South Bay. Retailers can purchase advertising space in the paper on a monthly contract basis for a period of 12 consecutive months. The advantage to the monthly contract is that the paper allows discounts for retailers who run features on a frequent basis. These discounts can be up to 50 percent, depending on the number of advertisements.

Also, the newspaper has a special entertainment insert that is ideal for restaurant advertisements. The insert, called "Lifestyle," features entertainment, food, and leisure activity

**Table II   Newspaper Reader Distribution
in the South Bay**

| Newspaper | Readership |
|-----------|------------|
| The Daily Breeze | 34.7% |
| The Beach Reporter | 17.4 |
| The Easy Reader | 15.5 |

*Source:* 1991 Scarborough Report.

news. Moreover, the paper has a special Friday edition that is dedicated to entertainment and restaurants.

### C. Promotional Fliers

Another promotional vehicle is the use of advertising fliers that are either stuffed in mailboxes or hand delivered to residents in the market area. Domino's Pizza uses this strategy on a regular basis with great results. The idea is to hire school-age kids that either deliver the fliers to residents' mailboxes or drop them off at their doorsteps. This is an inexpensive strategy to reach the target market with the costs being the printing of the advertisements and the hiring of the kids to deliver them. Therefore, El Flaco's marketing efforts will incorporate the use of fliers to supplement the advertising plan.

## VIII. IMPLEMENTATION AND CONTROL

The first step in developing controls is to project El Flaco's annual sales. From the sales estimate, we can then proceed to calculate develop additional financial controls which will lead towards an overall budget in the form of a pro forma balance sheet and profit and loss statement. Table III is a comparative analysis of sales of various food-service operations.

Using the categories in the table, El Flaco would fall somewhere between a "sit-down, short-order" restaurant and a "fast-service, family-service" restaurant category. The average sales range in these categories is $542,000 to $829,000.

**Table III   Comparative Food Service Sales**

| Type of Food Service | Average Sales per Year |
|---|---|
| Fried chicken take-out | $ 280,000 |
| Hamburger chain | 397,000 |
| Combined sit-down and lunch counter | 464,000 |
| Root beer, hot dog take-out | 104,000 |
| Hamburger take-out | 304,000 |
| Soft ice cream and hamburger take-out | 154,000 |
| Hamburger take-out | 394,000 |
| Sit-down lunch counter | 156,000 |
| *Quality Family Restaurants* | |
| Sit-down using convenience foods | 901,000 |
| Donuts and limited short order | 264,000 |
| Family sit-down cafeteria | 375,000 |
| Pizza | 276,000 |
| Sit-down, short order | 542,000 |
| Hot dog specialty, fast food | 236,000 |
| High level, quality personality restaurant | 1,350,000 |
| Family sit-down steak house | 2,000,000 |
| Fast service, inexpensive steaks, family service | 829,000 |
| Fine high quality restaurant | 1,250,000 |
| Quality seafood family restaurant | 1,525,000 |
| Fine restaurant, family and business people | 910,000 |

*Source:* Dewey A. Dyer, *So You Want to Start a Restaurant?*

Additionally, the *1987 Census of Retail Trade* for California indicates that the average sales for 133 eating establishments in Redondo Beach is $72 million dollars, which averages to $541,000 each. Moreover, El Flaco is planned to have a seating capacity of 60 (15 tables ✕ 4 seats).

El Flaco is planned to be open seven days a week for breakfast, lunch, and dinner with an average sales check of $10 including a beverage. Therefore, assuming full capacity and focusing only on the main meal periods, the restaurant will serve 180 individuals per day for total sales of $1,800. This calculates into a total annual sales volume of $657,000.

Since El Flaco is a new business and will need at least two years to attain its full sales potential the projected sales for the first year will be on the conservative side. However, the subsequent sales plan for the next two years will be projected based on a 10 percent increase per year. Therefore, El Flaco's first year's sales are projected at $550,000. Although this figure is conservative, it is a reasonable estimate taking into account available data and El Flaco's capacity.

The 1987-88 Edition of Dun & Bradstreet's *Industry Norms and Key Business Ratios* lists a number of industry standards for various account balances.[10] These are annualized total from the Bradstreet report for "Eating Places" of establishments with a sales volume of $626,000 per year.

The following sales and profit projections represent El Flaco's initial opening budgets. Although the figures may be under- or overinflated, they are a start towards gaining financial control over the new operations. As time passes and actual figures come in, these budgets will be revised accordingly.

## A. Income Norms

As Table IV indicates, a major cost factor for restaurants is in the category of wages and salaries. In view of this, El Flaco's waitress and bus boy personnel will consist primarily of part-time help. The use of part-time help provides additional control measures for this cost category in that their working hours can be adjusted according to sales volume.

**Table IV    Income Norms**

| Income Statement Norms for Eating Places | Percent to Sales |
|---|---|
| Cost of goods sold | 42.8% |
| Wages and salaries | 21.2 |
| Repairs | 1.7 |
| Bad debts | 0.1 |
| Rent | 5.4 |
| Taxes | 3.9 |
| Interest | 1.5 |
| Depreciation | 3.7 |
| Advertising | 3.0 |
| Benefits | 0.8 |
| Utilities | 2.5 |
| Supplies | 2.9 |
| Other expenses | 7.3 |
| Net profit before tax | 3.2 |
| Total | 100.0 |

*Source:* Dun & Bradstreet, *Industry Norms and Key Business Ratios,* 1987–88 ed.

Also of interest from Table IV is the very low pre-tax profit of 3.2 percent for restaurants of El Flaco's size (volume). This underscores the need to control expenses in order to maintain a profitable operation.

## B. Financial Ratios

It should be noted that the income norms in Table IV were compared with other sources such as the *Almanac of Business and Financial Ratios* by Leo Troy, and RMA's *Annual Statement Studies* for fiscal year ending 1990. For the most part, the restaurant industry standards from these publications did not conflict with each other. Most likely, this is due to the dining industry's longevity and business stability. This same double-checking approach was applied for all the subsequent pro forma statements, which were based on industry standards.

The financial ratios in Table V will be used as benchmarks to appraise El Flaco operating performance once the restaurant has opened. Although these ratios are industry averages, they can be used as key indicators of emerging problems which require corrective action.

## C. Balance Sheet Norms

As mentioned before, the industrial averages shown in Table VI will be used as starting points in developing El Flaco's pro forma financial reports. The approach is to begin with industry norms, then adjust them to actuals once operations begin.

Using the preceding data, the pro forma balance sheet and profit and loss statements for El Flaco are developed as follows.

**Table V    Industry Financial Ratios**

| Financial Ratios for Eating Places | Percent to Sales |
|---|---|
| *Solvency* | |
| Quick ratio | 0.7% |
| Current ratio | 1.2 |
| Current liabilities to net worth | 43.4 |
| Current liabilities to inventory | 270.3 |
| Total liabilities to net worth | 89.7 |
| Fixed assets to net worth | 99.4 |
| *Efficiency* | |
| Collection period | 5.5 |
| Sales to inventory | 62.5 |
| Assets to sales | 34.0 |
| Sales to NWC | 17.3 |
| Accounts payable to sales | 2.7 |
| *Profitability* | |
| Return on sales | 3.6 |
| Return on assets | 7.3 |
| Return on net worth | 15.1 |

*Source:* Dun & Bradstreet, *Industry Norms and Key Business Ratios,* 1987–88 ed.

**Table VI    Industry Balance Sheet Norms**

| Balance Sheet Norms for Eating Places | Percent to Sales |
|---|---|
| Cash | 16.1% |
| Accounts receivable | 4.1 |
| Notes receivable | 1.1 |
| Inventory | 7.2 |
| Other current | 5.2 |
| Total Current | 33.7 |
| Fixed assets | 35.5 |
| Other noncurrent | 30.8 |
| Total Assets | 100.0 |
| Accounts payable | 8.2 |
| Bank loans | 0.7 |
| Notes payable | 4.1 |
| Other current | 14.8 |
| Total Current | 27.8 |
| Other long term | 26.5 |
| Deferred credits | 0.2 |
| Net worth | 45.5 |
| Total Liabilities and Net Worth | 100.0 |

*Source:* Dun & Bradstreet, *Industry Norms and Key Business Ratios,* 1987–88 ed.

## D. Pro Forma Income Statement

Sales for the first year are projected to be $550,000 with a modest net profit of $14,080. However, as shown in Table VII it is projected that El Flaco's sales volume will increase at rate of 10 percent for a two-year period, peaking at $650,000 in 1995.

It is doubtful that sales will grow much beyond the 1995 projection. This is due to the restaurant's seating and operating capacity. The restaurant's location is being acquired on a lease basis which prohibits any building expansion to accommodate future sales growth.

## E. Pro Forma Balance Sheet

The pro forma balance sheet (Table VIII) indicates long-term notes of $49,555 and short term debt of $7,667. The long term debt consists of start-up costs of $35,000 for restaurant furnishings and kitchen equipment. The balance is to finance other miscellaneous start-up costs. The short-term debt is to finance preopening inventory purchases, advertising, and operating supplies.

## F. Break-Even Analysis

El Flaco's break-even point is calculated at an annual sales volume of $525,555. At an average meal ticket of $10, this means El Flaco would have to serve 52,555 patrons a year or 144 patrons a day. If the seating capacity is 60 then El Flaco's daily capacity is 180 patrons for the three-meal period which confirms the veracity of the break-even analysis (Table IX).

The "Other Variable Costs" calculation is based on using 7.5 percent of sales to include several expenses related to keeping the business open (reference, Brown, *How to Set Up, Operate, and Manage a Financially Successful Restaurant*). These other variable expenses include those shown in Table X.

**Table VII    Pro Forma Income Statement**

| El Flaco Three-Year Pro Forma Income Statement | 1993 | 1994 | 1995 |
|---|---|---|---|
| Net sales | $550,000 | $600,000 | $650,000 |
| Cost of operations | 235,400 | 256,800 | 278,200 |
| Gross Profit | $314,600 | $343,200 | $371,800 |
| Salaries and wages | 116,600 | 127,200 | 137,800 |
| Repairs | 9,350 | 10,200 | 11,050 |
| Bad debts | 550 | 600 | 650 |
| Rent | 29,700 | 32,400 | 35,100 |
| Taxes | 21,450 | 23,400 | 25,350 |
| Interest | 8,250 | 9,000 | 9,750 |
| Depreciation | 20,350 | 22,200 | 24,050 |
| Advertising | 16,500 | 18,000 | 19,500 |
| Benefits | 4,400 | 4,800 | 5,200 |
| Utilities | 13,750 | 15,000 | 16,250 |
| Supplies | 15,950 | 17,400 | 18,850 |
| Other expenses | 40,150 | 43,800 | 47,450 |
| Total Expenses | $297,000 | $324,000 | $351,000 |
| Pretax profit | 17,600 | 19,200 | 20,800 |
| Taxes | 3,520 | 3,840 | 4,160 |
| Net Profit after Tax | $ 14,080 | $ 15,360 | $ 16,640 |

**Table VIII   Pro Forma Balance Sheet**

| *El Flaco Three-Year*<br>*Pro Forma Balance Sheet* | *1993* | *1994* | *1995* |
|---|---|---|---|
| Cash | $ 30,107 | $ 32,844 | $ 35,581 |
| Accounts receivable | 7,667 | 8,364 | 9,061 |
| Notes receivable | 2,057 | 2,244 | 2,431 |
| Inventory | 13,464 | 14,688 | 15,912 |
| Other current | 9,724 | 10,608 | 11,492 |
| Total Current | 63,019 | 68,748 | 74,477 |
| Fixed assets | 66,385 | 72,420 | 78,455 |
| Other noncurrent | 57,596 | 62,832 | 68,068 |
| Total Assets | $187,000 | $204,000 | $221,000 |
| Accounts payable | $ 15,334 | $ 16,728 | $ 18,122 |
| Bank loans | 1,309 | 1,428 | 1,547 |
| Notes payable | 7,667 | 8,364 | 9,061 |
| Other current | 27,676 | 30,192 | 32,708 |
| Total Current | 51,968 | 56,712 | 61,438 |
| Other long term | 49,555 | 54,060 | 58,565 |
| Deferred credits | 374 | 408 | 442 |
| Net worth | 85,085 | 92,820 | 100,555 |
| Total Liabilities and Net Worth | $187,000 | $204,000 | $221,000 |

**Table IX   Break-Even Analysis Chart**

| *El Flaco Three-Year*<br>*Break-Even Analysis* | *1993* | *1994* | *1995* |
|---|---|---|---|
| Projected sales | $550,000 | $600,000 | $650,000 |
| Cost of operations | 231,000 | 252,000 | 273,000 |
| Other variable costs | 41,250 | 45,000 | 48,750 |
| Total variable costs | $272,250 | $297,000 | $321,750 |
| Variable costs % to sales | 49.5 | 49.5 | 49.5 |
| Fixed costs | $260,150 | $260,150 | $260,150 |
| Break-Even Point | $525,555 | $525,555 | $525,555 |

**Table X   Industry Expense Norms**

| *Direct Expense* | *Percent to Sales* |
|---|---|
| Advertising | .6 |
| Cleaning and maintenance | 1.4 |
| Laundry | 1.5 |
| Equipment maintenance | .2 |
| Promotion | .4 |
| Repairs | .4 |
| Restaurant supplies | 1.0 |

## G. Break-Even Graph

El Flaco's break-even point is illustrated by the following graph. The point at which the fixed costs line intercepts with total costs indicates the break-even point for El Flaco. Note that this point falls midway between volume levels of $500,000 and $600,000 which has previously been calculated at $525,555.

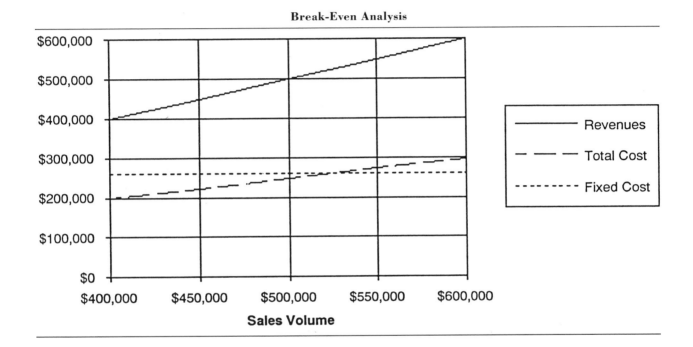

**Break-Even Analysis**

## H. Cash Flow Projections

The cash flow projections that follow indicate a need for some short-term borrowing at specific times during the year. This is mainly because of payments for interest and tax amounts which are due on a quarterly basis.

Research indicates that the restaurant industry sales volume is somewhat static throughout the year and does not peak like a retail department store would due to holiday shopping.[11] However, there does appear to be a slight peak during the summer vacation periods and towards the October through December fall holiday periods. Therefore, to arrive at a more accurate projection of monthly sales, these variances in monthly sales distributions were applied to develop the following monthly cash flow forecasts.

## I. Preopening Timetable

The timetable shown in Table XIV is a list of major milestones that must be met prior to opening El Flaco. The activities are arranged by earliest date order and include start and end dates. The table also includes some follow-up activities after El Flaco's opening which consist of reviewing operational plans and adjusting budgeted expense and income accounts to actual sales. As indicated, El Flaco's opening is scheduled for January 1, 1993.

### Table XI    1993 Cash Flow Forecast ($1,000)

| B.O.S by month | 6% | 7% | 7% | 7% | 8% | 8% | 9% | 9% | 9% | 10% | 12% | 100% |
|---|---|---|---|---|---|---|---|---|---|---|---|---|
| Month | Jan | Feb | Mar | Apr | May | Jun | July | Aug | Sept | Oct | Nov | Dec |
| Annual sales = $550 | | | | | | | | | | | | |
| Cash outflows | $33 | $39 | $39 | $39 | $47 | $44 | $44 | $50 | $50 | $55 | $55 | $63 |
| Purchases | 14 | 19 | 19 | 19 | 23 | 22 | 22 | 25 | 25 | 25 | 27 | 31 |
| Wages | 10 | 10 | 10 | 10 | 10 | 10 | 10 | 10 | 10 | 10 | 10 | 10 |
| Other expenses | 2 | 3 | 3 | 3 | 3 | 3 | 3 | 4 | 4 | 4 | 4 | 5 |
| Interest | | | 2 | | | 2 | | | 2 | | | 2 |
| Tax | | | 5 | | | 5 | | | 5 | | | 5 |
| Start-up costs | 35 | | | | | | | | | | | |
| Total Outflows | $ 62 | $32 | $39 | $32 | $37 | $42 | $35 | $38 | $45 | $38 | $41 | $53 |
| Net Cast Gain/Loss | $(29) | $ 7 | $ 0 | $ 7 | $10 | $ 2 | $ 9 | $11 | $ 4 | $11 | $14 | $10 |
| Desired cash level | 5 | 6 | 6 | 6 | 8 | 7 | 7 | 8 | 8 | 8 | 9 | 10 |
| Cumulative Surplus Cash | $(34) | $ (1) | $ (6) | $ 1 | $ 2 | $ (5) | $ 2 | $ 3 | $(4) | $ 3 | $ 5 | $ 0 |

### Table XII    1994 Cash Flow Forecast ($1,000)

| B.O.S by month | 6% | 7% | 7% | 7% | 8% | 8% | 9% | 9% | 9% | 10% | 12% | 100% |
|---|---|---|---|---|---|---|---|---|---|---|---|---|
| Month | Jan | Feb | Mar | Apr | May | Jun | July | Aug | Sept | Oct | Nov | Dec |
| Annual sales = $600 | | | | | | | | | | | | |
| Cash outflows | $36 | $42 | $42 | $42 | $51 | $48 | $48 | $54 | $54 | $54 | $60 | $69 |
| Purchases | 15 | 21 | 21 | 21 | 25 | 24 | 24 | 27 | 30 | 30 | 30 | 34 |
| Wages | 11 | 11 | 11 | 11 | 11 | 11 | 11 | 11 | 11 | 11 | 11 | 11 |
| Other expenses | 3 | 3 | 3 | 3 | 4 | 4 | 4 | 4 | 4 | 4 | 4 | 5 |
| Interest | | | 2 | | | 2 | | | 2 | | | 2 |
| Tax | | | 5 | | | 5 | | | 5 | | | 5 |
| Start-up costs | | | | | | | | | | | | |
| Total Outflows | $29 | $35 | $42 | $35 | $40 | $45 | $38 | $42 | $49 | $42 | $45 | $57 |
| Net Cast Gain/Loss | $ 7 | $ 7 | $ 0 | $ 7 | $11 | $ 3 | $10 | $12 | $ 5 | $12 | $15 | $12 |
| Desired cash level | 6 | 7 | 7 | 7 | 8 | 8 | 8 | 9 | 9 | 9 | 10 | 11 |
| Cumulative Surplus Cash | $ 1 | $ 0 | $ (7) | $ 0 | $ 3 | $ (5) | $ 2 | $ 3 | $(4) | $ 3 | $ 5 | $ 1 |

### Table XIII    1995 Cash Flow Forecast ($1,000)

| B.O.S by month | 6% | 7% | 7% | 7% | 8% | 8% | 9% | 9% | 9% | 10% | 12% | 100% |
|---|---|---|---|---|---|---|---|---|---|---|---|---|
| Month | Jan | Feb | Mar | Apr | May | Jun | July | Aug | Sept | Oct | Nov | Dec |
| Annual sales = $650 | | | | | | | | | | | | |
| Cash outflows | $40 | $46 | $46 | $46 | $56 | $53 | $53 | $59 | $59 | $59 | $66 | $76 |
| Purchases | 17 | 23 | 23 | 23 | 28 | 26 | 26 | 29 | 29 | 29 | 33 | 38 |
| Wages | 12 | 12 | 12 | 12 | 12 | 12 | 12 | 12 | 12 | 12 | 12 | 12 |
| Other expenses | 3 | 3 | 3 | 3 | 4 | 4 | 4 | 4 | 4 | 4 | 5 | 6 |
| Interest | | | 2 | | | 2 | | | 2 | | | 2 |
| Tax | | | 5 | | | 5 | | | 5 | | | 5 |
| Start-up costs | | | | | | | | | | | | |
| Total Outflows | $32 | $38 | $45 | $38 | $44 | $49 | $42 | $46 | $53 | $46 | $49 | $62 |
| Net Cast Gain/Loss | $ 8 | $ 8 | $ 1 | $ 8 | $12 | $ 4 | $11 | $14 | $ 7 | $14 | $17 | $14 |
| Desired cash level | 6 | 7 | 7 | 7 | 9 | 9 | 9 | 10 | 10 | 10 | 11 | 12 |
| Cumulative Surplus Cash | $ 2 | $ 1 | $ (6) | $ 1 | $ 3 | $ (5) | $ 2 | $ 4 | $ (3) | $ 4 | $ 6 | $ 2 |

Table XIV    Timetable for El Flaco Mexican Restaurant Opening Schedule 1992–1993

| Milestone | APR | MAY | JUN | JUL | AUG | SEP | OCT | NOV | DEC | JAN | FEB | MAR |
|---|---|---|---|---|---|---|---|---|---|---|---|---|
| Complete Lease Arrangements | 4/13 | | 6/8 | | | | | | | | | |
| Apply for Business License | 4/13 | | 6/12 | | | | | | | | | |
| Interior Planning and Design | | | 6/8 | 7/31 | | | | | | | | |
| Apply for Construction Permits | | | 6/15 | | 8/10 | | | | | | | |
| Order Restaurant Equipment | | | | 7/17 | | | 10/15 | | | | | |
| Order Operating Supplies | | | | 7/17 | | | 10/15 | | | | | |
| Order Kitcheon Supplies | | | | 7/16 | | | 10/15 | | | | | |
| Order Food Supplies | | | | | | | | 11/2 | 12/2 | | | |
| Hire Personnel | | | | | | | | 11/2 | | | | |
| Schedule Preopening Advertising | | | | | | | | 11/23 | | 1/1 | | |
| Restaurant Opening (from start to finish) | 4/1 | | | | | | | | | ★ 1/1 | | |
| Schedule Follow up Promotional Advertising | | | | | | | | | | 1/10 | | |
| Reevaluate Personnel Requirements | | | | | | | | | | | 2/1 | |
| Review and Update Business Plan | | | | | | | | | | | 2/2 | |

# IX. SUMMARY

## A. A Final Marketing Point

A key crucial area in operating a successful restaurant that has not been stressed enough is the importance of menu planning. The research findings indicate that although many restaurants can thrive without a fancy atmosphere or quality service, none can survive without exceptional food. Therefore, a major part of the planning process consists of menu design. According to the *Facilities Operations Manual,* prepared by the National Restaurant Association, the major points listed in Table XV should be considered when selecting menu items.[12]

Also, research indicates that the successful restaurants are those that strive to limiting their menu selections to those recipes and ideas which are compatible with the restaurant's atmosphere, decor, and anticipated clientele. Moreover, new restaurants should make attempts toward specialization and serve only menu items which they can prepare better than other establishments in the area.[13]

**Table XV    Important Menu Selection Points**

1. The menu item must be of superior quality.
2. The raw materials used to prepare the item must be available year round at stable prices.
3. The menu item must be affordable and demanded by the clientele.
4. The menu item must be acceptable to the preparation and cooking staff system used.
5. The raw materials used in preparing the menu item must be easily portioned by weight.
6. All menu items must have consistent cooking results.
7. All menu items must have a long shelf life.
8. All menu items must have similar cooking times.
9. The storage facilities must accommodate the raw materials used in preparing the menu items.
10. Menu items should be creative and not readily available in other restaurants.

Therefore, specializing seems to be the key towards building a successful restaurant business with a solid reputation for quality. Word-of-mouth advertising is the most effective form of advertising available and this means having trained staff and equipment to properly prepare and serve food items.

## B. Conclusion

One of the major challenges to El Flaco's success will be in the area of competition. Earlier in this report, it was pointed out that El Flaco would employ the use of coupon specials and price "specials" to lure and develop a customer base. However, it should be noted that many competitors use these same marketing tactics to attract customers.

With customer spending down, many restaurants are seeking an elusive mix of pricing, food quality, and service in an effort to create a perception of value in order to increase business. Research studies reveal that it is the *value concept* that establishes a restaurant's permanent reputation with the customer. During times in which restaurants offer discount coupons, they usually enjoy higher traffic patterns, but once the discounts are discontinued, customer counts drop back to prior levels or even lower.

Therefore, El Flaco's marketing efforts will place emphasis more on service and quality to bring in customers. The discount specials will be used solely as a way to introduce El Flaco to new customers and level out its business flow.

Adding value service and high quality products, therefore, will be the pillars of El Flaco's marketing efforts to guide it towards success. This means providing the patron with an enjoyable dining experience by offering a high quality product and service at a reasonable price. It should be noted that low prices do not necessarily mean low margins. This is because customers who come in for the budget item also tend to buy high margin items. Again, careful menu planning is the key towards profits.

In the area of service quality, while training employees to respond more quickly and politely is relatively inexpensive, it can lead to a better dining experience. This may mean allocating more money for labor expenses in order to put more cooks in the kitchen or waiters and waitresses on the floor. This strategy may lead to narrow margins initially, since patrons do not necessarily notice the difference immediately. However, over time it can increase customer traffic which, in turn, increases profits.

Above all, El Flaco's business plan is to develop an established loyal customer base and rely on word of mouth to spread its reputation as a great Mexican restaurant. El Flaco's management will remain committed to quality service and listen to its customer's suggestions to serve them better. This may include providing the customers with a suggestion box or with a comment section on the back of their saleschecks to note recommendations. By taking care of its customers' needs, El Flaco will prosper and become one of the most popular restaurants in the South Bay.

## ENDNOTES

1. Louis Rukeyser, *Louis Rukeyser's Business Almanac* (New York: Simon & Schuster, 1991), pp. 96–109.
2. Rukeyser, p. 106.
3. Robert Brown, *How to Set Up, Operate, and Manage a Financially Successful Restaurant* (Atlanta: Lauderhill, 1989), pp. 53–55.
4. Brown, p. 67.
5. *Business Week*, "Ponderosa: A Steakhouse Tries to Fatten Profits by Going Mexican" (Corporate Strategies Sec., April 25, 1986), p. 98.
6. *County and City Data Book*, Department of Commerce (Information Publications, 1989) p. 469.
7. *County and City Data Book*, p. 315.
8. Lawrence W. Tuller, *Financing the Small Business* (New York: Prentice Hall, 1991). pp. 113–114.
9. Tuller, p. 167.
10. *Industry Norms and Key Business Ratios*, Dun & Bradstreet (Dun & Bradstreet Credit Service, 1987–88 ed.), p. 155.
11. Robert Brown, p. 143.
12. *Facilities Operations Manual*. Prepared by the National Restaurant Association (Washington DC, 1989), Ch. 3, p. 44.
13. *Facilities Operations Manual*, pp. 69–71.

## BIBLIOGRAPHY

Brown, Robert. *How to Set Up, Operate, and Manage a Financially Successful Restaurant*. Atlanta: Lauderhill, 1989.

*Business Update*. Published by the Redondo Beach Chamber of Commerce, January 1992.

*California Cities, Towns & Counties: Basic Data Profiles for all Municipalities & Counties*. Palo Alto: Information Publications, 1989.

Cohen, William A. *Developing a Winning Marketing Plan*. New York: Wiley, 1987.

*County and City Data Book*. U.S. Department of Commerce.

Droms, William G. *Finance and Accounting for Nonfinancial Manager*. New York: Addison-Wesley, 1990.

Kotler, Phillip. *Marketing Management Analysis, Planning, Implementation and Control*. Englewood Cliffs, NJ: Prentice Hall, 1991.

*RMA Annual Statement Studies 1990*. Philadelphia: Robert Morris Associates, 1991.

Rukeyser, Louis. *Louis Rukeyser's Business Almanac*. New York: Simon & Schuster, 1991.

Sherry, John E. H. *The Laws of Innkeepers*. New York: Cornell, 1981.

Troy, Leo PhD. *Almanac of Business and Industrial Financial Ratios*. Englewood Cliffs, NJ: Prentice Hall, 1991 ed.

Tuller, Lawrence W. *Financing the Small Business*. New York: Prentice Hall, 1991.

Zemke, Ron, and Schaaf, Dick. *The Service Edge*. New York: Plume, 1990.

# APPENDIX

# How the Country Spent Its Retail Dollars and Total Number of Retail Establishments

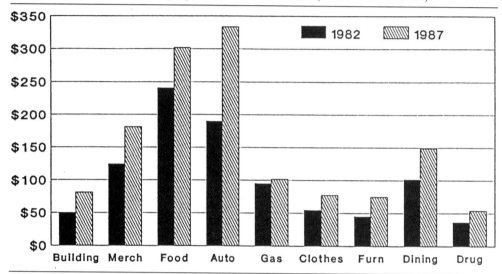

**How the Country Spent Its Retail Dollars (Billions of Dollars)**

*Source:* 1987 Census of Retail Trade.

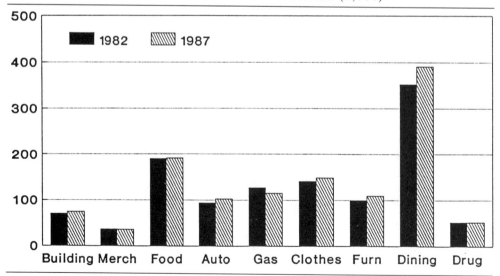

**Total Number of Retail Establishments (1,000)**

*Source:* 1987 Census of Retail Trade.

**How the Country Spent Its Retail Dollars (Billions of Dollars)**

| Kind of Business[1] | Establishments[2] (1,000) | | Sales (mil. dol.) | | Annual Payroll (mil. dol.) | | Paid Employees[3] (1,000) | |
|---|---|---|---|---|---|---|---|---|
| | 1982 | 1987 | 1982 | 1987 | 1982 | 1987 | 1982 | 1987 |
| Retail trade, total | 1,425 | 1,506 | 1,039,029 | 1,494,112 | 123,619 | 177,706 | 14,468 | 17,793 |
| Building materials and garden supplies stores | 70 | 74 | 49,939 | 81,487 | 6,221 | 9,760 | 504 | 668 |
| Building materials, supply stores | 36 | 38 | 34,827 | 60,525 | 4,179 | 6,929 | 307 | 432 |
| Hardware stores | 21 | 20 | 8,335 | 10,535 | 1,250 | 1,564 | 127 | 138 |
| Retail nurseries, lawn and garden supply stores | 8 | 11 | 2,873 | 5,411 | 456 | 822 | 47 | 71 |
| Mobile home dealers | 5 | 5 | 3,904 | 5,015 | 336 | 445 | 24 | 27 |
| General merchandise stores | 36 | 35 | 124,066 | 181,147 | 15,163 | 19,586 | 1,876 | 2,003 |
| Department stores (incl. leased depts.)[4,5] | 10 | 11 | 107,163 | 156,922 | (NA) | (NA) | (NA) | (NA) |
| Department stores (excl. leased depts.)[4,5] | 10 | 11 | 103,289 | 147,181 | 12,836 | 16,688 | 1,552 | 1,688 |
| Variety stores | 12 | 10 | 8,090 | 6,762 | 1,085 | 926 | 161 | 121 |
| Misc. general merchandise stores | 14 | 14 | 12,687 | 27,204 | 1,241 | 1,971 | 163 | 194 |
| Food Stores[4] | 190 | 191 | 240,520 | 301,847 | 23,530 | 29,819 | 2,348 | 2,855 |
| Grocery stores | 138 | 138 | 226,609 | 285,481 | 21,364 | 27,084 | 2,031 | 2,502 |
| Meat and fish (seafood) markets | 12 | 11 | 5,274 | 5,616 | 563 | 606 | 62 | 59 |
| Retail bakeries | 19 | 22 | 3,543 | 4,871 | 979 | 1,353 | 159 | 185 |
| Fruit and vegetable markets | 3 | 3 | 1,330 | 1,802 | 135 | 186 | 17 | 20 |
| Candy, nut, confectionery stores | 5 | 6 | 801 | 1,182 | 129 | 199 | 23 | 31 |
| Dairy products stores | 5 | 3 | 1,375 | 880 | 163 | 106 | 27 | 17 |
| Automotive dealers[6] | 94 | 103 | 189,677 | 333,420 | 16,731 | 28,688 | 1,035 | 1,373 |
| New and used car dealers | 28 | 28 | 154,726 | 280,529 | 12,309 | 22,205 | 699 | 940 |
| Used car dealers | 12 | 15 | 6,273 | 10,849 | 450 | 809 | 36 | 55 |
| Auto and home supply stores | 41 | 46 | 19,638 | 25,460 | 3,072 | 4,152 | 229 | 286 |
| Boat dealers | 4 | 5 | 2,870 | 6,824 | 304 | 620 | 23 | 35 |
| Recreational and utility trailer dealers | 3 | 3 | 2,767 | 5,687 | 231 | 453 | 16 | 26 |
| Motorcycle dealers | 5 | 4 | 2,877 | 3,475 | 308 | 382 | 27 | 27 |
| Gasoline service stations | 127 | 115 | 94,719 | 101,997 | 4,768 | 6,414 | 604 | 702 |
| Apparel and accessory stores[4] | 141 | 149 | 54,622 | 77,391 | 7,455 | 9,725 | 967 | 1,121 |
| Men's and boys' clothing stores | 19 | 17 | 7,735 | 8,869 | 1,224 | 1,361 | 123 | 115 |
| Women's clothing and specialty stores | 52 | 60 | 19,743 | 28,531 | 2,649 | 3,519 | 385 | 455 |
| Women's clothing stores | 45 | 52 | 18,002 | 25,868 | 2,383 | 3,150 | 351 | 419 |
| Family clothing stores | 19 | 18 | 13,451 | 21,117 | 1,671 | 2,362 | 219 | 268 |
| Shoe stores | 39 | 39 | 11,275 | 14,411 | 1,571 | 1,880 | 189 | 205 |
| Children's and infants' wear stores | 6 | 6 | 1,356 | 2,101 | 172 | 245 | 28 | 37 |
| Furniture and homefurnishings stores | 100 | 110 | 45,314 | 74,783 | 6,287 | 9,904 | 543 | 703 |
| Furniture stores | 32 | 33 | 17,223 | 25,997 | 2,608 | 3,828 | 214 | 247 |
| Homefurnishings stores | 27 | 32 | 8,848 | 16,374 | 1,320 | 2,389 | 124 | 176 |
| Household appliance stores | 12 | 11 | 5,697 | 8,332 | 697 | 953 | 59 | 65 |
| Radio, television, computer, and music stores | 30 | 34 | 13,545 | 24,080 | 1,662 | 2,734 | 146 | 215 |
| Computer and software stores | (NA) | 4 | (NA) | 2,651 | (NA) | 325 | (NA) | 22 |
| Eating and drinking places | 352 | 391 | 101,723 | 148,776 | 25,706 | 38,582 | 4,666 | 6,100 |
| Eating places[6] | 284 | 333 | 93,158 | 139,282 | 23,987 | 36,633 | 4,341 | 5,787 |
| Restaurants and lunchrooms | 135 | 155 | 47,136 | 66,364 | 12,935 | 18,796 | 2,291 | 2,822 |
| Refreshment places | 120 | 138 | 35,678 | 56,870 | 8,185 | 13,269 | 1,610 | 2,352 |
| Drinking places | 68 | 59 | 8,565 | 9,495 | 1,721 | 1,950 | 325 | 313 |
| Drug and proprietary stores | 52 | 52 | 36,242 | 53,824 | 4,605 | 6,476 | 496 | 574 |
| Miscellaneous retail stores | 264 | 286 | 102,207 | 139,440 | 13,150 | 18,754 | 1,430 | 1,694 |
| Liquor stores | 37 | 35 | 17,340 | 18,597 | 1,310 | 1,454 | 167 | 157 |
| Used merchandise stores | 19 | 18 | 3,798 | 4,305 | 730 | 823 | 80 | 81 |

*(continued)*

NA not available.
[1] Based on 1972 Standard Industrial Classification; see text, section 13.
[2] Represents the number of establishments in business at any time during year.
[3] For pay period including March 12.
[4] Includes sales from catalog order desks.
[5] Establishments defined as department stores with 25 employees or more.
[6] Includes other kinds of businesses, not shown separately.
[7] The abbreviation n.e.c. means not elsewhere classified.

*Source:* U.S. Bureau of the Census, *1987 Census of Retail Trade*, RC87-A-52.

### How the Country Spent Its Retail Dollars (Billions of Dollars)    (Continued)

| Kind of Business[1] | Establishments[2] (1,000) | | Sales (mil. dol.) | | Annual Payroll (mil. dol.) | | Paid Employees[3] (1,000) | |
|---|---|---|---|---|---|---|---|---|
| | 1982 | 1987 | 1982 | 1987 | 1982 | 1987 | 1982 | 1987 |
| Miscellaneous retail stores (continued) | | | | | | | | |
| Miscellaneous shopping goods stores | 108 | 123 | 32,524 | 49,460 | 4,623 | 6,481 | 566 | 706 |
| Sporting goods stores and bicycle shops | 20 | 22 | 6,718 | 10,077 | 844 | 1,218 | 96 | 121 |
| Book stores | 10 | 11 | 3,133 | 5,116 | 401 | 581 | 58 | 72 |
| Stationery stores | 5 | 5 | 1,495 | 1,814 | 257 | 287 | 28 | 27 |
| Jewelry stores | 24 | 28 | 8,352 | 11,994 | 1,433 | 1,921 | 132 | 163 |
| Hobby, toy, and game shops | 8 | 10 | 3,238 | 7,031 | 325 | 614 | 46 | 76 |
| Camera, photographic supply stores | 4 | 4 | 1,884 | 2,294 | 225 | 276 | 21 | 21 |
| Gift, novelty, souvenir shops | 24 | 32 | 4,620 | 7,459 | 694 | 1,055 | 110 | 151 |
| Luggage, leather goods stores | 2 | 2 | 589 | 839 | 94 | 122 | 11 | 11 |
| Sewing, needlework, and piece goods stores | 10 | 10 | 2,495 | 2,836 | 350 | 406 | 62 | 65 |
| Nonstore retailers | 23 | 23 | 20,155 | 33,894 | 2,942 | 4,523 | 274 | 318 |
| Catalog and mail-order houses | 8 | 7 | 11,254 | 20,347 | 1,194 | 1,932 | 103 | 123 |
| Merchandising machine operators | 6 | 5 | 4,727 | 5,692 | 935 | 1,090 | 84 | 74 |
| Direct selling establishments | 9 | 11 | 4,175 | 7,855 | 813 | 1,501 | 88 | 121 |
| Fuel and ice dealers | 13 | 13 | 16,818 | 14,250 | 1,405 | 1,834 | 95 | 100 |
| Florists | 24 | 27 | 3,416 | 4,810 | 711 | 1,019 | 104 | 125 |
| Tobacco stores and stands | 2 | 2 | 576 | 518 | 68 | 57 | 9 | 7 |
| News dealers and newsstands | 2 | 2 | 500 | 703 | 60 | 90 | 9 | 10 |
| Miscellaneous retail stores, n.e.c.[6,7] | 35 | 44 | 7,078 | 12,902 | 1,301 | 2,472 | 127 | 191 |
| Optical goods stores | 11 | 14 | 1,729 | 3,415 | 404 | 811 | 34 | 54 |

# 3

# BUSINESS PLAN FOR
# THE CHU TUTORING SERVICE

*Developed by*
**Tom Urbanski**

# Table of Contents

# Tables

# Chart and Figures

## I.  INTRODUCTION

Immigration into the United States is increasing yearly. Most Asians that come to the United States rely on education and hard work to increase their social status. They want their children to succeed in school. However, often their children are limited English speakers. They need specialized instruction to excel in English as well as to understand other subjects they are being taught.

The mission of the Chu Tutoring Service is to provide superior academic opportunities for children and young adults through the implementation of progressive tutoring services.

Helen Chu-Urbanski moved to the United States from Taipai, Taiwan when she was five years old. She did not speak English. She spoke Mandarin (Chinese). In less than two years she had become proficient in English and has no discernable accent today. After gaining a sociology degree at the University of California at Los Angeles, she began to teach bilingual kindergarten students in Hollywood. The majority of her class is "limited English proficient" (LEP) students. She has taught for five years and been very successful at teaching her students English and other primary subjects.

Helen would like to continue to teach LEP students when we relocate to Atlanta. However, the school systems in both Los Angeles and Atlanta have very structured pay scales. This does not allow Helen to negotiate a salary for her services. Beginning a tutoring service would allow Helen to exploit a need in the marketplace and earn a salary that does not have a ceiling on it.

Tutoring services are already established in Atlanta. The Atlanta phone book lists 46 such services. However, very few of these companies cater to the needs of the LEP students and immigrants. Most of the services deal with speech impediments or basic skills.

## II.  SITUATION ANALYSIS

## 1.  The Situational Environ

### A.  Demand and Demand Trends

There is sufficient demand to support 46 tutoring services in Atlanta. This is the number of companies listed in the telephone directory. There are no relevant statistics issued that focus primarily on tutoring services. However, we will use two methods to estimate demand. First, we will focus on trends that are listed in periodicals. Second, a market survey will be performed by phoning the tutoring services in the Atlanta area.

"Baby boomers are well-educated; consequently, they spend freely on educational toys, videos, and tutoring services for their children."[1] Baby boomers make up the largest segment of the U.S. population.

"There has been a flood of new immigrants and capital into the US from Asia, and this has multiplied the economic, cultural, and social needs of Chinese-Americans. An estimated 36,000 Chinese immigrants have come to the US annually since 1980."[2]

Results of a market survey appear in Appendix D. The results will be covered in detail in the section "The Competitor Environ." Looking at this questionnaire, we can see that there are two national firms offering services similar to ours in the Atlanta area. We will proceed on the assumption that because there are healthy competitors in the marketplace, demand must be present.

### B.  Social and Cultural Factors

Since our company's primary target market will be Chinese-Americans, we will concentrate our study on this racial group. However, it should be noted that we will market our services to other Asian-Americans.

Chinese immigration has increased steadily since the repeal of the Chinese Exclusion Act in 1943 and the abolition of national origin quotas in 1965.

Early Chinese immigrants came mostly from the southern provinces of China. They came to the United States because of economic hardship at home and the prospect of quick wealth in California in the late 1840s (gold rush era). Due to social and political turmoil in the early twentieth century, Chinese from other areas and provinces in China immigrated.

[1] Susan B. Garland, "Those Aging Boomers," *Business Week,* 20 May 1991: 106.
[2] Todd W. Bressi, "Chinatowns Stand Their Ground," *Planning,* Nov. 1987: 12.

Today, immigrants tend to come from the People's Republic of China, Taiwan, Hong Kong, and Southeast Asia. "The composition of these recent immigrants differs from that of past generations. There are fewer laborers; professionals and technicians emerge as the most numerous groups of new Chinese immigrants."[3] These Chinese tend to emigrate from the following sources:

1. Refugees.
2. Hong Kong.
3. Taiwanese children.

Many Chinese have fled their countries as refugees. Included in the Vietnamese "boat people" are ethnic Chinese. Many of these refugees remain immersed in Chinese culture and traditions.

Hong Kong Chinese who are apprehensive about 1997, when the British government will return the colony to Chinese control, are leaving and moving to the United States.

Taiwanese children who are sent by their parents to live with relatives in the United States to escape rigorous school systems in Taiwan and to take advantage of the U.S. educational system, are yet another source of Chinese-Americans.

While there are many forms of spoken Chinese, Mandarin is the most prevalent language and has been adopted as the official language of the People's Republic of China. It is also referred to as the "national language."

Educating children with cultural and linguistic needs presents a challenge. Also, working with Chinese parents and their special needs children is a highly complex job that requires cultural knowledge, sensitivity, and a high degree of professionalism.

"Nearly ⅓ of Chinese-Americans still live in Chinatowns, whose populations are kept stable by the arrival of newcomers who outnumber those who migrate out to the suburbs."[4] In Atlanta, there are two Chinatown areas. The first

[3] Alice Lee, MS, "A Socio-Cultural Framework for the Assessment of Chinese Children with Special Needs," *Topics in Language Disorders* 9(3), (1989): 39.
[4] Susumu Awanohara, "Tyros, Triads, Tycoons," *Far Eastern Economic Review,* 18 July 1991: 50.

is located in the downtown area. The second is approximately 10 miles northeast of downtown Atlanta, in the city of Chamblee which is within Gwinnett county. Figure 1 highlights these two areas of high Chinese-American concentration.

The new trend is towards establishing satellite settlements. The Chinese population is becoming less centralized. This is the case in Atlanta, where a large number of Chinese and other Asians are moving into the surrounding counties of Atlanta. The demographic information presented in the following section will substantiate this argument.

## C. Demographics

There are many sources that offer demographic information concerning our target market. The sources used include the 1990 census, the 1980 census, and the Atlanta Chamber of Commerce.

The United States Census Bureau provides more detailed information concerning separate ethnic groups. However, the most recent census, taken in 1990, has not yet reported the detailed information concerning racial groups other than population.

The 1980 census detail can be used as a base and detailed information concerning Atlanta's population can be projected using 1990 detail.

The Atlanta Chamber of Commerce is another source for demographic information. The majority of the information that they provide is not detailed enough to identify a specific target market. For example, all Asian-Americans are grouped into one population group. This group consists of Japanese-Americans, Filipino-Americans, and other groups including Chinese-Americans. More detail is needed and the Census Bureau can supply this information.

Table 1 shows the number of Asians living in the three-county area that our company will target. The change in population growth between 1980 and 1990 has been dramatic and has continued to increase. In 1980, the Atlanta MSA had approximately 12,000 Asian-Americans. By 1990, Dekalb County alone, surpassed this figure. The final column of Table 1 shows that the Asian-American population growth over the past decade has been 448.1 percent.

Figure 1    Locations of Chinatowns in Atlanta's MSA

Table 1    Atlanta's Asian-American Population Growth

| County | 1980 Population | 1990 Population | % Increase 1980–1990 |
|---|---|---|---|
| Dekalb | 4,324 | 16,266 | 276.2% |
| Fulton | 2,802 | 8,380 | 199.1 |
| Gwinnett | 1,059 | 10,219 | 865.0 |
| 3-County Total | 8,185 | 44,865 | 448.1 |

*Source:* U.S. Department of Commerce, Census Bureau, 1980 and 1990.

Tables 2, 3, and 4 show the racial breakdown of the population of the Dekalb, Fulton, and Gwinnett counties, respectively. These are taken from the 1990 U.S. census.

The total population in Dekalb, Fulton, and Gwinnett counties is projected to increase by a rate of 6.7, 4.9, and 19.3 percent, respectively, between now and 1994. This means a growing market.

### Table 2 Dekalb County Population by Racial Groups

| Race | Population |
| --- | --- |
| White (800–869, 971) | 292,310 |
| Black (870–934, 972) | 230,425 |
| American Indian, Eskimo, or Aleut (000–599, 935–970, 973–975): | |
| American Indian (000–599, 973) | 925 |
| Eskimo (935–940, 974) | 19 |
| Aleut (941–970, 975) | 54 |
| Asian or Pacific Islander (600–699, 976–985): | |
| Asian (600–652, 976, 977, 979–982, 985): | |
| Chinese (605–607, 976) | 3,186 |
| Filipino (608, 977) | 485 |
| Japanese (611, 981) | 803 |
| Asian Indian (600, 982) | 3,687 |
| Korean (612, 979) | 3,435 |
| Vietnamese (619, 980) | 1,856 |
| Cambodian (604) | 621 |
| Hmong (609) | 222 |
| Laotian (613) | 672 |
| Thai (618) | 287 |
| Other Asian (601–603, 610, 614–617, 620–652, 985) | 896 |
| Pacific Islander (653–699, 978, 983, 984): | |
| Polynesian (653–659, 978, 983): | |
| Hawaiian (653, 654, 978) | 45 |
| Samoan (655, 983) | 21 |
| Tongan (657) | 0 |
| Other Polynesian (656, 658, 659) | 2 |
| Micronesian (660–675, 984): | |
| Guamanian (660, 984) | 25 |
| Other Micronesian (661–675) | 0 |
| Melanesian (676–680) | 21 |
| Pacific Islander, not specified (681–699) | 2 |
| Other race (700–799, 986–999) | 5,838 |

*Source:* 1990 Census of Population and Housing Summary, U.S. Census Bureau.

### Table 3 Fulton County Population by Racial Groups

| Race | Population |
| --- | --- |
| White (800–869, 971) | 309,901 |
| Black (870–934, 972) | 324,008 |
| American Indian, Eskimo, or Aleut (000–599, 935–970, 973–975): | |
| American Indian (000–599, 973) | 956 |
| Eskimo (935–940, 974) | 13 |
| Aleut (941–970, 975) | 12 |
| Asian or Pacific Islander (600–699, 976–985): | |
| Asian (600–652, 976, 977, 979–982, 985): | |
| Chinese (605–607, 976) | 2,053 |
| Filipino (608, 977) | 375 |
| Japanese (611, 981) | 674 |
| Asian Indian (600, 982) | 1,268 |
| Korean (612, 979) | 1,204 |
| Vietnamese (619, 980) | 1,418 |
| Cambodian (604) | 454 |
| Hmong (609) | 0 |
| Laotian (613) | 291 |
| Thai (618) | 116 |
| Other Asian (601–603, 610, 614–617, 620–652, 985) | 424 |
| Pacific Islander (653–659, 978, 983, 984): | |
| Polynesian (653–659, 978, 983): | |
| Hawaiian (653, 654, 978) | 46 |
| Samoan (655, 983) | 22 |
| Tongan (657) | 0 |
| Other Polynesian (656, 658, 659) | 4 |
| Micronesian (660–675, 984): | |
| Guamanian (660, 984) | 25 |
| Other Micronesian (661–675) | 4 |
| Melanesian (676–680) | 0 |
| Pacific Islander, not specified (681–699) | 2 |
| Other race (700–799, 986–999) | 5,681 |

*Source:* 1990 Census of Population and Housing Summary. U.S. Census Bureau.

### D. Economic and Business Conditions

In recent years, Atlanta and the surrounding counties have experienced strong growth. The Atlanta Metropolitan Statistical Area (MSA) currently ranks ninth in the United States with 2.8 million people. This represents a 40 percent increase over the past 10 years.

The service industry in the Atlanta MSA experienced a decrease in jobs over the past year.

The number of new businesses relocating or expanding into Metropolitan Atlanta is illustrated by Chart 1 on page 3·10. Historical data and future projections show that Atlanta's business base is increasing and is expected to continue increasing.

### E. Technology

Technologically advanced teaching tools will be used by the company's instructors. Laptop

**Table 4   Gwinnett County Population by Racial Groups**

| Race | Population |
|---|---|
| White (800–869, 971) | 320,971 |
| Black (870–934, 972) | 18,175 |
| American Indian, Eskimo, or Aleut (000–599, 935–970, 973–975): | |
| American Indian (000–599, 973) | 688 |
| Eskimo (935–940, 974) | 4 |
| Aleut (941–970, 975) | 23 |
| Asian or Pacific Islander (600–699, 976–985): | |
| Asian (600–652, 976, 977, 979–982, 985): | |
| Chinese (605–607, 976) | 2,092 |
| Filipino (608, 977) | 463 |
| Japanese (611, 981) | 610 |
| Asian Indian (600, 982) | 2,132 |
| Korean (612, 979) | 2,423 |
| Vietnamese (619, 980) | 965 |
| Cambodian (604) | 208 |
| Hmong (609) | 62 |
| Laotian (613) | 309 |
| Thai (618) | 277 |
| Other Asian (601–603, 610, 614–617, 620–652, 985) | 576 |
| Pacific Islander (653–699, 978, 983, 984): | |
| Polynesian (653–659, 978, 983): | |
| Hawaiian (653, 654, 978) | 59 |
| Samoan (655, 983) | 2 |
| Tongan (657) | 0 |
| Other Polynesian (656, 658, 659) | 0 |
| Micronesian (660–675, 984): | |
| Guamanian (660, 984) | 17 |
| Other Micronesian (661–675) | 6 |
| Melanesian (676–680) | 1 |
| Pacific Islander, not specified (681–699) | 17 |
| Other race (700–799, 986–999) | 2,830 |

Source: 1990 Census of Population and Housing Summary, U.S. Census Bureau.

computers will be purchased and used because they offer convenience, portability, and functionality.

Personal computers and the laptop computers will be used with educational software that will allow interactive communication with the students.

An example of a software package that will be used is IBM's Linkway program. Features included in this software include graphics, calendars, to-do lists, and flash card utilities. The flash card section can be used for arithmetic, spelling, and language interaction. The graphics can be used for art. Finally, the calendar and to-do lists can be used by the instructors themselves to organize their instruction.

Computer printers will be used in conjunction with the computers. These are already owned and will be part of the capital investment into the firm.

### F.   Politics

No foreseeable political forces will hinder our company's operations.

### G.   Laws and Regulations

A business license will have to be attained. This will cost our company approximately $200.

Also our tutors will be credentialed by state school boards. Employment will be based on this qualification.

## 2.   The Neutral Environ

### A.   Financial Environments

A large capital investment will be unnecessary because our main product is service oriented and will not require building or plant expenses. However, it will still be necessary to hold costs down. In order to keep costs at a desirable level, the most economical sales levels will not be able to be pursued aggressively. At higher sales levels, economies of scale could be taken advantage of and costs could be spread amongst more customers. This would lead to higher profit per customer.

### B.   Government Environments

One issue that should be noted concerning the governmental environment is immigration reform. The Chinese Exclusion Act of 1943 was repealed in 1965. That same year, the abolition of the national origin quotas occurred. Today, there are no strong threats to stop immigration from Asian countries.

### C.   Media Environments

A negative portrayal of Asians in the media over the past year could have a negative effect on the company. Asian-Americans are often

**Chart 1**
**New Businesses Relocating or Expanding into Metropolitan Atlanta**

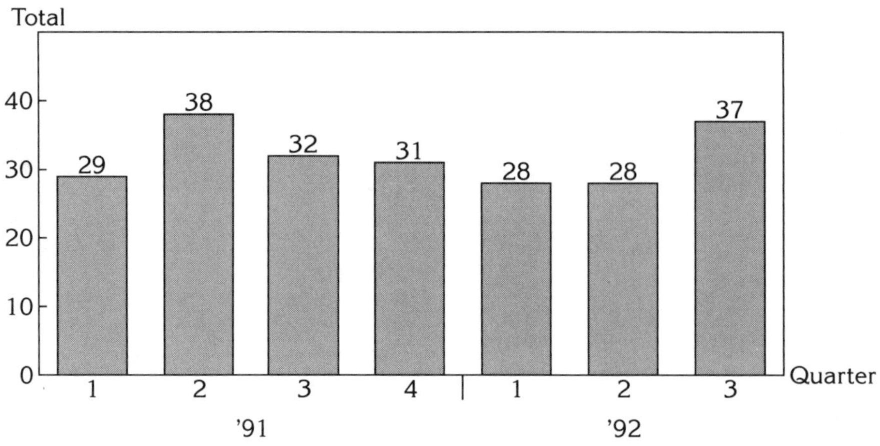

Source: Atlanta Chamber of Commerce, Research Department.

perceived to all be in the same racial group. As a result, anti-Japanese sentiment that has been prevalent over the past year could be directed towards a company with a Chinese and Japanese-sounding name. However, since the majority of our customers will be from the Asian community, this problem will not be directly felt.

### D. Special Interest Environments

No special interest groups can be identified that would cause a serious threat to our company. Tutoring services, in general, are not influenced by special interest groups. Individual parents may request specific services for their children, but this will be handled on a case-to-case basis.

## 3. The Competitor Environ

To identify the characteristics of the competition, the following sources were used:

1. Atlanta Metro Area phone book.
2. Phone survey of tutoring services.
3. Discussions with employees at the Chinese community center.

In order to get honest responses, I posed as a prospective customer who had a child needing tutoring services consistent with our company's niche. Our child was a LEP student.

The sample results of a questionnaire of tutoring services appear in Appendix D. The survey consisted of telephone calls to 46 tutoring services. Of these 46 companies, some were no longer operating, some could no longer be reached at the phone numbers listed in the phone book, while still others did not offer services that they advertised in the phone book.

The survey consisted of the following questions:

1. Does your company provide ESL instruction?
2. Are there any Chinese-speaking tutors working for your company?
3. How much are your fees?
4. Are your tutors certified?
5. Are computers used as an instructional tool?
6. Do you offer in-home tutoring?
7. How large is your company?
8. What is the teacher-to-student ratio when instructing the students?

The questions in the survey were intended to determine several factors pertinent to our company. We wanted to know if any other company pursued our target market, how much they charged, the size of their company, the characteristics of their services, and the characteristics of their personnel.

Appendix D has the results of the phone questionnaire for the eight competitors that are most similar to our company. The key categorizes the responses as follows:

A. For questions 1, 2, 5, and 6—
  Y Yes, the company does offer this service.
  N No, the company does not offer this service.
  NA No answer, the company did not respond to this question.

B. For question 3—
  L The fees for 40 hours of service are under $950.
  M The fees are between $950 and $1150.
  H The fees are over $1150.

C. For question 4—
  C The tutors are certified.
  UC The tutors are not certified.

D. For question 7—
  NT The service is part of a national chain.
  LC The service is a local company.
  NB The service is a neighborhood service.

E. For question 8—
  L The student-to-teacher ratio is 1 on 1.
  M The student-to-teacher ratio is 2 students to one teacher.
  H The student-to-teacher ratio is three or more students to 1 teacher.

Of all the companies surveyed, Total Tutoring was the most similar company. It offers English-as-a-second-language (ESL) instruction, certified teachers, and computerized instruction. However, it does not offer in-home services and does not cater to Asian-Americans.

Additional competition that Chu Tutoring Service will face in the Atlanta tutoring market will come mainly from schools, churches, and Chinese neighborhood community centers.

The school competition will occur from public and private schools.

Chinese neighborhood community centers did not offer English tutoring. They did offer tutoring in Chinese. They tended to emphasize traditional Chinese services and not services that would help their customers assimilate into mainstream society.

Competition from churches will be difficult to combat because their pricing is relatively very low or nonexistent. Mountain West Church is an example of this trend towards very inexpensive services.

## 4. The Company Environ

The services that our company will furnish will be educational tutoring services. Helen Chu-Urbanski has five years of experience teaching grade school and a bachelor's degree in sociology.

The company will require an initial $10,000 capital investment. This will come from Helen Chu-Urbanski's personal finances.

School supplies and books will be purchased at local educational supply stores in the Atlanta area.

## III.  THE TARGET MARKET

The target market that the Chu Tutoring Service will focus on is made up of Asian-Americans who need tutoring services for their children or for themselves. After two years of targeting these customers, our service will begin to market to a more general market.

The markets pursued will be limited to a 2½-county area as shown in Figure 2. This includes Gwinnett county, Dekalb county, and Fulton county. Due to transportation time restrictions, we cannot offer in-home services outside this area.

## IV.  PROBLEMS AND OPPORTUNITIES

The major problems that exist for our company are:

1. Creating a customer base.
2. Parents denying that their child needs special academic attention.

Opportunities include:

1. An untapped market niche—Chinese-Americans.

Figure 2   Three-County Target Market in Atlanta's MSA

2. Ability to communicate with customers in their native tongue.

Creating a customer base will be the first problem faced. By advertising and word of mouth, a niche within the market will be captured.

The second problem, parents not wanting to admit that their child needs special attention will be dealt with using a lot of empathy. It would be a mistake to suggest to most Chinese parents that their child needs special attention.

This would be an embarrassment to their family and would result in lost sales. We will play down the fact that their child needs special attention while stating our services.

## V.   BUSINESS OBJECTIVES AND GOALS

The Chu Tutoring Service will have modest sales goals in its first year of operation. This year will be used to gain experience and to discover and remedy any unforeseen problems with operations, and to begin preparations to market the product heavily for the second year of operation.

By the third year of operation, the company will provide full-time employment for Helen Chu-Urbanski and a second full-time tutor. As the company grows, the target market will be expanded if needed to fill the tutoring schedules of both employees.

## VI.   MARKETING STRATEGY

Our strategy is to enter an already existing market with a flank attack strategy. We will concentrate our strengths against our competitors' weaknesses. Our strengths will involve our level of specialization. Our competitors do not offer the level of specialization to compete against us in this niche. We will market our product to Asian-Americans with an emphasis on Chinese-Americans.

The pricing strategy will be close to what our competitors are charging because of the industry characteristics. First, tutoring services are established already in our market. Second, our product could be copied by another firm simply by employment of a specialist in our area. Last, there are many competitors, approximately 40, in our market already without a large, distinguishable amount of product differentiation.

To summarize our marketing strategy, the following list is offered:

1. Price—close to market price.
2. Initially market to specific niche—Asian-Americans.
3. Increase market share by offering additional services—tutoring to the whole market not just Asian-Americans.

## VII.   MARKETING TACTICS

Advertisements will be put into two separate media. First, the Gwinnett and Dekalb county phone books will be used to advertise our services. This will cost the company $135 per month to advertise with a one-inch advertisement with art work (Chinese alphabet). Second, the Chinese newspaper, The *Chinese Community Newspaper* will be used. The Chinese newspaper is issued twice each month and a one-inch ad in the business section will cost only $17 per month. In both instances, both Chinese characters and English words will be used to advertise.

A third source, word of mouth, will be instrumental in advertising our company. Business cards will be used to advertise our services. These cards will be $35 for 500 cards. The cards will have raised letters and a professional appearance.

In the third year of operation, when the growth of our company allows for a larger advertising budget, brochures will be produced and will be sent to all customers inquiring about our services. Presently, 500 color brochures cost approximately $164. Since our financial projections are in constant dollars, we will use this figure in our financial reports.

The following actions will need to be taken to accomplish our marketing tactics:

1. Listen to customers' feedback.
2. Know our benefits and services and be able to discuss them with potential customers.
3. Show commitment to quality.
4. Stress customer service among all employees.
5. Build a referral network.
6. Continue to advertise with business cards, telephone directory ads, and newspaper advertisements.

## VIII.   IMPLEMENTATION AND CONTROL

Pro forma balance sheets and income statements are provided in Appendix A. Because our firm is service oriented, we will not have many balance sheet accounts to control. All investments in equipment and cash proceeds will directly affect retained earnings. By 1995, our company will have grown by 45% from our 1993 level.

These financial projections take into account the following assumptions:

1. The number of customers in years 1, 2, and 3 will be 3, 5 and 8, respectively.

2. Approximately 5% interest will be earned on cash reserves.
3. All projections are in constant dollars.

Appendix B includes pro forma income statements thru 1995. A break-even analysis using the projected income reveals that the break-even point on our $10,000 investment will come in year 2. This is including both wages and net income into total earnings. This may be unconventional, but the purpose of our company is to provide employment and earn equity in the firm.

A cash flow analysis is contained in Appendix C. This contains sources and outflows of cash that our company will experience over the next three years. The advertising expenses include the costs of brochures, business cards, telephone directory ads, and newspaper advertisements. The cost of the telephone will be high in the first year due to the purchase of an answering machine and the initial setup costs associated with installing a new telephone line. Supplies will include office supplies. Equipment mainly includes the cost of computers.

## IX. SUMMARY

The Chu Tutoring Service will result in two very important benefits for Helen Chu-Urbanski. She will have employment through the life of the company and as the company grows, equity will build up in the service.

The company will eventually expand into a broader target market. Initially, keeping in mind the growing Asian-American population, the firm will position itself in a niche that will fuel its early growth.

As people strive to improve their social standing through education, the Chu Tutoring Service will assist them in satisfying their needs.

## BIBLIOGRAPHY

Awanohara, Susumu. "Tyros, Triads, Tycoons," *Far Eastern Economic Review,* 18 July 1991: 50–51.

Bressi, Todd W. "Chinatowns Stand Their Ground," *Planning,* Nov. 1987: 12–16.

Cohen, William A., and Reddick, Marshall E. *Successful Marketing for Small Business.* New York: Amacom, 1981.

Davidson, Jeffrey P. *Marketing on a Shoestring.* New York: John Wiley & Sons, Inc., 1988.

Davidson, Jeffrey P. *The Marketing Sourcebook for Small Business.* New York: John Wiley & Sons, Inc., 1989.

Garland, Susan B. "Those Aging Boomers," *Business Week,* 20 May 1991: 106–112.

Kotler, Philip. *Marketing Management,* 7th ed. Englewood Cliffs, NJ: Prentice Hall, Inc., 1991.

Lee, Alice. "A Socio-Cultural Framework for the Assessment of Chinese Children with Special Needs," *Topics in Language Disorders,* 9(3), (1989): 38–44.

Matsuda, Maryon. "Working with Asian Parents: Some Communication Strategies," *Topics in Language Disorders* 9(3), (1989): 45–53.

# APPENDIX A

# Balance Sheets
# The Chu Tutoring Service

|  | Sept. 1993 | Sept. 1994 | Sept. 1995 |
|---|---|---|---|
| *Assets* | | | |
| Cash | $ 9,009 | $11,020 | $11,374 |
| Supplies | 300 | 450 | 450 |
| Equipment | 2,500 | 2,500 | 5,300 |
| Total Assets | $11,809 | $13,970 | $17,124 |
| *Liabilities* | | | |
| Accounts payable | $    500 | $    500 | $    500 |
| Total Liabilities | $    500 | $    500 | $    500 |
| *Equity* | | | |
| Retained earnings | $11,309 | $13,470 | $16,524 |
| Total Liabilities and Equity | $11,809 | $13,970 | $17,124 |

# APPENDIX B

# Income Statements
# The Chu Tutoring Service

|  | Sept. 1992 | Sept. 1993 | Sept. 1994 |
|---|---|---|---|
| *Revenues* |  |  |  |
| Tuition | $9,855 | $16,425 | $26,280 |
| Interest | 580 | 675 | 720 |
| *Expenses* |  |  |  |
| Wages | 7,560 | 12,000 | 21,600 |
| Supplies | 200 | 330 | 450 |
| Equipment | 2,500 | 300 | 2,500 |
| Transportation | 400 | 660 | 900 |
| Advertising | 388 | 549 | 437 |
| Telephone | 380 | 300 | 600 |
| Net Income | $ -993 | $ 2,961 | $ 513 |
| Taxes | 0 | 977 | 169 |
| N.I. After Taxes | $ -993 | $ 1,984 | $ 344 |
| *Note:* Net Income + Salary | $6,567 | $13,984 | $13,864 |

# APPENDIX C

# Cash Flow Analysis
# The Chu Tutoring Service

**Sept 1992 to Aug 1993**

|                            | Sep      | Oct     | Nov     | Dec     | Jan      | Feb      |
|----------------------------|----------|---------|---------|---------|----------|----------|
| Beginning Balance          | $10,000  | $9,689  | $9,044  | $8,394  | $ 7,742  | $10,310  |
| *Sources*                  |          |         |         |         |          |          |
| Tuition                    | 3,285    | 0       | 0       | 0       | 3,285    | 0        |
| Interest                   | 50       | 50      | 46      | 43      | 45       | 51       |
| Total Sources              | $ 3,335  | $  50   | $  46   | $  43   | $ 3,330  | $   51   |
| *Outflow*                  |          |         |         |         |          |          |
| Salaries                   | 630      | 630     | 630     | 630     | 630      | 630      |
| Supplies                   | 67       | 0       | 0       | 0       | 67       | 0        |
| Equipment                  | 2,500    | 0       | 0       | 0       | 0        | 0        |
| Transportation             | 33       | 33      | 34      | 33      | 33       | 34       |
| Advertising (inc. postage) | 201      | 17      | 17      | 17      | 17       | 17       |
| Telephone                  | 215      | 15      | 15      | 15      | 15       | 15       |
| Taxes                      | 0        | 0       | 0       | 0       | 0        | 0        |
| Total Outflow              | $ 3,646  | $ 695   | $ 696   | $ 695   | $  762   | $  696   |
| Ending Balance             | $ 9,689  | $9,044  | $8,394  | $7,742  | $10,310  | $ 9,665  |

**Sept 1992 to Aug 1993**

|                            | Mar     | Apr     | May      | Jun      | Jul      | Aug      |
|----------------------------|---------|---------|----------|----------|----------|----------|
| Beginning Balance          | $9,665  | $9,024  | $ 8,375  | $10,940  | $10,300  | $9,657   |
| *Sources*                  |         |         |          |          |          |          |
| Tuition                    | 0       | 0       | 3,285    | 0        | 0        | 0        |
| Interest                   | 54      | 46      | 42       | 55       | 52       | 48       |
| Total Sources              | $  54   | $  46   | $ 3,327  | $  55    | $  52    | $  48    |
| *Outflow*                  |         |         |          |          |          |          |
| Salaries                   | 630     | 630     | 630      | 630      | 630      | 630      |
| Supplies                   | 0       | 0       | 66       | 0        | 0        | 0        |
| Equipment                  | 0       | 0       | 0        | 0        | 0        | 0        |
| Transportation             | 33      | 33      | 34       | 33       | 33       | 34       |
| Advertising (inc. postage) | 17      | 17      | 17       | 17       | 17       | 17       |
| Telephone                  | 15      | 15      | 15       | 15       | 15       | 15       |
| Taxes                      | 0       | 0       | 0        | 0        | 0        | 0        |
| Total Outflow              | $ 695   | $ 695   | $  762   | $  695   | $  695   | $  696   |
| Ending Balance             | $9,024  | $8,375  | $10,940  | $10,300  | $9,657   | $9,009   |

**Sept 1993 to Aug 1994**

|  | Sep | Oct | Nov | Dec | Jan | Feb |
|---|---|---|---|---|---|---|
| Beginning Balance | $ 9,009 | $12,677 | $11,644 | $10,602 | $ 9,558 | $13,874 |
| *Sources* | | | | | | |
| Tuition | 5,475 | 0 | 0 | 0 | 5,475 | 0 |
| Interest | 45 | 64 | 55 | 53 | 48 | 69 |
| Total Sources | $ 5,520 | $ 64 | $ 55 | $ 53 | $ 5,523 | $ 69 |
| *Outflow* | | | | | | |
| Salaries | 1,000 | 1,000 | 1,000 | 1,000 | 1,000 | 1,000 |
| Supplies | 110 | 0 | 0 | 0 | 110 | 0 |
| Equipment | 300 | 0 | 0 | 0 | 0 | 0 |
| Transportation | 55 | 55 | 55 | 55 | 55 | 55 |
| Advertising (inc. postage) | 362 | 17 | 17 | 17 | 17 | 17 |
| Telephone | 25 | 25 | 25 | 25 | 25 | 25 |
| Taxes | 0 | 0 | 0 | 0 | 0 | 0 |
| Total Outflow | $ 1,852 | $ 1,097 | $ 1,097 | $ 1,097 | $ 1,207 | $ 1,097 |
| Ending Balance | $12,677 | $11,644 | $10,602 | $ 9,558 | $13,874 | $12,846 |

**Sept 1993 to Aug 1994**

|  | Mar | Apr | May | Jun | Jul | Aug |
|---|---|---|---|---|---|---|
| Beginning Balance | $12,846 | $11,813 | $ 9,798 | $14,114 | $13,088 | $12,056 |
| *Sources* | | | | | | |
| Tuition | 0 | 0 | 5,475 | 0 | 0 | 0 |
| Interest | 64 | 59 | 48 | 71 | 65 | 65 |
| Total Sources | $ 64 | $ 59 | $ 5,523 | $ 71 | $ 65 | $ 65 |
| *Outflow* | | | | | | |
| Salaries | 1,000 | 1,000 | 1,000 | 1,000 | 1,000 | 1,000 |
| Supplies | 0 | 0 | 110 | 0 | 0 | 0 |
| Equipment | 0 | 0 | 0 | 0 | 0 | 0 |
| Transportation | 55 | 55 | 55 | 55 | 55 | 55 |
| Advertising (inc. postage) | 17 | 17 | 17 | 17 | 17 | 17 |
| Telephone | 25 | 25 | 25 | 25 | 25 | 25 |
| Taxes | 0 | 977 | 0 | 0 | 0 | 0 |
| Total Outflow | $ 1,097 | $ 2,074 | $ 1,207 | $ 1,097 | $ 1,097 | $ 1,097 |
| Ending Balance | $11,813 | $ 9,798 | $14,114 | $13,088 | $12,056 | $11,024 |

**Sept 1994 to Aug 1995**

|                            | Sep      | Oct      | Nov      | Dec      | Jan      | Feb      |
|----------------------------|----------|----------|----------|----------|----------|----------|
| Beginning Balance          | $11,002  | $15,025  | $13,155  | $11,275  | $ 9,386  | $16,096  |
| *Sources*                  |          |          |          |          |          |          |
| Tuition                    | 8,760    | 0        | 0        | 0        | 8,760    | 0        |
| Interest                   | 55       | 75       | 65       | 56       | 45       | 58       |
| Total Sources              | $ 8,815  | $   75   | $   65   | $   56   | $ 8,805  | $   58   |
| *Outflow*                  |          |          |          |          |          |          |
| Salaries                   | 1,800    | 1,800    | 1,800    | 1,800    | 1,800    | 1,800    |
| Supplies                   | 150      | 0        | 0        | 0        | 150      | 0        |
| Equipment                  | 2,500    | 0        | 0        | 0        | 0        | 0        |
| Transportation             | 75       | 75       | 75       | 75       | 75       | 75       |
| Advertising (inc. postage) | 217      | 20       | 20       | 20       | 20       | 20       |
| Telephone                  | 50       | 50       | 50       | 50       | 50       | 50       |
| Taxes                      | 0        | 0        | 0        | 0        | 0        | 0        |
| Total Outflow              | $ 4,792  | $ 1,945  | $ 1,945  | $ 1,945  | $ 2,095  | $ 1,945  |
| Ending Balance             | $15,025  | $13,155  | $11,275  | $ 9,386  | $16,096  | $14,209  |

**Sept 1994 to Aug 1995**

|                            | Mar      | Apr      | May      | Jun      | Jul      | Aug      |
|----------------------------|----------|----------|----------|----------|----------|----------|
| Beginning Balance          | $14,209  | $12,332  | $10,271  | $16,987  | $15,127  | $13,258  |
| *Sources*                  |          |          |          |          |          |          |
| Tuition                    | 0        | 0        | 8,760    | 0        | 0        | 0        |
| Interest                   | 68       | 53       | 51       | 85       | 76       | 61       |
| Total Sources              | $   68   | $   53   | $ 8,811  | $   85   | $   76   | $   61   |
| *Outflow*                  |          |          |          |          |          |          |
| Salaries                   | 1,800    | 1,800    | 1,800    | 1,800    | 1,800    | 1,800    |
| Supplies                   | 0        | 0        | 150      | 0        | 0        | 0        |
| Equipment                  | 0        | 0        | 0        | 0        | 0        | 0        |
| Transportation             | 75       | 75       | 75       | 75       | 75       | 75       |
| Advertising (inc. postage) | 20       | 20       | 20       | 20       | 20       | 20       |
| Telephone                  | 50       | 50       | 50       | 50       | 50       | 50       |
| Taxes                      | 0        | 169      | 0        | 0        | 0        | 0        |
| Total Outflow              | $ 1,945  | $ 2,114  | $ 2,095  | $ 1,945  | $ 1,945  | $ 1,945  |
| Ending Balance             | $12,332  | $10,271  | $16,987  | $15,127  | $13,258  | $11,374  |

# APPENDIX D

# Questionnaire

| | Q.1 | Q.2 | Q.3 | Q.4 | Q.5 | Q.6 | Q.7 | Q.8 |
|---|---|---|---|---|---|---|---|---|
| Berlitz | N | N | H | UC | N | Y | NT | L |
| Educational Resources | N | N | M | C | Y | N | NT | M |
| Mountain West Church | Y | N | L | UC | N | N | NB | L |
| Total Tutoring | Y | N | M | C | Y | N | LC | L |
| Alexander Smith | N | N | H | C | N | N | LC | L |
| Kiara Tutoring Center | Y | N | M | C | N | Y | LC | H |
| A Plus Learning Labs | N | Y | H | C | N | N | LC | H |

Q.1 Provide E.S.L. Instruction?
Q.2 Chinese-speaking tutors?
Q.3 Fees?
Q.4 Tutors certified?
Q.5 Use computer instruction?
Q.6 In-home tutoring?
Q.7 Size?
Q.8 Teacher : Student ratio?

Key
Y—Yes
N—No
NA—Failed to answer
L—Low
M—Moderate
H—High

C—Certified
UC—Uncertified
NT—National
LC—Local
NB—Neighborhood

# 4

# BUSINESS PLAN FOR ALTERNATIVE POOL HALL

*Developed by*
**Bernadette Gines,
Bryan Sue,
Frances Vien,
Joshua Que, and
Shant Koumriqian**

# Executive Summary

"The Alternative Pool Hall" is scheduled to be open on June 1, 1993 in the Montrose Shopping Park. It will start out as a partnership entity. The partners include Bernadette Gines, Bryan Sue, Frances Vien, Joshua Que, and Shant Koumriqian. We plan to expand the pool hall in 1995. The purpose of this business plan is to present the plan to the future investors of our pool hall, so that we will be able to expand our pool hall to serve the increasing demand of the community.

We are going to proceed with the project through the contribution of $40,000.00 from each partner. This will be sufficient to start the pool hall. With this initial investment, we will be able to start up and will look forward to expanding. Therefore, we present this business plan so that we can begin to accept financial investments for our expansion.

# Table of Contents

## I.  INTRODUCTION

We have prepared this business plan to open up a pool hall. According to the *New York Times,* "The pool industry claims that more than 38 million Americans play the game."[1] This is nearly twice the number of tennis players or golfers. Due to lack of entertainment centers encompassing the Northern Glendale, La Canada, La Crescenta, and Montrose areas, we feel that there is an opportunity to open up a pool hall in this area.

## II.  SITUATION ANALYSIS

According to Howard Zambert, general manager of Golden Cue in Glendale (who has been in the industry for seven years), "Classy pool halls have become very popular recently." Mr. Zambert's statement is supported by *The Wall Street Journal* which states "one new pool hall opens every week."[2] According to the general manager of Charles Billiards of Glendale and an article in the *New York Times,* "the demand and popularity for pool halls has been increasing since 1986 after the release of the movie *The Color of Money.*"[3] All the pool halls cater to the older single crowds, generally those ages 21 and over. All of these pool halls serve alcohol and do not admit anyone under the age of 18.

### A.  Neutral Environment

Much emphasis has been given lately to the subject of family values. The Republican party felt this was a strong issue during the 1992 Presidential election. It has become a popular issue related to the deterioration of the family unit. Drug and alcohol abuse has been reaching peak levels, especially among teenagers. Youth involvement in gangs has been increasing as well as alcohol-related injuries and death. Many of these problems can be linked to the deteriorating family units.

   Our pool hall will tailor to society's interest in the family values ideology. By doing this, we will create an environment for those who do not want to be around intoxicated people and cigarette smoke. The pool hall will also create a place for youth under the drinking age of 21. Some establishments offer alcohol and allow minors in their premises. The fact that they are around the alcohol might influence them to use it in the future. Some minors may ask people over 21 to purchase the alcohol for them, while others may be able to purchase it for themselves by using a fake identification. By not serving alcohol, our pool hall will promote the campaign "Say No to Drugs." Also, we will not contribute to the intoxicating of customers and then sending them off to drive home as many other establishments do.

   Our pool hall will set a family-type environment where teenagers, young adults, and families can enjoy a game of pool. This will cater to the surrounding community, which contains a large percentage of family households. It will be a place where teenagers can go instead of loitering in the streets and perhaps causing trouble. By designing our pool hall to have a family setting, parents will be more likely to allow their children to spend their time there. Parents will be assured that their children are in a safe place, instead of staying on the streets or going to parties where an abundance of alcohol and drugs are available.

---

[1] "Clean Pool." *New York Times* (Feb. 23, 1992), p. 28 (1).
[2] "Upscale Pool Halls Click with the Night Club Crowds." *The Wall Street Journal* (March 26, 1992), p. PA1(5).
[3] "Pool: It's Upwardly Mobile and It's on a Run." *New York Times* (Feb. 1, 1991), p. C4 (1).

## B.   Competitor Environment

We feel that our competition may be any goods or services that consumers would rather spend their money on for entertainment purposes. We also feel that there is no competition that we must directly compete with because there are no pool halls in our target area. However, there are two bowling alleys, four video rental stores, one video game arcade, and several restaurants. Both bowling alleys serve alcohol and attract an older and less sophisticated crowd. The video arcade promotes individual entertainment because many games are played alone. Also the arcade tends to be a "hangout" that attracts gang-affiliated people. Video rental stores offer a form of entertainment for those who do not want to leave their homes. Restaurants typically are a place to go before or after the consumers have gone somewhere else for entertainment. Thus, we will not face much competition from restaurants. Since there are no movie theaters in our target area, we will not have to worry about this type of competition in the short run.

## C.   Company Environment

We have a few advantages in promoting our pool hall. Three of our partners play pool at least once a week. Thus, it gives us an advantage of knowing what a typical customer wants in a pool hall. Another advantage is that we can decrease our advertising costs because one of our partners owns a print shop.

All of the partners of the company have recently graduated from the area high schools. Experiencing the lack of entertainment options during our own high school years will help us to relate to the needs of our younger customers. Another factor that will give us an advantage is that we still have close contacts to most of the current students and faculty of the local high schools. This will allow us to more effectively promote our business and attract new customers. We will have these same advantages toward the college and university students, because all of us are attending universities and have many close friends at various universities who can help to promote our pool hall.

Also, all of us still live at home and are not responsible for a family. We have no mortgages or payments to make. This will allow us to concentrate all of our effort in the business. It is not critical that we make large profits immediately because we have no other financial obligations. We can take all the revenues from the business and reinvest it to improve the pool hall.

## III.   TARGET MARKET

## A.   Demographic

Every industry and market that promotes a product can be divided or subdivided into various segments or target markets toward which it will be directed. Our particular segment includes the age group between 16 and 35 of both genders who prefer an alternative environment, that is, an alcohol- and smoke-free environment.

In reference to Exhibit 1, the shaded area represents the population of our target area cities of Northern Glendale, La Canada, La Crescenta, and Montrose. The first bar represents the age group of 16–20 which has a population of 8,234. The second bar represents the age group of 21–24 which has a population of 12,539. The third bar represents the age group of 25–35 which has a population of 39,631. The sum of these three groups gives us 44 percent of the total population.

We are targeting high school students and college students who prefer a nonalcoholic and nonsmoking environment. Therefore, in relation to the total population of

**Exhibit 1   Collective Data from 1992
California's Cities, Towns and Counties. Basic
Data Profiles for all Municipalities and Counties**

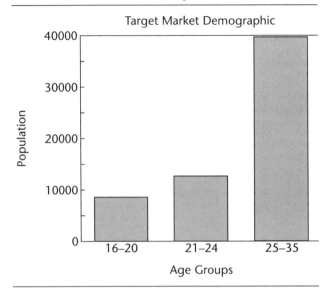

60,404, 30.8 percent attend high school and 24.8 percent are attending the first three years of college. This gives us a total of 55.6 percent who are students. Having a marketing tactic of targeting specific high schools and colleges will be of great advantage to us.

The household income is a major factor because it shows how much our potential customers could spend on entertainment or recreation. The household income encompassing Northern Glendale, La Canada, La Crescenta, and Montrose is relatively high. Only 5.2 percent of the households make below $5,000 annually; 75 percent of the households make between $20,000 and $60,000 annually; 16 percent of the households make over $75,000 annually. The residential value is also relatively high: ranging between $200,000 and $600,000.[4] For these reasons, our target market encompasses Northern Glendale, La Canada, La Crescenta, and Montrose area.

## B.  Psychographic

We believe that a person's occupation also plays an important factor on how a consumer will spend his or her disposable income. According to an article in *American Demographics*, "Discretionary income grows as one's educational attainment or career rises."[5] It is to our advantage that within our target area 67.7 percent of the population hold a white-collar job. This gives the household members a greater amount of disposable income for entertainment and recreation.

## C.  Behavioristic

We also believe that the consumer's behavior plays an important factor on what an individual would spend his or her income on. According to the 1990 Consumer Expenditure Survey, women who live alone spend an average of $569 a year on entertainment,

---

[4] Susan Krafft. "The Demographics of Extra Money," *American Demographics* (May 1991), p. 20 (1).
[5] Ibid.

**Exhibit 2    Annual Household Income of Northern Glendale, La Canada, La Crescenta and Montrose**

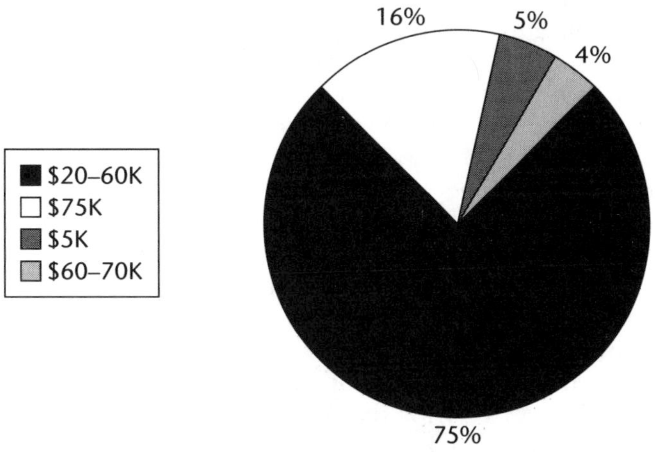

16%    5%    4%

- ■ $20–60K
- □ $75K
- ▨ $5K
- ▤ $60–70K

75%

compared with $1,019 for men. Two-thirds of all entertainment spending by people who live alone goes for fees and admissions, and televisions, radios, and sound equipment. Single women spend an average of $182 a year on fees and admissions, while single men spend $295. Fees and admissions include fees for participant sports; fees for club memberships; and admission to sporting events, movies, and theater events. In relation to Exhibit 3, an average single under 25 spends $1,397 annually. On the other hand, singles ranging between 25 and 35 spend $2,073 annually for entertainment.

Over 40 percent of the entertainment spending of women under the age 25 goes for fees and admissions. Over 50 percent of the entertainment of men under the age of 25 goes for fees and admissions. It's this very predictable statistic, in fact, that makes running a pool hall possible and profitable. Therefore, our target market is consumers between the ages of 18 and 35.

## IV.    PROBLEMS AND OPPORTUNITIES

There are a few problems that we should encounter with the location of the pool hall since the pool hall is located close to a residential area. For instance, curfew is set at

**Exhibit 3    Average Annual Spending on Entertainment by Single Men and Women**

|  | Fees and Admissions | TV's, Radios, Sound Equipment | Pets and Toys | Other Supplies |
|---|---|---|---|---|
| *Men* | | | | |
| Under 25 | $306 | $392 | $ 44 | $177 |
| 25 to 35 | 380 | 411 | 96 | 266 |
| *Women* | | | | |
| Under 25 | $207 | $142 | $ 44 | $ 74 |
| 25 to 35 | 253 | 296 | 120 | 251 |

*Source:* Collective data from "Entertainment Singles," *American Demographics,* August 1991.

10:30 P.M. All police officers will be carefully looking out for people loitering the streets. We will alleviate this problem by keeping everyone inside after 10:30 P.M. Noise level is another problem. We plan to insulate the walls and turn off the music after 10:30 P.M. These problems may cause us to close earlier than we plan causing most teenagers and young adults to resort to other forms of entertainment, which would have a tremendous effect on our profits. Another problem is being located within a conservative area. Most parents will tend to discourage their children from going to a pool hall. In the past the image of a pool hall was that of a underground place where hustlers and drunks were frequently seen. Hopefully, our pool hall will change the old image of smoky pool halls. Our main opportunity in opening a pool hall will be that there are no competitors in the market at this time. Most of the pool halls are targeted toward the young adults 21 and over and allow smoking or serving of alcoholic beverages.

Although there are no other pool halls like ours in the surrounding areas, we will be competing with other forms of entertainment, for example, bowling, arcades, movie theaters, and video rentals. For a couple of friends to see a movie costs an average of $6.75 per ticket equaling $13.50 for two people. This does not include refreshments such as nachos, popcorn, and drinks. Also, a movie lasts for about two hours giving a certain time limit. On the other hand, two friends can come to our pool hall and spend less than $15.00 for over two hours, which also includes their drinks.

In summary, we have compared our company to many other entertainment sources. Our conclusion is that spending time at a pool hall is less expensive and more enjoyable.

## V.  BUSINESS OBJECTIVES AND GOALS

Our pool hall will introduce to the community an alternative source of entertainment besides bowling, video arcades, and watching a movie. The area we will be focusing on includes Northern Glendale, La Canada, La Crescenta, and the Montrose communities. Our objective is to have a $129,000 net profit in the second year after introduction.

The main goal of our plan is to attract the people under the age of 21 because as residents of the area, we noticed the need for a place to relax instead of loitering on the streets. Another goal that we wish to achieve is to attract the young adults 21 and over who prefer a nonalcoholic and smoke-free environment. Because of these two important factors, the pool hall will also establish a source of entertainment for the entire family.

## VI.  MARKETING STRATEGY

In today's society, consumers are more aware of the problems caused by alcohol consumption. California Senate Bill 2599, which was formalized by the governor, calls for extensive planning at state and local levels, and for mobilization of community effort, to eliminate alcohol and drug use in California. Because of this, our strategy is to target those who prefer a nonalcoholic and nonsmoking environment.

We have compared ourselves to five different pool halls. We noticed that they vary from an unclean and below-average environment, to the clean and expensive. An example of a below-average pool hall is "Georges" in Glendale, which had a very smoky atmosphere. On the other hand, "Hollywood Athletic Club" is very clean and is considered a high-class pool hall. We have decided to position ourselves in between the two. We set our price above that of the below-average pool hall, reason being that our pool hall will consist of brand-new tables and our environment will be smoke-free. We are charging our customers lower than the price of the above-average pool hall because our target is to attract the youths. We feel the youths wouldn't have sufficient amount of income to support the habit of playing pool if our prices were equal to that of a high-class pool hall.

## VII.  MARKETING TACTICS

### A.  Price

Our hourly charge after 6:00 P.M. is $5.00. However, with a student identification, our discount price is $4.50 after 6:00 P.M. Before 6:00 P.M. the hourly charge for all customers is $4.00. We add $1.00 for each additional player.

### B.  Place

We are located at the Montrose Shopping Park, 2565 Honolulu Blvd. The Center is surrounded by a conservative and affluent community.

### C.  Product

We are providing a family-setting pool hall that does not serve alcohol. The pool hall consists of 20 tables, 4½ feet × 9 feet, with a computerized lighting system, a big screen TV, the latest video games, pinball, and fussball. We offer a nonsmoking and nonalcoholic pool hall environment with various soft drinks and prepackaged snacks.

### D.  Promotion

We will advertise our product through flyers, school newspapers, and through word of mouth. We will also offer pool classes in high schools and colleges.

## VIII.  CONTROL AND IMPLEMENTATION

Without implementation and control, a great business plan would fail. Implementation is an important part of the business management process. In order to have a successful implementation, business management must motivate and communicate to its employees the organizational goals and the importance of focusing on quality and service. We have decided not to hire additional employees but instead divide the task of operating the pool hall among the partners. Thus, there will be no need to motivate or communicate the organizational goals to our employees. All of the partners will help in determining the organizational goals and will know that we must focus on quality and service.

To properly control the business activities of the pool hall, we will establish some performance standards. We will measure our performance by the percentage increase in yearly sales. We would like to obtain at least a 10 percent increase in sales each year after the introduction. If we do not achieve this standard, we will have to reconsider some of our marketing tactics and strategy. We will have to rescan our environment and make proper changes in our price, advertising expenditures, and possibly redirect our position towards a different target market. Although we would not be content, we may have to change our image to attract those customers in more profitable markets that we originally decided not to serve.

## IX.  SUMMARY

In summary, we would like to reemphasize a few points. First of all, the popularity and the demand for pool halls have increased drastically since the movie *The Color of Money* in 1986. Second, there are a few entertainment facilities encompassing Northern Glendale, La Canada, La Crescenta, and Montrose for younger adults who are prohibited by law to consume alcohol. Last, consumers are more aware of their health and what alcohol and smoking can do to them. All of these three points are a good measure for an opportunity. Therefore, we have decided to open up a nonalcoholic and nonsmoking pool hall in Montrose to serve those consumers who prefer to be in a healthy environment for entertainment.

## X.  BIBLIOGRAPHY

*California's Cities, Towns & Counties Basic Data Profiles for All Municipalities and Counties.* 1992. Edith R. Hornor. Information Publications, Palo Alto, Ca.

"Clean Pool," *The New York Times Magazine,* Feb. 23, 1992, p. 28 (1).

"Entertainment Singles," *American Demographics,* August 1990, p. 6 (2).

Krafft, Susan. "The Demographics of Extra Money," *American Demographics,* May 1991, p. 20 (1).

*Montrose-Verdugo City Chamber of Commerce Directory.* 1992–1993.

"Pool: It's Upwardly Mobile and It's on a Run," *New York Times,* Feb. 1, 1991, p. C4 (1).

"Upscale Pool Halls Click with the Night Club Crowds," *The Wall Street Journal,* March 26, 1992, p. A1 (5).

## XI.  APPENDIX

The tables for this Appendix appear on pages 4·11 through 4·14.

## The Alternative Pool Hall Profit/Loss Statement for Fiscal Year Ended May 31, 1994

| | 06/93 | 07/93 | 08/93 | 09/93 | 10/93 | 11/93 | 12/93 | 01/94 | 02/94 | 03/94 | 04/94 | 05/94 | Total |
|---|---|---|---|---|---|---|---|---|---|---|---|---|---|
| Sales Revenue | $11,050 | $11,050 | $11,603 | $11,603 | $11,603 | $12,155 | $12,155 | $12,763 | $13,401 | $14,741 | $14,741 | $15,478 | $152,342 |
| Less: Operating expenses | | | | | | | | | | | | | |
| Rent | $ 3,000 | $ 3,000 | $ 3,000 | $ 3,000 | $ 3,000 | $ 3,000 | $ 3,000 | $ 3,000 | $ 3,000 | $ 3,000 | $ 3,000 | $ 3,000 | $ 36,000 |
| Utilities | 1,300 | 1,300 | 1,300 | 900 | 900 | 900 | 1,300 | 1,300 | 900 | 900 | 900 | 1,300 | 13,200 |
| Advertising | 500 | 500 | 500 | 500 | 350 | 350 | 350 | 350 | 350 | 350 | 300 | 300 | 4,700 |
| Supplies | 590 | 590 | 590 | 590 | 590 | 590 | 590 | 590 | 590 | 590 | 590 | 590 | 7,080 |
| General and administrative expenses | 300 | 300 | 300 | 300 | 300 | 300 | 300 | 300 | 300 | 300 | 300 | 300 | 3,600 |
| Depreciation expense* | 9,583 | 9,583 | 9,583 | 9,583 | 9,583 | 9,583 | 9,583 | 9,583 | 9,583 | 9,583 | 9,583 | 9,583 | 114,996 |
| Total Operating Expenses | $15,273 | $15,273 | $15,273 | $14,873 | $14,723 | $14,723 | $15,123 | $15,123 | $14,723 | $14,723 | $14,673 | $15,073 | $179,576 |
| Net Profit/Loss** | $ (4,223) | $(4,223) | $(3,671) | $(3,271) | $(3,120) | $(2,568) | $(2,968) | $(2,360) | $(1,322) | $ 18 | $ 68 | $ 405 | $(27,234) |

**Depreciate the start-up costs of $115,000 for 12 months.
**Partnership has no tax liabilities.

**The Alternative Pool Hall Profit/Loss Statement for Fiscal Year Ended May 31, 1995**

| | 06/94 | 07/94 | 08/94 | 09/94 | 10/94 | 11/94 | 12/94 | 01/95 | 02/95 | 03/95 | 04/95 | 05/95 | Total |
|---|---|---|---|---|---|---|---|---|---|---|---|---|---|
| Sales Revenue | $15,478 | $15,478 | $15,478 | $15,478 | $16,252 | $16,252 | $16,252 | $16,252 | $16,252 | $16,252 | $16,252 | $16,252 | $191,928 |
| Less: Operating expenses | | | | | | | | | | | | | |
| Rent | $ 3,000 | $ 3,000 | $ 3,000 | $ 3,000 | $ 3,000 | $ 3,000 | $ 3,000 | $ 3,000 | $ 3,000 | $ 3,000 | $ 3,000 | $ 3,000 | $ 36,000 |
| Utilities | 1,300 | 1,300 | 1,300 | 900 | 900 | 900 | 1,300 | 1,300 | 900 | 900 | 900 | 1,300 | 13,200 |
| Advertising | 300 | 300 | 200 | 200 | 200 | 250 | 250 | 200 | 200 | 200 | 250 | 250 | 2,800 |
| Supplies | 590 | 590 | 590 | 590 | 590 | 590 | 590 | 590 | 590 | 590 | 590 | 590 | 7,080 |
| General and administrative expenses | 300 | 300 | 300 | 300 | 300 | 300 | 300 | 300 | 300 | 300 | 300 | 300 | 3,600 |
| Total Operating Expenses | $ 5,490 | $ 5,490 | $ 5,390 | $ 4,990 | $ 4,990 | $ 5,040 | $ 5,440 | $ 5,390 | $ 4,990 | $ 4,990 | $ 5,040 | $ 5,440 | $ 62,680 |
| Net Profit/Loss* | $ 9,988 | $ 9,988 | $10,088 | $10,488 | $11,262 | $11,212 | $10,812 | $10,862 | $11,262 | $11,262 | $11,212 | $10,812 | $129,248 |

*Partnership has no tax liabilities.

**The Alternative Pool Hall Breaking Even**

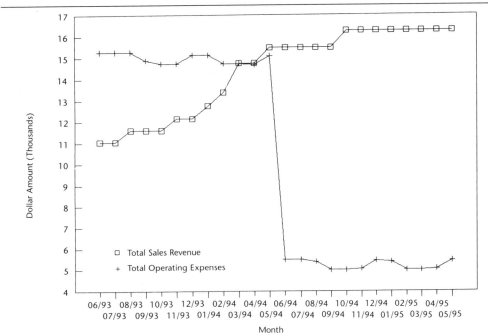

**The Alternative Pool Hall Net Profit/Loss**

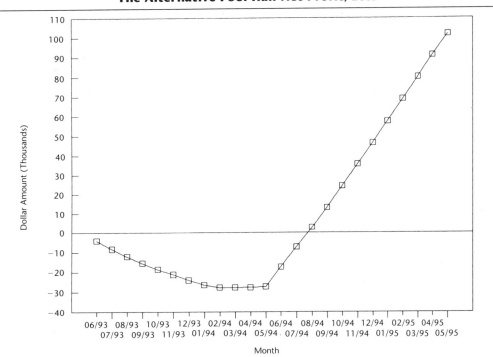

## Map of Montrose and Surrounding Areas

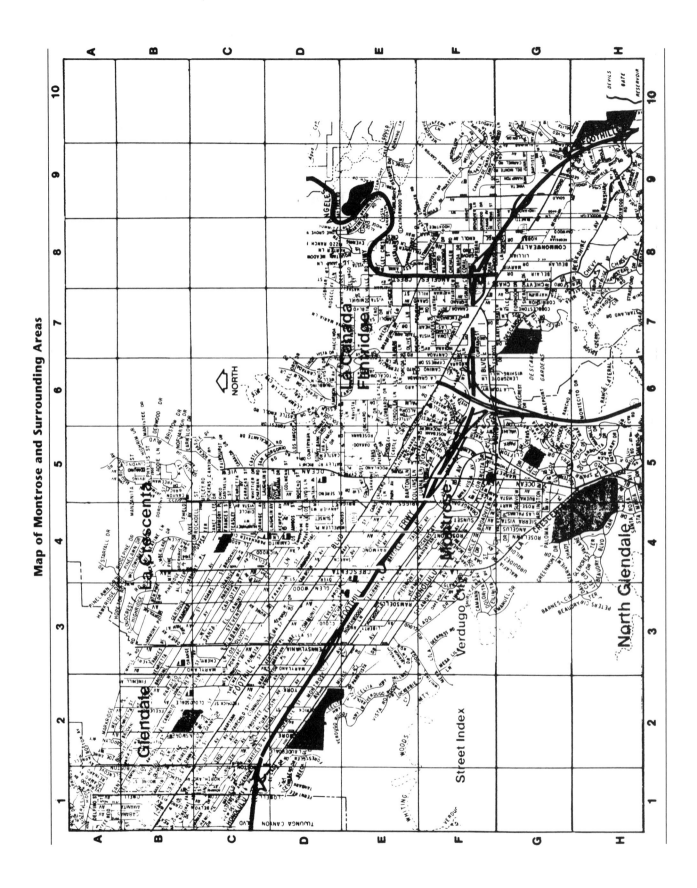

NORTH

Street Index

# 5

# BUSINESS PLAN FOR PROFESSIONAL FITNESS

*Developed by*
**Iain Mozoomdar**

# EXECUTIVE SUMMARY

*Professional Fitness* will be an upscale health club located in the City of San Marino, California, and will be targeted at the over-40 age group. This club will offer state-of-the-art equipment and facilities. The aerobic room of Professional Fitness will be soundproofed to ensure that nonaerobic class participants can work out or relax with minimum discomfort. The club will be equipped with high-end weight resistance machines, exercise bicycles, stair climbers, treadmills, cross-country ski machines, satin-finished dumbbells and barbells, and a sauna in both the male and female locker rooms. The club will also provide child-care for members when they work out and will also house a health bar, pro shop, and an attractive members' lounge.

The decision to target the over-40 market was made so as to capitalize on the ongoing transition of the health club industry from an industry that primarily targeted the under-30 market, to one that focuses on the over-40, and family market. Currently, an increased emphasis is being placed on enhancing the quality of life for seniors through the use of specially designed weight training programs. Researchers have found these programs to be very effective in battling the physical and mental deterioration of the body as one moves into the "golden years."

The main differential advantage offered by Professional Fitness will be the unmatched level of personal service and pampering that will be extended to the clients. The aging of the American population, an increased health awareness, and the lack of another such upscale, over-40 facility in the primary trading area of the club will also contribute to the success of the club. The club is expected to have a potential market of 58,258 people. These potential clients will be geographically located from San Marino and the surrounding cities of Pasadena, South Pasadena, Arcadia, Alhambra, Monterey Park, Glendale and La Canada Flintridge.

The start-up costs for the club are estimated to be $1,274,055. The club will charge an initiation fee of $675 and monthly dues of $75. This pricing strategy is conservatively expected to attract 1,200 clients in the first year, 1,800 in the second, and 2,300 by the end of the third year. The club will offer a limited membership of 2,500 people. The expected return on investment will be 15.1 percent in year one, 22.8 percent in year two, and 33.1 percent in year three. The club will break even with 1,096 members and is expected to achieve this within the first year. The estimated dollar gross sales figure for the first year is $1,371,040.31 and this is expected to increase to $2,570,343.27 by the end of the third year.

# TABLE OF CONTENTS

# LIST OF TABLES

# LIST OF FIGURES

# I.  INTRODUCTION

## A.  Statement of Purpose

The purpose of this business plan is to document the credibility and feasibility of opening an upscale, health club in the City of San Marino, California—Professional Fitness. This upscale club will offer a soundproofed aerobic room, state-of-the-art weight stations, exercise bicycles, stair climbers, treadmills, cross-country ski exercisers, free weights, a sauna in both locker rooms, massage facilities, health bar, pro shop, an upscale member lounge, and a child-care center.

## B.  Background

Over the past decade, numerous varieties of health clubs have popped up all over America. Every major city has at least one major health club specializing in total body fitness. The booming movie industry in Southern California has played a major role in making California the most health-conscious state in the country. Southern California's climate and long summer days coupled with mild winters encourage an outdoor-oriented lifestyle. Be it trekking, sun tanning, biking, competitive sports, or just plain "loafing"; Southern Californians want to look their best, hence the sprouting of fitness oriented clubs all over the Southland.

The American Medical Association (AMA) has also placed a stronger emphasis on health and fitness for the aging population (40 and above) over the past five years. This factor has also played a great part in the health club boom. Other factors will be discussed in more detail in the environmental analysis sections.

## C.  Scope

This business plan will include an analysis of the situation, neutral, competitor, and company environments; the target market to be reached; opportunities and threats faced by Professional Fitness; marketing objectives, strategy, and tactics; financial implementation and control.

## D.  Limitations/Delimitations

A time constraint requiring the entire business plan to be completed within 10 weeks causes the content and detail of the business plan to be narrowed in focus.

## E.  Methods

This business plan consists of applied research since the strategies and tactics of this plan are going to be used by the owners and management of Professional Fitness to gain a competitive edge over its competitors. The data for the plan is mainly collected through secondary research and financial data is based on calculated estimates. Some of the results and conclusions used in the competitor analysis section were collected via a questionnaire instrument.

## F.  Assumptions

It is assumed that the economic environment of the primary trading area remains constant and also that the current low interest rate will prevail. It is also assumed that the current lifestyle trends of Southern Californians remain unchanged and that the viable fitness-oriented market segment continues to grow at the same rate.

## G.  Preview

This business plan is to be presented in the following format:

       I.      Situation analysis.

      II.     Target market.

      III.    Opportunities and threats.

      IV.    Business goals and objectives.

      V.     Marketing strategy.

      VI.    Marketing tactics.

      VII.   Implementation and control.

      VIII.  Summary.

A copy of the questionnaire used to evaluate the competitor environment of World Gym, Pasadena, is included in the Appendix.

## II.  SITUATION ANALYSIS

This section is to be divided into the following parts:

    A. Situational environment.

    B. Neutral environment.

    C. Competitor environment.

    D. Company environment.

## A.  The Situational Environment

The situational environment for Professional Fitness is to be analyzed using the following format:

    1. Demand and demand trends.

    2. Social and cultural factors.

    3. Demographics.

    4. Economic and business conditions.

    5. State of technology for fitness equipment.

    6. Laws and regulations.

### 1.  Demand and Demand Trends

There are many factors that are affecting the demand for an upscale health club in San Marino. One of the most important factors is the life cycle of the health club industry. This industry grew at an increasing and phenomenal rate from the late 1970s to about 1989; since then, the

**Figure 1    Life Cycle of the Health Club Industry**

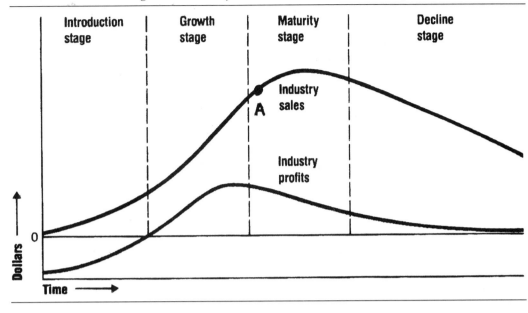

industry is growing, however at a decreasing rate. On the product life-cycle chart, as illustrated in Figure 1, the industry would roughly be at point A.

According to *Club Industry*, a trade publication, from 1982 to 1987, the industry grew at the rate of up to 15 percent a year.[1] In 1987, there were an estimated 10,000 clubs around the country. Also, in 1987, an estimated 30 million Americans had memberships to at least one health club, up from 20 million in 1982.[2] These clubs ranged from aerobics-only to multipurpose facilities. In 1988, consumer spending on health clubs, massages, and the like, increased to a record high of 25 percent over 1987 and became the fastest growing category in personal care.[3]

In 1989, there were an estimated 30,000 clubs all over the country, thanks to a slew of company-owned fitness clubs. These company-owned clubs ranged from a basic weight room with a few free weights and machines, where employees would work out during their lunch break; to comprehensive athletic facilities, like that of corporate giants AT&T, Saatchi & Saatchi Advertising, and Tenneco.[4]

In 1990, an industry estimate by *Club Industry*, showed that there were just under 33,000 clubs in the country, an increase of under 10 percent.[5] Also, in 1990, Americans spent $5.3 billion on health club memberships and $1.73 billion on exercise equipment.[6]

The slight slowdown in the industry has been due in part to the recession which has been plaguing the United States since the middle of 1990. Investment and real estate loans have become increasingly difficult to obtain. The collapse of the savings and loan industry has also caused banks and investors to become more "tight-fisted."

Consumers of health club memberships are also becoming much more selective and educated in choosing a health club. This is due in part to the large number of clubs available, and

---

[1]Laura Loro, "Health Clubs Stretch Markets," *Advertising Age*, May 16, 1988: 38.
[2]Dennis Rodkin, "Health Clubs Sweat the Details in Ads," *Advertising Age*, Dec. 3, 1989: 39.
[3]Vivian Brownstein, "Consumers Will Help the Economy Stay in Shape Next Year," *Fortune*, Oct. 23, 1989: 32.
[4]Brian O'Reily, "New Truths about Staying Healthy," *Fortune*, Sep. 25, 1989: 58.
[5]"Health Clubs Cool Down," *Club Industry*, Mar. 1991: 17.
[6]Eleanor Branch, "Making Your Fitness Their Business," *Black Enterprise*, Sep. 1991: 83.

also to the natural progression of any industry as it moves into the maturity stage of its life cycle. The industry has now become so competitive that a large number of clubs not emphasizing personal service and custom-tailored fitness programs have gone bankrupt. In fact, Marc Onigman, the editor of *Club Industry*, admitted that the battle is usually fought and won on the service side and that an increasing number of clubs are "servicing the daylights out of members" just to stay in business.[7]

### 2. *Social and Cultural Factors*

Since the 1970s, health clubs have been a very popular way to meet people of the opposite sex and to make new friends. In fact, at one point in the mid-1970s, coed gyms began to take the place of singles bars! Over the past four years, health clubs that had initially focused only on the young adult market, and those that primarily marketed breathtaking physiques have seen their market shrink dramatically due to the aging of the baby boomers. According to the Census Bureau, the number of people between the ages of 18 and 34 is projected to shrink by 11 percent during the 1990s.[8] The executive director of the Association of Quality Clubs (AQC), John McCarthy, stated that the industry was in a phase of major transition, from being one that focused primarily on the under-30 market; to an industry that focuses on the corporate market, families, and the 40-plus group.[9] This shift is not away from the aerobically toned baby boomers, but rather it is aimed towards improving health at all ages.

In a recent study of the 40-plus market, the AQC found that nearly 50 percent of those surveyed did exercise at least three times a week, and nearly 75 percent of the respondents stated that they had become more concerned about their health. But, interestingly enough, only 10 percent of those surveyed belonged to a health club.[10]

In fact, advertisers are starting to recognize that ads that feature well-built, male Chippendale dancers and sexy, shapely, 22-year-old female models are scaring away millions of potential male and female customers who cannot expect to look that way. Thus, clubs like the Health & Tennis chain, are featuring an increasing number of older celebrities such as Cher, Victoria Principal, and Farrah Fawcett in their advertisements as they seem more credible to potential members.[11]

The new buzz word for health clubs is now wellness. Since the emphasis has now been shifted to the older age groups, many health clubs are evolving into comprehensive health centers, that are as concerned with the emotional and medical well-being of their members as they are with flabby thighs and love handles. This transformation has occurred as the consumer of the 1990s is, in general, demanding that clubs be concerned with the whole person.[12] Thus, most upscale clubs now offer seminars in stress management, nutrition, and smoking cessation. Some of these clubs are even affiliating with physicians, cardiologists, and plastic surgeons to provide medical services for their clients.

Over the past three years, an increasing number of executive women have started weight training. Women, who for years have dedicated themselves to slimmer thighs and flatter stomachs, have finally acknowledged the need for upper-body strength. For example, Darcy Troy, a Yale graduate and investment banker, said it was "the coolest thing. . . . one minute, nothing.

---

[7]Loro, p. 28.

[8] Judith Waldrop, "Feeling Good," *American Demographics*, May 1990: 6.

[9]Rodkin, p. 38.

[10]"Health Clubs Look Beyond the Baby Boomers," *Changing Times*, Feb. 1990: 95.

[11]Loro, p. 28.

[12]Janice M. Horowitz, "From Workouts to Wellness," *Time*, July 30, 1990: 64.

Next minute, muscles."[13] These women have found that upper-body strength improves posture, protects against backache and bone loss, and improves confidence.

This increase in the number of serious women weight trainers has given rise to a new kind of health club: women-only clubs. In addition to the normal aerobic floors and other amenities, these clubs usually have specially designed weight machines and poundages that are geared towards a woman's frame size and strength capabilities. This phenomenon, according to *Club Industry* magazine features editor, Dan Tobin, is due to the fact that women who were in their early 20s during the heyday of the fitness boom in the early 1980s, are now in their early-to-mid-30s and are now less interested in joining a health club for social reasons.[14]

Finally, it seems to be currently "chic" to be able to remain fit, healthy, and physically strong during the "golden years," that is, ages 60 and beyond. A survey conducted by the Gallup Organization for the *American Health* magazine showed that the most rapidly growing segment of fitness enthusiasts is aged 50 or older. This segment increased by 46 percent from 1984 to 1986.[15]

A 43-question health survey was administered by *New Choices* magazine in June 1989 and one-half of the 5,600 subscribers who responded to the survey were aged 63 or older. Eighty percent of the respondents took at least one step to improve their health in 1989. The most popular methods included regular exercise and a good diet—low in fat, high in fiber, and plenty of fresh fruits and vegetables. Almost one-quarter (24 percent) of the respondents attend exercise classes, ski, or lift weights regularly. Three-quarters of the respondents felt younger and fitter than their actual chronological age.[16] In general, the respondents were determined to take advantage of their capacity to live healthier and longer than ever before.

## 3. *Demographics*

Selected demographics for San Marino and surrounding cites are shown in the following tables. These demographics include population breakdown, size of the respective age groups, and the median age of the population. These statistics will be used later to help determine the target market for Professional Fitness.

**Table I    Selected Population Breakdown**

|  | Total Population | White | % | Black | % | Asian | % |
|---|---|---|---|---|---|---|---|
| San Marino | 12,959 | 8,559 | 66.1 | 32 | 0.3 | 4,189 | 32.3 |
| Pasadena | 137,501 | 79,312 | 57.6 | 25,064 | 18.2 | 11,593 | 8.4 |
| South Pasadena | 23,936 | 16,711 | 69.8 | 745 | 3.1 | 5,086 | 21.3 |
| Arcadia | 48,277 | 34,512 | 71.5 | 374 | 0.8 | 11,321 | 23.5 |
| Glendale | 180,038 | 133,270 | 74.0 | 2,334 | 1.3 | 25,453 | 14.1 |
| Alhambra | 82,106 | 33,498 | 40.8 | 1,643 | 2.0 | 31,313 | 38.1 |
| Monterey Park | 60,738 | 16,245 | 26.7 | 374 | 0.6 | 34,898 | 57.5 |
| La Canada Flintridge | 19,378 | 16,645 | 85.9 | 81 | 0.4 | 2,397 | 12.4 |

*Source:* U.S. Census Bureau, 1990 Population and Housing Census.

[13]Dorothy Schefer, "The New Body Building," *Vogue*, May 1989: 368.
[14]Laura Broadwell, "Girls Just Wanna Work Out," *Women's Sports & Fitness*, Sep. 1990: 47.
[15]Waldrop, p. 6.
[16]Carin Rubenstein, "Here's to Your Health," *New Choices for the Best Years*, Jan. 1990: 37–38.

**Table II   Age Groups and Median Age of Residents**

|  | Aged 25–44 | Aged 45–54 | Aged 55–59 | Aged 60–64 | Median Age |
|---|---|---|---|---|---|
| San Marino | 2,996 | 2,097 | 782 | 742 | 41.4 |
| Pasadena | 48,124 | 12,339 | 4,859 | 4,910 | 32.7 |
| South Pasadena | 9,157 | 2,764 | 1,046 | 959 | 35.0 |
| Arcadia | 12,793 | 9,848 | 4,865 | 4,217 | 38.9 |
| Glendale | 64,075 | 19,397 | 7,820 | 7,614 | 34.3 |
| Alhambra | 29,346 | 7,119 | 2,907 | 3,093 | 32.1 |
| Monterey Park | 18,982 | 5,870 | 3,007 | 3,113 | 33.9 |
| La Canada Flintridge | 4,837 | 3,110 | 1,161 | 982 | 40.8 |

*Source:* U.S. Census Bureau, 1990 Population and Housing Census.

### 4.   Economic and Business Conditions

As mentioned in the subsection on demand trends, the United States has been in a recession since the middle of 1990. This recession is unlike most other recessions in that it has hit white-collar workers as hard or harder than the blue-collar workers. Southern California has been hit especially hard this time around due to the large reductions in defense and aerospace spending. Within the past two years, over one million jobs have disappeared in California.

The business section of the *Los Angeles Times* recently reported that 220,000 jobs have been lost per month over the past six months. The level of the consumer confidence index has also decreased to a level of 46.3, its lowest level since December 1974.[17] This monthly index measures how consumers feel about the economy and its future prospects and its low level indicates that the consumer may not be willing to spend enough to pull the economy out of its tailspin.

Although the index of consumer spending is not inspiring, economic data obtained from the months of January and February 1992 indicates that a national recovery is underway. These indicators show that consumers are not acting as depressed as they feel, the real estate segment is responding to lower financing costs, car sales have picked up slightly, and the industrial sectors seem to be gaining back a portion of their lost momentum.[18]

Despite the recession, the cities of San Marino and Pasadena are doing quite well. A comparison of the 1990 and 1991 *Survey of Buying Power* published annually by the *Sales and Marketing Management* magazine, shows that in Pasadena the percentage of households with an effective buying income (EBI) of $50,000 or greater increased from 25.9 percent in 1990 to 28.5 percent in 1991. The group with an EBI of $35,000 to $49,999 also increased from 14.7 percent to 15.5 percent during this period of time. This increase in the percentage of households with an EBI of $35,000 and over is also seen in Arcadia, Alhambra, Glendale, and Monterey Park. In all these cities, the percentage increase in households with an EBI of $50,000 and over is significantly greater than the percentage increase of the $35,000 to $49,999 group for 1990 to 1991. Thus, the business conditions for the primary trading area of Professional Fitness are very encouraging.

### 5.   State of Technology

The fitness equipment that is to be installed in Professional Fitness requires very little maintenance. Weight-resistance machines such as Cybex, Nautilus, David, and Flex require simple

[17]Michael Mandel, "Bummed-Out in America," *Business Week*, Mar. 16, 1992: 34.
[18]James C. Cooper and Kathleen Madigan, "Cross Your Fingers, Knock Wood: That May Be a Recovery out There," *Business Week*, Mar. 16, 1992: 31.

maintenance monthly. This maintenance consists of oiling and cleaning the cables and cams. Due to the low humidity in this area, rust would not be a worrisome factor. The spring-loaded mat that is to be used for aerobic classes would most likely require replacement every three to five years, depending on the level of usage. The saunas also require very little maintenance. The treated wood used in the construction of the sauna has to be inspected yearly and additional treatment or replacement of the panels might be needed.

### 6.  *Laws and Regulations*

For zoning purposes, the city of San Marino falls within the C-1 commercial zone. Health clubs are considered establishments that possess "characteristics of such unique and special form as to make impractical an advance classification of "permitted" or "prohibited" use in the C-1 zone."[19] Thus, each establishment has to apply for a conditional use permit on an individual basis. City Hall officials gave guaranteed assurance that the required permits and business licenses for an upscale health club could be easily obtained. The required permits also include a building safety inspection permit and a fire and health safety permit. These licenses and permits would cost approximately $1,730.

A separate conditional use permit is also required for any renovations of the leased site in excess of 20 percent of its value, over the period of five years. Approval for the renovation or remodeling plans shall be granted within 30 days of the application. Landscaping the exterior of the building and screening of parking spaces need the approval of the Planning Commission. Parking spaces that use concrete surfacing or asphalt placed on soil treated with weed control require further approval by the city.

## B.   The Neutral Environment

The neutral environment is to be analyzed using the following three categories:

1.  Financial environments.
2.  Government environments.
3.  Media environments.
4.  Special interest environments.

### 1.  *Financial Environments*

Interest rates have currently dropped to their lowest levels in over 15 years. The prime rate reported in the March 16, 1992, issue of *Business Week* index is 6.50 percent. Banks and other traditional lending institutions have vastly curtailed new business and other capital investment loans. Venture capitalists are currently also very careful about where they invest their money. However, good projects with minimal risks are still being funded, providing investors with competitive returns.

Funds needed to finance Professional Fitness can be obtained from either of three banks in the Pasadena area: Citizen's Bank, First Interstate Bank, or Bank of America. In general, these institutions quoted rates of 1 to 4 percent above prime for an unsecured, 8-year business loan amount of $375,000. The actual rate, be it prime-plus-one or prime-plus-four depends on the credit standings of the business lender. There is also a 1- to 2-point closing cost depending on

---

[19]Los Angeles County City Ordinance, Article III—C-1 Commercial Zone, Sect. 23.14 (C), p. 220.

the type of loan (secured or unsecured) and financial institution chosen. Funds from venture capitalists can also be sought at a competitive rate of 14 percent APR.

## 2.   *Government Environments*

Initially, in 1985, the Federal Trade Commission (FTC), the government "watchdog" for unscrupulous consumer trade practices, decided not to issue industry-wide rules that would have regulated health clubs. The FTC based their 1985 decision on the fact that the pervasiveness of fraud and abuse cases was not occurring nationwide. Thus, the FTC decided to act on a case-by-case basis.[20]

Since 1988, an increasing number of complaints lodged against numerous health clubs have also caused the FTC to step in and close down a large number of clubs. These complaints have ranged from "hard-sell" sales techniques and misleading contracts to deceptive advertisement. A large number of health clubs have been sued by patrons charging that serious injuries were caused by unskilled instructors and poor equipment maintenance.[21]

Many states including California, have now legislated formal regulations concerning the operation of health clubs and spas.[22] In general, the regulations mandate the following:

- A "cooling-off" period, during which a consumer can obtain a full refund of the paid membership fee. California law mandates this period to be 3 business days.

- A limit on the length of contract period. Some states forbid lifetime contracts.

- Cancellation rights for members, in the event that the club relocates or that the member becomes disabled.

- A surety bond amount ranging from as low as $50,000 in several states to as high as $200,000 in Maryland to cover losses in the event that the club folds. California legislates a bond amount of $100,000.

## 3.   *Media Environments*

Over the past three years, there has been increasing coverage in such media as documentaries, magazines, and research journals on fitness for the older population; on the positive effects of weight-bearing exercises on bone density, and on the importance of good nutrition. This attention has resulted in positive publicity for the health club industry. The health club industry has received some bad publicity through lawsuits brought about by unsatisfied members and the closing of unscrupulous clubs by the FTC.

A widely publicized experiment performed by Tufts University researchers on nursing home participants aged between 86 and 96 years old yielded extremely positive and conclusive results. The participants, most of whom suffered from either arthritis, hypertension, or heart disease, were put on a weight training program to strengthen their legs. After only two months on the program, all the participants either doubled, tripled, and even quadrupled their leg strength. Two of the participants had even gained enough leg strength to discard their canes![23]

Medical researchers have also found the best way to prevent the onset of osteoporosis in women is to develop maximum bone mass prior to bone loss. In the past, women have largely avoided strength training and have preferred to stick with aerobic toning only, because of a perceived social stigma attached to developing muscle mass. Researchers have found that strength

---

[20]Margaret Engel, "Beware of Fitness Club Contracts," *Glamour*, Aug. 1987: 92.
[21]Walecia Konrad, "Health Clubs: Exercise Caution," *Business Week*, June 6, 1988: 142.
[22]"Is Your Health Club Healthy?" *Changing Times*, Sep. 1989: 116.
[23]Vic Sussman, "Muscle Bound," *U.S. News and World Report*, May 20, 1991: 88.

training, especially in women, can have an extremely beneficial effect on bone strength and density; and are thus emphatically stressing the importance of a specially designed strength training program for women.[24]

In addition to regular physical activity, the importance of a diet low in saturated fat and high in fiber, fruit, and vegetables is also currently stressed in a variety of media.[25]

### 4.  *Special Interest Environments*

Four influential special interest groups include the American College of Sports Medicine, the National Health Club Association, the Association of Quality Clubs, and the Institute for Aerobics Research.

In 1978, the *American College of Sports Medicine* (ACSM) equated fitness with aerobic exercise and recommended aerobic exercise three to five days weekly for 15 to 60 minutes for all healthy adults. Due to current proven research on the benefits of strength training, these 1978 guidelines were revised in 1990 to include a twice-weekly routine of 8 to 10 different weight-bearing exercises to strengthen the legs, back, and chest—in addition to the three to five weekly aerobic workouts.[26] The ACSM also certifies instructors in preventive and rehabilitative health and fitness. This revised recommendation of the ACSM serves as a great opportunity for the health club industry to expand its market.

The *National Health Club Association* (NHCA) is primarily a "trade union" for health clubs nationwide. It costs $180 in yearly dues. There are currently over 2,000 privately owned clubs in the NHCA. Some of the benefits include SBA loan assistance, health insurance plans for owners and staff, group liability insurance plans, sales training seminars, and management workshops.

The *Association of Quality Clubs* (AQC) assures that its member clubs adhere to a strict code of ethics. Affiliation with the AQC ensures club members that the club has attained a certain level of service and competence. Currently, there are around 1,550 clubs nationwide affiliated with the AQC. Most of these are upscale clubs that offer members seminars in weight reduction, stress management, and proper nutrition.

The *Institute of Aerobic Research* is the primary agency that certifies aerobic-class instructors. Certifications are available for physical fitness specialists and group exercise leaders.

## C.  The Competitor Environment

Professional Fitness has three main competitors. These health clubs are all located in the neighboring city of Pasadena. These clubs consist of the following:

1. Brignole Health and Fitness.
2. Pasadena Athletic Club.
3. World Gym, Pasadena.

### 1.  *Brignole Health and Fitness*

This health club is located on De Lacey Street in Pasadena. It has been in operation since 1985. This club will be the *primary competitor* of Professional Fitness. Brignole's offers a spring-loaded aerobic mat in the aerobics room; eight Lifecycles and Stairmasters; one tanning bed; a weight

---

[24]Kenneth H. Cooper, M.D., "Fighting Back Against Bone Loss," *The Saturday Evening Post*, Mar. 1991: 32.
[25]Susan Zarrow, "The New Diet Priorities," *Prevention*, Sep. 1991: 36.
[26]Cooper, p. 32.

room consisting of Flex resistance machines and free weights, dumbbells ranging from 3 pounds to 125 pounds; two squat cages, for intense thigh exercises (squats); a snack bar; and pro shop.

This club primarily targets the under 40, "yuppie" market and plans to merge with Sports Connection in the near future. This club is also going to be relocated to a larger facility, possibly in another neighboring city. Although the club is touted to be operated and owned by Mr. Doug Brignole, a top amateur bodybuilder during the years of 1986 to 1988, this is not true. Brignole's is actually owned by a group of seven investors. These actual owners employ Mr. Brignole as the manager and pay him in addition to his salary, a small royalty to use his name for the club. Mr. Brignole does not have any formal marketing, management, or financial background and used to be employed as a waiter in a Pasadena restaurant.

The annual membership fees have increased from $330 in 1987 to $550 presently with no initiation fee. The membership fee includes a personal training program and two free workouts with a trainer. The turnover at Brignole's is approximately 25 to 30 percent annually. Currently, the club boasts a membership of around 2,800 members.

Brignole's enjoys an enviable reputation with the members attending its aerobic classes and this can be considered as its greatest strength. Most aerobic instructors that teach at Brignole's are certified by the Institute of Aerobic Research and have won at least one award in nationwide or regional aerobic contests. Brignole Health and Fitness also offers child-care services, at no charge for the first hour, to its members.

Brignole's has three major weaknesses: untrained weight-lifting instructors, poor service attitudes, and poorly maintained weight-lifting equipment.

All of the instructors at Brignole's are male and none of them are certified by any reputable agency, most of them are not even certified. These instructors are able to spot a person during a lift, but have very little knowledge of the mechanics or proper form for the lift. The manager and the instructors also have a poor service attitude. They tend to give more personal service to female members who dress fashionably and are young, affluent, and attractive than to the average member, male or female. In other words, the level of personal service given to members is biased.

Finally, Brignole's has managed to turn away about one-half of its serious bodybuilders over the past five years, due to its poorly maintained and outdated equipment. It promised its members in 1989 that most of the weight resistance machines would be given a complete overhaul and updated. This promise was never fulfilled through 1991.

### 2.  Pasadena Athletic Club

This club has been in operation for almost 20 years, opening in 1973 and is located at Walnut Street in Pasadena. This club would not be in direct competition with Professional Fitness as it concentrates on a different market segment. It offers purely aerobic-oriented amenities and does not have a weight training room. The club offers 3 tennis courts, 6 racquetball courts, an Olympic-sized pool, an indoor basketball court, sauna and dry-steam rooms, and a Jacuzzi. It also offers aerobic classes throughout the day.

A nonrefundable, nontransferable, one-time initiation fee of $400 is charged for families and $300 for singles. The monthly membership dues for family membership is $65 and $43 for singles. This fee buys you unlimited usage of the facilities that operate from 6 A.M. to 11 P.M. on the weekdays and from 7 A.M. to 10 P.M. on weekends. There is presently a 13-month waiting period for membership at this club for new members. The total number of memberships is currently limited to 2,500.

Pasadena Athletic Club is primarily a family oriented club as opposed to a singles club as are most health clubs. An informal survey at the club showed that members were very satisfied with the personal service that they received and the amenities available.

The strengths of Pasadena Athletic Club include personable service, a great variety of different amenities, and long operating hours, even on the weekends. Weaknesses include a lack of instructors and pool safety personnel, a long waiting period for membership, and the unavailability of child-care services.

### 3. *World Gym, Pasadena*

This is a hard-core weight-lifting and bodybuilding gymnasium located on Altedena Drive in Pasadena. Although this club only opened on September 28, 1991, it already boasts a membership of around 1,200 members. Membership fees are $389 annually with no initiation fee. The club is open from 5:30 A.M. to 11 P.M. on the weekdays and 7 A.M. to 7 P.M. on weekends.

World Gym has a land area of 10,000 square feet and does not have an aerobics room. The club offers state-of-the-art weight-lifting and bodybuilding equipment including Cybex and Flex weight resistance machines. It also has 10 Lifecycles, 8 Stairmasters, 2 treadmills, and an extensive variety of dumbbells, barbells and weight racks. This club would not also be in direct competition with Professional Fitness as it targets primarily serious weight lifters and the under-40 market.

An effectiveness study was carried out on World Gym, Pasadena, in November 1991. A questionnaire (see Appendix) was used to gauge the level of satisfaction of its members with regard to the gym's offerings in terms of price, personnel, and equipment.[27] In general, the members were very satisfied with the level of service and equipment offered by the club. Almost one-third of the members were over 40 and three-quarters of the members lived within a six-mile radius of the club. There is also a three-to-one ratio of male to female members.

Strengths of World Gym include long operating hours, very personable owners and management, great equipment and training atmosphere. Its weaknesses include not having a formal business plan, no planned specific target market of its members and also, a lack of a specific and directed promotion campaign.

## D.  The Company Environment

Professional Fitness is to be positioned as an upscale health club in the City of San Marino. It will offer state-of-the-art weight resistance machines, exercise bicycles, stair climbers, treadmills, cross-country ski simulators, saunas, and aerobic area.

The club will also provide child-care facilities with no time limit as long as the member is working out on the premises. The club will also offer the services of a licensed, professional masseuse at a subsidized rate. The pro shop will carry fashionable workout gear targeted at the over-40 market. The snack bar will carry healthy food items, such as yogurt, low-fat cottage cheese, protein and fruit shakes, sandwiches and the like, that are low in fat, sugar, and cholesterol and generally abide by the guidelines put forth by the American Heart Association (AHA).

The club is to be managed by a certified physical fitness specialist. He or she would preferably have a degree in physical education from an accredited university and a minimum of two years experience in managing an upscale health club. Marketing, management and financial consultants will be used when necessary. All aerobic or weight instructors and personal trainers must be certified by a reputable certification agency such as the American College of Sports Medicine or the Institute of Aerobic Research. At least one staff, trained and certified by the

---

[27]Iain Mozoomdar, "A Study to Determine the Effectiveness of World Gym, Pasadena," (unpublished), Nov. 1991.

American Red Cross in CPR, will be present at all times. The club will also periodically conduct seminars on stress reduction, nutrition, and time management, with emphasis on the over-40 population. Seminars in yoga and meditation will also be offered. The club will limit its membership to 2,500 people. Ideally, this figure will be obtained within the span of three years.

The club is to be financed by a limited partnership of six partners. The cost of each partnership unit is $150,000. Each partner is guaranteed a sum of $1,500 per month with additional income distributions based on yearly gross sales figures. Additional financing would come from either an unsecured, eight-year business loan from a traditional lending institution or from a group of venture capitalists with a guaranteed return of 14 percent APR.

The strengths of Professional Fitness include a superior service attitude; knowledgeable, trained, and dedicated staff; and a nonthreatening and comfortable training atmosphere.

The weaknesses of Professional Fitness include the lack of a management consultant and a financial consultant on the permanent staff, the nonavailability of an Olympic-sized pool and Jacuzzi, a possible waiting period needed for new members after three years, and the difficulty of finding land needed for expansion of the club in San Marino, if necessary.

## III. THE TARGET MARKET

Professional Fitness is to be located in the city of San Marino, California. There are two main reasons for choosing this city for the location of Professional Fitness.

The city of San Marino has, for the past two decades, been perceived to be a rich, upper-class town. This perception of San Marino is perfect for the positioning of Professional Fitness. This is to be positioned as an upscale health club and should thus be located in an upper-class neighborhood. According to the latest census results available with per capita income statistics (1988), the per capita income for San Marino for the period of 1979 to 1987 increased 68.5 percent, from $21,485 to $36,196. The per capita income for Beverly Hills in 1987 was $36,690, only 1.4 percent higher than San Marino. These figures clearly confirm that the perceived wealth of San Marino residents is not without foundation. San Marino is chosen also because it is surrounded by affluent cities such as Pasadena, South Pasadena, and Arcadia.

Assuming that the per capita income increases at the rate of 8.5 percent a year, the per capita income in 1991 for San Marino residents should be around $46,233. This health club is thus going to target executives who earn at least $40,000 annually.

As mentioned in the section on competitor environment, a study on the effectiveness of World Gym, Pasadena, revealed that although one-half of their members were above 30 years old; surprisingly, about one-third of their members were over 40. This finding proves that there is a viable market segment of older consumers. This finding is also in agreement with a large amount of published literature as mentioned in Section I. Thus, Professional Fitness shall target clients from the over-40 age groups.

The clientele of Professional Fitness shall be targeted towards individual consumers and corporate consumers. This club will not, however, entice groups of executives from a particular firm using special group rate discounts. Group rate discounts will damage the image of Professional Fitness as being an upscale club.

Geographically, the clientele is to be targeted from the primary areas of San Marino, Pasadena, South Pasadena, and Arcadia. Secondary areas to be targeted include Alhambra and Monterey Park to the south, Glendale to the east, and La Canada Flintridge to the west. This geographic targeting is immensely important as the previous study on World Gym showed that over 75 percent of their clientele lived within a six-mile radius of the gymnasium. Another study conducted by the American Service Finance company in 1989 also showed that 80 percent of a club's members come from within a 15-minute drive radius.[28]

The ethnic groups to be targeted include Caucasians, Asians, and blacks. The highest earning ethnic group are Asians. Historically, a large majority of executive health club patrons have been Caucasians. American-born Chinese and other Asians have assimilated the American fitness lifestyle and patronize executive health clubs with the same frequency as the Caucasians. Over the past decade, an increasing number of black executives are beginning to patronize upscale health clubs. This could be due to the fact that, as an ethnic group, their income has also been steadily increasing over the same period of time.

From the population and age breakdowns in Section I, there are approximately 139,206 people aged 40 and over, and are either Caucasian, Asian or black in the target market. From the percentages quoted by the *1991 Survey of Buying Power,* there are on average 46.5 percent of the people with an effective buying income of $35,000 or over in San Marino and the surrounding seven cities. Thus the market potential for Professional Fitness consists of 64,731 people. According to the survey by the Association of Quality Clubs (Section I), only about 10 percent of them belong to a health-club-penetrated market. Thus, conservatively, Professional Fitness will have an *effective target market* of approximately *58,258 people.* This is a conservative estimate, as people aged 65 and over were not included.

In summary, the typical customer profile of professional fitness shall include:

- Age group            40 and over.
- Income               $40,000 and over annually.
- Sex                  Male or female.
- Education            College graduates.
- Occupation           White-collar workers—executives, or retirees.
- Family life cycle    Full nest III, empty nest I, and empty nest II.[29]
- VALS Scale           Achievers or Experientials.[30]
- Benefits sought      Prestige, quality, and service.
- Location             San Marino, Pasadena, South Pasadena, Arcadia, Alhambra, Monterey Park, Glendale, and La Canada Flintridge.

## IV. OPPORTUNITIES AND THREATS

### A. Opportunities

Professional Fitness is presented with the following opportunities:

- There are at present no upscale health clubs specializing in aerobic and weight training in San Marino.
- There are no clubs in the immediate vicinity that specialize in providing upscale exercise facilities for the over-40 segment.

---

[28]"American Service Finance Renewal Study (1989)," *National Health Club Association,* 1991 (reprinted with permission).
[29]Philip Kotler, *Marketing Management* (Englewood Cliffs, NJ: Prentice Hall, 1991), 7th ed., p. 171.
[30]Ibid., p. 173.*

- Current research by the AMA and the ACSM prove that weight training is beneficial for all ages, regardless of sex and physical condition.
- Only 10 percent of people over 40 belong to a health club.
- The current demographic shift of the American population is projected to cause the 18-to-34 age group to shrink 11 percent during the 1990s.

First, since there are presently no upscale health clubs in San Marino, Professional Fitness would be able to position itself easily in the market without facing stiff competition and entry barriers from other upscale club providers. The club would also be able to maintain an effective physical and psychological separation between itself and its three main competitors in Pasadena.

Second, there is no club in the primary trading area of Professional Fitness that specializes in clients aged 40 and over. This relatively untapped niche presents new and profitable market opportunities for the maturing health club industry. This segment also has special needs that can be adequately fulfilled by Professional Fitness. Some of the special requirements include the hiring of older instructors, specialized programs to serve the mature consumer, the "extra" personal service, or pampering expected by the older consumer, and so on.

Third, current medical research, as mentioned in Section I, also helps educate and motivate the older consumer. This club presents the opportunity for older consumers in the primary trading area to enhance the quality of their life, and to enter the golden years armed with the necessary physical strength to combat painful and debilitating diseases such as arthritis and osteoporosis.

Fourth, since a survey conducted by the Association of Quality Clubs showed that only 10 percent of people aged 40 and over belong to a health club, there is a viable and reachable market segment for the club.

Finally, the aging population also ensures that the over-40 market will expand in the 1990s and into the year 2000. Thus, the effective target market will increase beyond the estimated 58,258 people.

## B.   Threats

Threats faced by Professional Fitness include the following:

- Increased federal, state, or city regulations.
- Lawsuits against the club.
- Entry of new competitors.
- Decline in the overall health club industry.

First, increased regulations could potentially affect the profit motive of the club. The management of the club has to be alert for changes in the legal environment—environment scanning—and do their utmost best to adapt to it.

Second, if lawsuits are brought against the club by members, the club will try to settle out of court to avoid excessive negative publicity. Ideally, this situation can be completely avoided through the use of qualified and trained personnel, and well-maintained equipment.

The last two threats—entry of new competitors and a decline in the industry—are inevitable. Professional Fitness will thus strive to maintain the goodwill of its customers through exceptional personal service and dedication. The club will also fiercely defend its position as an upscale club to enhance its prestigious appeal.

## V.  BUSINESS OBJECTIVES AND GOALS

### A.  Mission Statement

Professional Fitness shall provide an exceptional level of personal service and state-of-the-art equipment to our clients while maintaining a return of investment of 15 percent in the first year of operation. All of our clients and customers will be treated equally and with utmost respect regardless of race, sex, or religious preferences. Business operations will be conducted in a legal, ethical, and safe manner as described by federal laws, California state laws, and all applicable county and city ordinances.

### B.  Objectives of the Firm

- Establish a limited partnership under the laws of the State of California.
- Achieve and maintain a return on investment of 20 percent by the end of year 2.
- Break even within 18 months.
- Achieve a minimum market share of 3.5 percent by year three.
- Achieve a minimum average sales volume of 100 memberships per month in year 1.
- Achieve $1,300,000 in sales by the end of year 1.
- Achieve $2,000,000 in sales by the end of year 2.

## VI.  MARKETING STRATEGY

As mentioned earlier, the health club industry's growth has slowed down from approximately 15 percent annually to just under 10 percent. Thus, although the industry is still growing, its sales are increasing at a decreasing rate, and it has thus reached the maturity stage of its life cycle. The industry has, until recently, been focusing primarily on the 18-to-34 age group.

Professional Fitness is to pursue a *market-nicher* strategy. It is also going to be positioned as a quality/price specialist—high-quality equipment and impeccable service, high-price end of the industry; and an end-user specialist—over-40 segment. This strategy is very attractive to Professional Fitness due to its relatively limited capital resources. Niche marketing has also proven to be successful for firms in mature industries. An ideal market niche has the following characteristics:

- Sufficient growth potential.
- Sufficient size and buying power.
- Negligible interest to major competitors.

In addition, the "nicher" firm needs to have the capacity and resources available to serve the niche effectively, and be able to defend its position through built-up customer goodwill.[31]

As was explained in the previous sections, the over-40 segment has sufficient growth potential, size, and buying power. Also, the three competitors of Professional Fitness are currently

---

[31]Ibid., pp. 395–396.

not pursuing this segment. This club will be specifically designed to provide the manpower and resources needed to serve the segment and protect its position through built-up goodwill.

Since the industry is in its maturity phase, this club will be designed also to effectively serve the early majority and to compete in a monopolistic competition-based market structure. Thus, product differentiation is crucial for the long-term survival of the club and will be discussed in detail in the next section.

Professional Fitness will also try to increase its market penetration by encouraging the adoption of individual, tailor-made programs of weight training and aerobic classes that enhance the quality and preservation of life as the consumer ages, in place of other generic aerobic activities such as jogging, tennis, or golf. Hence, joining Professional Fitness will be a wiser and more educated choice than an upscale athletic or racket club, such as the Pasadena Athletic Club.

This strategy would most likely evoke a defensive response from Pasadena Athletic Club (PAC) and other such facilities. Due to its business experience, PAC might try to engage in price competition and attempt to use the superb-value strategy—offering high quality at a low price. While this strategy would be effective with a majority of products, health club consumers in Pasadena and its neighboring cities are typically upscale customers with relatively inelastic price sensitivities. Thus offering a lower price would most likely damage PAC's prestige factor and in effect, possibly lower its market share instead of increasing it.

Due to this customer profile and price inelasticity, Professional Fitness will not compete in price competition, rather it will defend its competitive position by enhancing the prestige and exclusiveness of the club; in short—"snob appeal." The level of personal service, ambience, and state-of-the-art technology will be emphasized.

## VII.  MARKETING TACTICS

The market-nicher strategy of Professional Fitness is to be implemented using the four tactical variables of:

> A. Product.
> B. Price.
> C. Promotion.
> D. Distribution.

### A.  Product

The heart of Professional Fitness is its personable staff and state-of-the-art equipment. This subsection is to be discussed using the following categories:

> 1. Equipment and facilities.
> 2. Staff.
> 3. Hours of operation.

#### 1.  Equipment and Facilities

One of the objectives of this club is to promote "health club addiction." This can be achieved in part by the offering of state-of-the-art equipment and excellent facilities. Weight resistance machines made by Cybex, David, Flex, and Nautilus will be offered. Satin-finished barbells and dumbbells will be purchased from Ironman Inc. The saunas will be made by an American leader in the field—Hex Equipment. Standard and recumbent type exercise bicycles will be offered, and purchased from Universal Inc. and Nautilus, respectively. The stair climbers will also be purchased from Universal Inc. Treadmills will be ordered from Quinton Fitness Equipment, known for its attractive state-of-the-art machines. Finally, cross-country ski exercisers that promote superior total-body aerobic workouts will be purchased from NordicTrack. Three massage tables will also be provided, along with the services of a professional masseuse at a special club rate for members.

Cybex weight machines come in an attractive white finish. The workmanship on these machines is superb, and they are designed according to stringent engineering standards. These machines offer a high degree of safety, reliability, and durability as well as a state-of-the-art appearance. In addition, Cybex machines offer an unparalleled degree of smoothness through their range of movement, and are ideal for people with joint stiffness or prior injuries. These machines are also angled correctly so as to lessen the chance of injury due to bad posture during a lift.

A unique feature of David weight machines is that, in addition to standard models, the company offers an extensive line of equipment designed primarily for women. These machines have lighter poundages and are designed for people that stand under 5 feet 7 inches. David machines are extensively used by women-only clubs all over the country. Professional Fitness will purchase some of these specially designed weight machines to cater to the needs of its female members and older members.

Flex and Nautilus machines are both attractively designed in blue or gray finishes. Both these companies offer state-of-the-art equipment that is functional, durable, and upscale. These companies also include a lifetime warranty on their machines and free scheduled maintenance by factory personnel for a period of two years. These machines also provide extremely smooth operation throughout their range of motion.

All the preceding machines use sealed ball bearings that help prolong the life of the machines by sealing out dirt and other environmental contaminants. These machines will also enhance the upscale appearance of the club.

The saunas made by Hex Equipment feature high-quality treated wood. As wood treatment is of utmost importance in the construction of the sauna, the company prides itself in having the "best-treated wood in America." These saunas also feature individually adjustable heat controls located inside each sauna. This feature is also extremely useful in the prevention of heatstroke and dizziness. Most saunas are controlled externally and its occupants have no mechanical control over the interior temperature except to manually open the door when the heat becomes overbearing.

The standard and recumbent exercise bicycles made by Universal and Nautilus feature state-of-the-art technology and appearance. These machines are made for heavy commercial use. Recumbent bicycles are ideal for older members as they provide more comfortable seats that follow the natural curvature of the spine and thus offer better lower lumbar support. These machines also provide attractive computer controls and intensity level readouts.

Like its exercise bicycle, stair climbers offered by Universal also provide intensity readouts and a computer-controlled hydraulic stepping mechanism that is designed not to overly stress the knees and ankles. NordicTrack's cross-country ski machines also provide smooth operation that reduces harmful stress on the joints. Finally, treadmills offered by Quinton Fitness are used in exclusive corporate clubs nationwide and also in NASA's astronaut training facility. They also feature a state-of-the-art appearance and technology.

The aerobic room will be partitioned off from the weight-training section of the club. A state-of-the-art sound system will be offered and a custom-made, spring-loaded mat will be ordered to lessen the intensity of impact on the knee joints. This room will be soundproofed to ensure maximum comfort for other members not attending aerobic classes. This would also enhance the prestigious appeal of the club.

Professional Fitness will also provide a child-care center staffed by certified child-care professionals. This center is to be used by members while they are working out. No time limits shall be imposed on the members.

A health bar serving foods low in fat, sugar, and cholesterol, and high in fiber will also be offered. This bar will serve low-fat yogurt, sherbet, protein shakes, and other such foods. Fresh juices and sandwiches will also be served.

A professional masseuse will also be available at a special club rate for members. Sixty-minute massages usually cost between $45 and $80 dollars. The club hopes to negotiate a price of $30 to $35 for its members.

The pro shop will feature the latest workout fashions targeted at the over-40 market. The member lounge will offer a large-screen television, laser disc player, videocassette recorder, and comfortable sofas for members. Members will be encouraged to use the lounge for informal business meetings and social purposes.

### 2. Staff

As mentioned in the subsection on company environment, Professional Fitness will only employ certified fitness personnel. The hired fitness personnel will be trained to provide exceptional personal service and formulate correct, custom-tailored exercise programs for the clientele. The club is to be managed by a physical fitness specialist. He or she must have a degree in physical fitness from an accredited university and at least two years experience managing an upscale health club.

The manager will report to the board of directors, comprising the six partners. The manager will be given full authority to implement any training program for the fitness instructors employed by the club. Although the manager will also be given the autonomy to manage the club as he or she sees fit, the manager needs to report on the progress of any improvement plans or staff training schedule to the board of directors monthly. The board of directors will only intervene when it feels that the ongoing plans or training programs are contrary to the prestigious and sophisticated image and positioning of the club.

The manager will be paid an annual salary of $30,000 initially. A salary increase based on a good performance appraisal is possible after nine months. The manager will also receive additional monetary incentives if the club performs well financially after the first year of operation. The other employees will be started at a rate of $10 per hour based on a standard 40-hour week. This basic rate will be raised to $11 in the second year of the club's operations. Standard overtime pay will also be given. This rate will be one and one-half times hourly wage for weekdays and two times hourly wage for nonscheduled weekends. Employees will be required to work on some weekends.

Employees will be instructed in personal service, operating procedures, and personal hygiene. Uniforms will also be provided by the club to the staff. Laundry and dry-cleaning expenses will be the responsibility of the employee.

### 3. Hours of Operation

The club will be open seven days a week, from 5 A.M. to 11 P.M. on weekdays (Monday to Friday) and 7 A.M. to 10 P.M. on weekends. These hours are determined based on the research done on World Gym, Pasadena.

## B. Price

Professional Fitness is to be priced as an upscale club. The use of a premium pricing strategy will be employed—high price and high quality. This strategy is very viable in the health club market in this geographic area due to the relatively inelastic price sensitivities of the upscale consumer.

As mentioned in the subsection on competitor environment, PAC is the only fitness club in the immediate area that charges an initiation fee. PAC charges a $300 initiation fee and monthly dues of $43 for single members and $400 initiation and $65 monthly for families. This strategy has worked well for PAC as it has been pursuing good-value strategy—low price coupled with medium quality product.

Professional Fitness will charge a $675 initiation fee and monthly dues of $75 for its members. It will also have a maximum membership of 2,500 members. This price range is justified as the club is to be positioned to promote and enhance a country club atmosphere and ambiance. The club would not price itself out of the market with this price either, as exclusive clubs in Los Angeles charge as much as $2,000 in initiation fees.

The club expects to attract 1,200 members in its first year, 1,800 in the second, and 2,300 in the third year with this price. This is a conservative estimate as World Gym, Pasadena boasts a membership of 1,200 members in just 5½ months of operation.

Monthly expected cash flows, pro forma income statements, and balance sheets for a period of 36 months using this estimate will be shown in the next section—financial implementation and control.

Various membership scenarios follow:

- Optimistic

  Year 1: 1,600 members
  Year 2: 2,100 members
  Year 3: 2,500 members

- Conservative

  Year 1: 1,200 members
  Year 2: 1,800 members
  Year 3: 2,300 members

- Pessimistic

  Year 1:   900 members
  Year 2: 1,500 members
  Year 3: 2,000 members

## C. Promotion

The promotion campaign that is to be used to launch Professional Fitness will be divided into two segments:

1. Precommercialization phase including the Grand Opening.
2. Regular promotional mix for the first two years of operation.

### 1. Precommercialization Phase

The promotional campaign that is to be used in this phase is to last a period of 13 weeks. The Grand Opening, which is to last an entire week, occurs in the last week of this phase. The promotional budget for this entire phase is $100,000. The promotion mix that is to be used includes direct mail, print and radio media advertising, sales promotion, and publicity. The advertising platform will be designed to emphasize the high degree of personal service and the exclusive "country club" ambiance of the club, the importance of improving the quality of life as one ages, and the benefits of feeling younger instead of looking younger. These issues will be the central theme for all the components of the promotion mix.

Direct mail will be used to reach corporate customers. This campaign will start at week 1 and continue through till the grand opening. Color brochures will be sent out to selected businesses in all eight cities, especially in Glendale, Pasadena, and La Canada Flintridge, at the rate of 250 per week.

Print advertising and spot-radio advertising will be used. Advertisements will be placed in the *Los Angeles* magazine; the *Star News*, the Pasadena daily newspaper; and the Southern California Community newspapers for the cities of San Marino, Alhambra, Monterey Park, South Pasadena, and Arcadia. The *Los Angeles* magazine is chosen as it has a readership of over 1 million upscale readers, 70 percent of them who are over 35. This magazine also has the capability of offering a four-color display advertisement instead of black and white. The *Star News* has a readership of around 45,000 in the Pasadena, San Marino, and South Pasadena areas and about one-half of them are aged 40 and over. The Southern California Community Newspapers are weekly papers published every Thursday, and can be custom designed to reach the targeted cities previously mentioned. These papers have a readership of around 73,000, one-half of which are businesses.

Spot radio will also be used to target older audiences. KKGO 105.1 FM is the only classical music station in Los Angeles and has a listenership of 550,000 people spanning Ventura to San Bernardino counties. The station states that over 80 percent of its audience are upscale consumers, aged 35 and over. Advertisements will also be placed on K-BIG 104.3 FM. This station boasts a listenership of over 1 million weekly; about 40 percent of them are aged between 35 and 54.

Publicity releases will also be issued to various news stations. The publicity campaign will promote a cause-related marketing plan: A $25 donation will be given to either the Green Peace ecological movement or the Los Angeles Mission for every new member that joins Professional Fitness. The donation will be made quarterly. This campaign will also help the club's corporate social image and standing in the community.

The Grand Opening will take place on the last week of the phase—the thirteenth week. This event will be designed to last for an entire week. During the Grand Opening, the public relations personnel from the Los Angeles Mission and Green Peace will be invited to give promotional talks on their respective organizations. This event will also hopefully draw out fitness celebrities such as Arnold Schwarzenegger, Lou Ferrigno, and others. Snacks and entertainment will also be provided.

Sales promotion, in the form of a sweepstakes, will also be used during the Grand Opening. A five-day/four-night cruise for two to either Mexico or Hawaii will be offered daily throughout the seven days. The Grand Opening will last from Sunday to Saturday the following week.

The breakdown of costs of this precommercial campaign and Grand Opening is shown in this section. A Gnatt chart for the implementation of this campaign is also shown.

## 2. Regular Promotion Mix

The cost of the promotion mix for the first three years of operation amounts to $108,000 yearly or $9,000 per month. This mix is identical to that of the precommercialization phase, with the exception of times and frequency of advertising. For example, ads will be placed in the *Los Angeles* magazine every other month—six times per year. Sweepstakes will be offered only once a year, on the yearly anniversary of the club. The cost of this regular promotion mix and a Gnatt chart for its implementation are also shown in the following pages.

## D.  Distribution

Professional Fitness is a direct service facility. Thus, to promote the upscale and sophisticated image that the club desires, the interior of the facility has to be decorated accordingly.

The interior of the club is to be designed using a subdued color scheme of a combination of pastel blue, pale green, pink, and ivory as these colors tend to be preferred by educated people, and also seem to sell well throughout the country.[32]

The furniture and lighting fixtures will have an upscale appearance and complement the rest of the club's decor. The aim is to provide a facility that is conducive to upscale consumers. Furthermore, towels and other essential toiletries will be also provided for the clients.

### Promotion Campaign for Precommercialization Phase and Grand Opening

| | |
|---|---:|
| **Direct Mail** | |
| $4.00 per mailing × 3,250 mailings | $ 13,000.00 |
| **Print Advertising** | |
| Newspapers | |
| *Star News* | |
| 6 × ½-page ads @ $1,770.75 | 10,624.50 |
| *Southern California Community Newspapers (SCCN)* | |
| 6 × ½-page ads @ $1,315.20 (Thursdays) | 7,891.20 |
| Magazines | |
| *Los Angeles* | |
| 3 × 4-color, ½-page ads @ $4,800 (monthly) | 14,400.00 |
| **Radio Advertising** | |
| KKGO 105.1 FM - Classical | |
| 3 months × 48 spots/month @ $125 per 30-seconds | 18,000.00 |
| K-BIG 104.3 FM | |
| 3 months × 48, 30-second spots/month @ $5,000 | 15,000.00 |
| **Sales Promotion** | |
| 7 × 5-day/4-night cruise for two to Mexico/Hawaii | |
| @$1,000—awarded during Grand Opening | 7,000.00 |
| **Grand Opening** | |
| 7 days × $500 per day | 3,500.00 |
| Subtotal | $ 89,415.70 |
| Outside services—ad agency and miscellaneous | 10,584.30 |
| Total | $100,000.00 |

---

[32]Marshall E. Reddick, *Entrepreneurship* (Los Angeles: California State University, Los Angeles, 1990), p. 143.

**Figure 2   Precommercialization Promotion Mix
Costs Allocation**

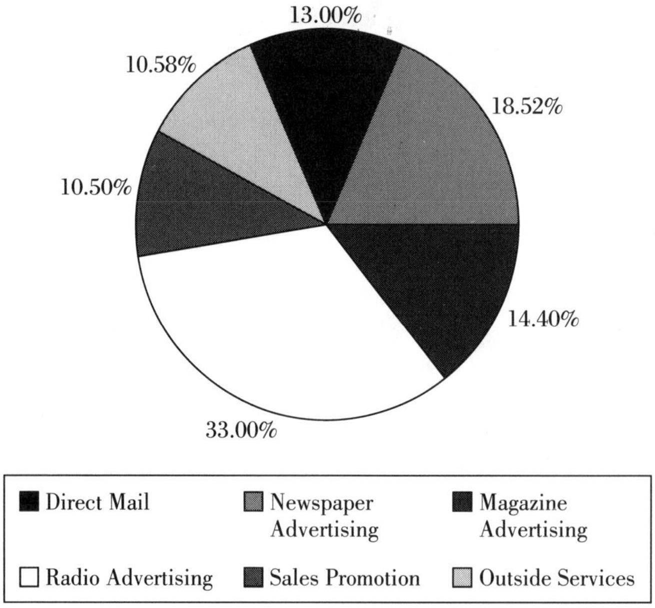

| | | |
|---|---|---|
| ■ Direct Mail | ▩ Newspaper Advertising | ■ Magazine Advertising |
| □ Radio Advertising | ■ Sales Promotion | ▨ Outside Services |

**Gnatt Chart for Precommercialization Promotion Mix**

| PROMOTION | WEEK | | | | | | | | | | | | |
|---|---|---|---|---|---|---|---|---|---|---|---|---|---|
| | 1 | 2 | 3 | 4 | 5 | 6 | 7 | 8 | 9 | 10 | 11 | 12 | 13 |
| Direct Mail | ▓ | ▓ | ▓ | ▓ | ▓ | ▓ | ▓ | ▓ | ▓ | ▓ | ▓ | ▓ | ▓ |
| | | | | | | | | | | | | | |
| Star News | | | ▓ | | | | ▓ | | ▓ | | ▓ | | ▓ |
| | | | | | | | | | | | | | |
| SCCN | | ▓ | | ▓ | | ▓ | | ▓ | | | ▓ | | |
| | | | | | | | | | | | | | |
| L.A. Magazine | | | | | ▓ | | | ▓ | | | | ▓ | |
| | | | | | | | | | | | | | |
| KKGO 105.1 FM | ▓ | ▓ | ▓ | ▓ | ▓ | ▓ | ▓ | ▓ | ▓ | ▓ | ▓ | ▓ | ▓ |
| | | | | | | | | | | | | | |
| K-BIG 104.3 FM | ▓ | ▓ | ▓ | ▓ | ▓ | ▓ | ▓ | ▓ | ▓ | ▓ | ▓ | ▓ | ▓ |
| | | | | | | | | | | | | | |
| Sweepstakes | | | | | | | | | | | | | ▓ |

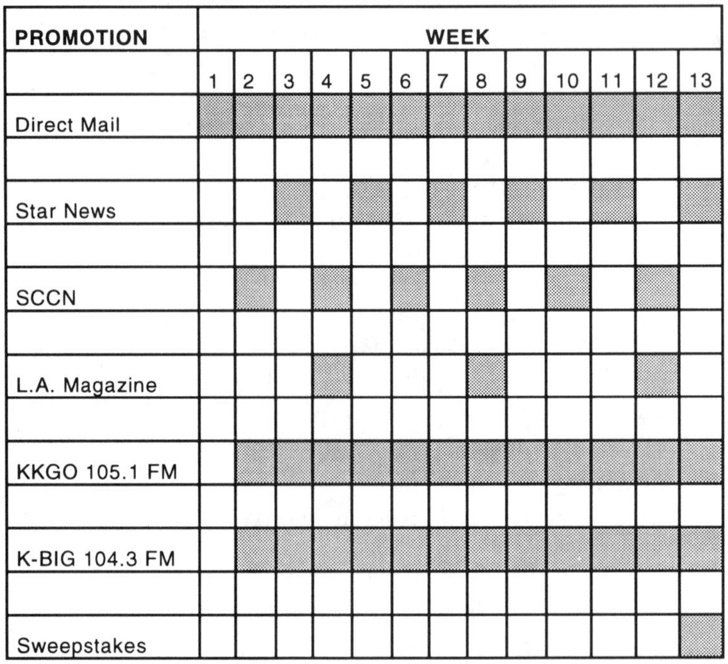

**Promotion Campaign for Year 1 to Year 3 of Professional Fitness**

| | |
|---|---:|
| **Direct Mail** | |
| $4.00 per mailing × 1,200 mailings | $    4,800.00 |
| **Print Advertising** | |
| Newspapers | |
| *Star News* (2 times per month for 6 months) | |
| 12 × ¼-page ads @ $881.60 | 10,579.20 |
| *Southern California Community Newspapers (SCCN)* | |
| 26 × ¼-page ads @ $621.30 (Thursdays) | 16,153.80 |
| Magazines | |
| *Los Angeles* | |
| 6 months × 4-color, ½-page ads @ $4,515 | 27,090.00 |
| **Radio Advertising** | |
| KKGO 105.1 FM - Classical | |
| 6 months × 24 spots/month @ $125 per 30-seconds | 18,000.00 |
| K-BIG 104.3 FM | |
| 6 months × 24, 30-second spots/month @ $2,500 | 15,000.00 |
| **Sales Promotion** | |
| 1 × 2-week cruise for two to Europe | |
| @$4,500—awarded during Anniversary Party | 4,500.00 |
| **Anniversary Party (AP)** | |
| 1 × $3,500 per event | 3,500.00 |
| Subtotal | $  99,623.00 |
| Outside services—ad agency and miscellaneous | 8,377.00 |
| Total | $108,000.00 |

**Figure 3     Regular Promotion Mix Costs Allocation**

Direct Mail     Newspaper Advertising     Magazine Advertising

Radio Advertising     Sales Promotion     Outside Services

Gnatt Chart for Promotion Mix of Year 1 to Year 3

| PROMOTION | MONTH | | | | | | | | | | | |
|---|---|---|---|---|---|---|---|---|---|---|---|---|
| | 1 | 2 | 3 | 4 | 5 | 6 | 7 | 8 | 9 | 10 | 11 | 12 |
| Direct Mail | ▨ | ▨ | ▨ | ▨ | ▨ | ▨ | ▨ | ▨ | ▨ | ▨ | ▨ | ▨ |
| Star News | ▨ | | ▨ | | ▨ | | ▨ | | ▨ | | ▨ | |
| SCCN | | ▨ | | ▨ | | ▨ | | ▨ | | ▨ | | ▨ |
| L.A. Magazine | | ▨ | | ▨ | | ▨ | | ▨ | | ▨ | | ▨ |
| KKGO 105.1 FM | ▨ | | ▨ | | ▨ | | ▨ | | ▨ | | ▨ | |
| K-BIG 104.3 FM | | ▨ | | ▨ | | ▨ | | ▨ | | ▨ | | ▨ |
| Sweepstakes | ▨ | | | | | | | | | | | |

If this club is extremely profitable after three years, there is a possibility that the club might start an upscale health club franchise. This move will only take place after the Board of Directors incorporates the company, thus obtaining the rights to issue stock and sell bonds.

## VIII.  IMPLEMENTATION AND CONTROL

This section will cover the financial implementation and control aspects of the club and will be separated into the following six sections:

    A.  Start-up costs.
    B.  Break-even analysis.
    C.  Pro forma cash flows (monthly).
    D.  Pro forma income statements.
    E.  Return on investment (ROI).
    F.  Pro forma balance sheets.

### A.  Start-Up Costs

The start-up cost for Professional Fitness is shown in this section. The total start-up cost is $1,274,055. Thus, a bank loan of $374,055 will be required. With the prevailing low interest rate, the assumption is that an unsecured, 8-year business loan is obtainable at a rate of prime plus two, that is, 8.5 percent. This assumed rate will be used in all future interest calculations.

**Start-Up Costs**

| | |
|---|---:|
| Remodeling and Equipment | |
|     Equipment and furniture | $  400,000 |
|     Remodeling and air-conditioning/heating system | 675,000 |
|     Computer system | 10,000 |
|     Inventory and supplies | 15,000 |
| Advertising | |
|     Precommercialization promotion campaign | 100,000 |
| Deposits and Other Fees | |
|     Lease of 12,000 square feet @ $1.20 per sq. ft., | |
|         3 months prepaid lease + last month + 1 month security deposit | 72,000 |
|     Utilities deposit | 325 |
|     Legal fees | |
|         Fire and health safety, city permits, and business license | 1,730 |
| Total Start-Up Costs | $1,274,055 |
|     Partners' equity | (900,000) |
| Loan Amount | $  374,055 |

The outlay required for the precommercialization promotional campaign and Grand Opening is calculated as part of start-up and fixed costs.

## B.   Break-Even Analysis

Since Professional Fitness makes a donation of $25 to charity for every new member that joins the club, the effective initiation fee is $650. The yearly dues for each member amount to $900 ($75 × 12). Thus, each new member pays an effective total of $1,550 for the first year of membership. Most of this fee represents fixed cost, the only variable amount being staff salaries. Out of each new member's $1,550 approximately 25 percent of it goes towards staff salaries. Thus:

$$\text{Break-even volume} = \text{Fixed cost} \backslash \text{Price} - \text{Variable cost}$$

$$= \$1,274,055/(\$1,550 - \$387.5)$$

$$= 1,096 \text{ members}$$

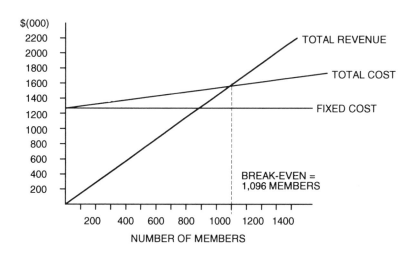

## C.   Pro Forma Monthly Cash Flows

Pro forma monthly cash flows have been computed for 36 months. The health club industry in Southern California is relatively constant except for the months of January and May. There is usually an increase over normal membership numbers during these two months. In January, people usually get very motivated about their New Year's resolutions to lose weight, and hence an increase in memberships into health clubs. In May, people want to trim down before the summer months actually arrive so that they can fit into the previous year's swimsuits! For the rest of the year, the demand is relatively constant.

The following assumptions are made in the monthly cash flow calculations:

- The club is to open on November 1, 199X. This is done so that the club gets two whole months to smooth out initial "kinks," before January arrives.

- The conservative membership assumption is used: 1,200 members in year 1; 1,800 in year 2; 2,300 in year 3.

- There is a constant level of memberships sold in year 1 for every month except for January and May. There will be 90 memberships sold every month for 10 months, and 150 memberships each month in January and May.

- Interest paid on the 8-year $374,055 loan amounts to $5,383.45 monthly at 8.5 percent APR. Monthly lease payments amount to $14,400. This lease payment starts on Month 4, as there was three months' prepaid rent.

- In year 2, the club gets a 70 percent renewal rate and 30 percent of year 1's members drop out. An assumption made is that the club loses this 30 percent of year 1's members at a constant monthly rate. For example, by the end of year 2, the club will have $0.7 \times 1,200 = 840$ members that signed up in year 1. The 360 members that dropped out did so at a rate of 30 members a month. In order to have 1,800 members by the end of year 2, 960 new members signed up in year 2. The new members joined the club at the constant rate of 75 per month for ten months and 105 members each in January and May. Thus, at the end of year 2, the club will have 840 members in their second year and 960 new members in their first year. This same 70 percent retention/30 percent loss is also used in year 3.

- A second manager is hired in year 2. The club is also assumed to maintain a staff-to-client ratio of 50 to 1. Thus, by the end of the second year, the club will employ 36 staff to service the expected 1,800 members.

## Pro Forma Monthly Cash Flow for Professional Fitness for Month 1 to Month 6

|  | 1 | 2 | 3 | 4 | 5 | 6 |
|---|---|---|---|---|---|---|
| **REVENUES** | | | | | | |
| Initiation Fees | $58,500.00 | $58,500.00 | $97,500.00 | $58,500.00 | $58,500.00 | $58,500.00 |
| Monthly Dues | 6,750.00 | 13,500.00 | 20,250.00 | 31,500.00 | 38,250.00 | 45,000.00 |
| Total Revenues | $65,250.00 | $72,000.00 | $117,750.00 | $90,000.00 | $96,750.00 | $103,500.00 |
| **EXPENSES** | | | | | | |
| Salaries | $27,140.00 | $27,140.00 | $27,140.00 | $37,700.00 | $37,700.00 | $37,700.00 |
| Rent | 0.00 | 0.00 | 0.00 | 14,400.00 | 14,400.00 | 14,400.00 |
| Advertising | 9,000.00 | 9,000.00 | 9,000.00 | 9,000.00 | 9,000.00 | 9,000.00 |
| Maintenance | 1,500.00 | 1,500.00 | 1,500.00 | 1,500.00 | 1,500.00 | 1,500.00 |
| Administration | 1,000.00 | 1,000.00 | 1,000.00 | 1,000.00 | 1,000.00 | 1,000.00 |
| Supplies | 1,000.00 | 1,000.00 | 1,000.00 | 1,000.00 | 1,000.00 | 1,000.00 |
| Insurance | 3,000.00 | 3,000.00 | 3,000.00 | 3,000.00 | 3,000.00 | 3,000.00 |
| Utilities | 2,500.00 | 2,500.00 | 2,500.00 | 2,750.00 | 2,750.00 | 2,750.00 |
| Depreciation | 6,833.33 | 6,833.33 | 6,833.33 | 6,833.33 | 6,833.33 | 6,833.33 |
| Loan Interest | 5,383.45 | 5,383.45 | 5,383.45 | 5,383.45 | 5,383.45 | 5,383.45 |
| Outside Services | 5,000.00 | 5,000.00 | 5,000.00 | 5,000.00 | 5,000.00 | 5,000.00 |
| Total Expenses | $62,356.78 | $62,356.78 | $62,356.78 | $87,566.78 | $87,566.78 | $87,566.78 |
| **NET PROFIT (LOSS)** | **$2,893.22** | **$9,643.22** | **$55,393.22** | **$2,433.22** | **$9,183.22** | **$15,933.22** |

## Pro Forma Monthly Cash Flow for Professional Fitness for Month 7 to Month 12

|  | 7 | 8 | 9 | 10 | 11 | 12 |
|---|---|---|---|---|---|---|
| **REVENUES** | | | | | | |
| Initiation Fees | $97,500.00 | $58,500.00 | $58,500.00 | $58,500.00 | $58,500.00 | $58,500.00 |
| Monthly Dues | 51,750.00 | 63,000.00 | 69,750.00 | 76,500.00 | 82,500.00 | 90,000.00 |
| Total Revenues | $149,250.00 | $121,500.00 | $128,250.00 | $135,000.00 | $141,000.00 | $148,500.00 |
| **EXPENSES** | | | | | | |
| Salaries | $37,700.00 | $37,700.00 | $37,700.00 | $45,240.00 | $45,240.00 | $45,240.00 |
| Rent | 14,400.00 | 14,400.00 | 14,400.00 | 14,400.00 | 14,400.00 | 14,400.00 |
| Advertising | 9,000.00 | 9,000.00 | 9,000.00 | 9,000.00 | 9,000.00 | 9,000.00 |
| Maintenance | 1,500.00 | 1,500.00 | 1,500.00 | 1,500.00 | 1,500.00 | 1,500.00 |
| Administration | 1,500.00 | 1,500.00 | 1,500.00 | 1,500.00 | 1,500.00 | 1,500.00 |
| Supplies | 1,500.00 | 1,500.00 | 1,500.00 | 1,500.00 | 1,500.00 | 1,500.00 |
| Insurance | 3,000.00 | 3,000.00 | 3,000.00 | 3,000.00 | 3,000.00 | 3,000.00 |
| Utilities | 3,000.00 | 3,000.00 | 3,000.00 | 3,000.00 | 3,000.00 | 3,000.00 |
| Depreciation | 6,833.33 | 6,833.33 | 6,833.33 | 6,833.33 | 6,833.33 | 6,833.33 |
| Loan Interest | 5,383.45 | 5,383.45 | 5,383.45 | 5,383.45 | 5,383.45 | 5,383.45 |
| Outside Services | 5,000.00 | 5,000.00 | 5,000.00 | 5,000.00 | 5,000.00 | 5,000.00 |
| Total Expenses | $88,816.78 | $88,816.78 | $88,816.78 | $96,356.78 | $96,356.78 | $96,356.78 |
| **NET PROFIT (LOSS)** | **$60,433.22** | **$32,683.22** | **$39,433.22** | **$38,643.22** | **$44,643.22** | **$52,143.22** |

## Pro Forma Monthly Cash Flow for Professional Fitness for Month 13 to Month 18

| | 13 | 14 | 15 | 16 | 17 | 18 |
|---|---|---|---|---|---|---|
| **REVENUES** | | | | | | |
| Initiation Fees | $48,750.00 | $48,750.00 | $68,250.00 | $48,750.00 | $48,750.00 | $48,750.00 |
| Monthly Dues | 93,375.00 | 96,750.00 | 102,375.00 | 105,750.00 | 109,125.00 | 112,500.00 |
| Total Revenues | $142,125.00 | $145,500.00 | $170,625.00 | $154,500.00 | $157,875.00 | $161,250.00 |
| **EXPENSES** | | | | | | |
| Salaries | $57,772.00 | $57,772.00 | $57,772.00 | $63,580.00 | $63,580.00 | $63,580.00 |
| Rent | 14,400.00 | 14,400.00 | 14,400.00 | 14,400.00 | 14,400.00 | 14,400.00 |
| Advertising | 9,000.00 | 9,000.00 | 9,000.00 | 9,000.00 | 9,000.00 | 9,000.00 |
| Maintenance | 1,500.00 | 1,500.00 | 1,500.00 | 1,500.00 | 1,500.00 | 1,500.00 |
| Administration | 2,000.00 | 2,000.00 | 2,000.00 | 2,000.00 | 2,000.00 | 2,000.00 |
| Supplies | 2,000.00 | 2,000.00 | 2,000.00 | 2,000.00 | 2,000.00 | 2,000.00 |
| Insurance | 3,500.00 | 3,500.00 | 3,500.00 | 3,500.00 | 3,500.00 | 3,500.00 |
| Utilities | 3,250.00 | 3,250.00 | 3,250.00 | 3,250.00 | 3,250.00 | 3,250.00 |
| Depreciation | 6,833.33 | 6,833.33 | 6,833.33 | 6,833.33 | 6,833.33 | 6,833.33 |
| Loan Interest | 5,756.85 | 5,756.85 | 5,756.85 | 5,756.85 | 5,756.85 | 5,756.85 |
| Outside Services | 5,000.00 | 5,000.00 | 5,000.00 | 5,000.00 | 5,000.00 | 5,000.00 |
| Total Expenses | $111,012.18 | $111,012.18 | $111,012.18 | $116,820.18 | $116,820.18 | $116,820.18 |
| **NET PROFIT (LOSS)** | **$31,112.82** | **$34,487.82** | **$59,612.82** | **$37,679.82** | **$41,054.82** | **$44,429.82** |

## Pro Forma Monthly Cash Flow for Professional Fitness for Month 19 to Month 24

| | 19 | 20 | 21 | 22 | 23 | 24 |
|---|---|---|---|---|---|---|
| **REVENUES** | | | | | | |
| Initiation Fees | $68,250.00 | $48,750.00 | $48,750.00 | $48,750.00 | $48,750.00 | $48,750.00 |
| Monthly Dues | 118,125.00 | 121,500.00 | 124,875.00 | 128,250.00 | 131,625.00 | 135,000.00 |
| Total Revenues | $186,375.00 | $170,250.00 | $173,625.00 | $177,000.00 | $180,375.00 | $183,750.00 |
| **EXPENSES** | | | | | | |
| Salaries | $69,388.00 | $69,388.00 | $69,388.00 | $75,696.00 | $75,696.00 | $75,696.00 |
| Rent | 14,400.00 | 14,400.00 | 14,400.00 | 14,400.00 | 14,400.00 | 14,400.00 |
| Advertising | 9,000.00 | 9,000.00 | 9,000.00 | 9,000.00 | 9,000.00 | 9,000.00 |
| Maintenance | 1,500.00 | 1,500.00 | 1,500.00 | 1,500.00 | 1,500.00 | 1,500.00 |
| Administration | 2,250.00 | 2,250.00 | 2,250.00 | 2,250.00 | 2,250.00 | 2,250.00 |
| Supplies | 2,250.00 | 2,250.00 | 2,250.00 | 2,250.00 | 2,250.00 | 2,250.00 |
| Insurance | 3,500.00 | 3,500.00 | 3,500.00 | 3,500.00 | 3,500.00 | 3,500.00 |
| Utilities | 3,500.00 | 3,500.00 | 3,500.00 | 3,500.00 | 3,500.00 | 3,500.00 |
| Depreciation | 6,833.33 | 6,833.33 | 6,833.33 | 6,833.33 | 6,833.33 | 6,833.33 |
| Loan Interest | 5,756.85 | 5,756.85 | 5,756.85 | 5,756.85 | 5,756.85 | 5,756.85 |
| Outside Services | 6,000.00 | 6,000.00 | 6,000.00 | 6,000.00 | 6,000.00 | 6,000.00 |
| Total Expenses | $124,378.18 | $124,378.18 | $124,378.18 | $130,686.18 | $130,686.18 | $130,686.18 |
| **NET PROFIT (LOSS)** | **$61,996.82** | **$45,871.82** | **$49,246.82** | **$46,313.82** | **$49,688.82** | **$53,063.82** |

**Pro Forma Monthly Cash Flow for Professional Fitness for Month 25 to Month 30**

| | 25 | 26 | 27 | 28 | 29 | 30 |
|---|---|---|---|---|---|---|
| **REVENUES** | | | | | | |
| Initiation Fees | $52,000.00 | $52,000.00 | $78,000.00 | $52,000.00 | $52,000.00 | $52,000.00 |
| Monthly Dues | 137,625.00 | 140,250.00 | 145,875.00 | 148,500.00 | 151,125.00 | 153,750.00 |
| Total Revenues | $189,625.00 | $192,250.00 | $223,875.00 | $200,500.00 | $203,125.00 | $205,750.00 |
| **EXPENSES** | | | | | | |
| Salaries | $85,676.00 | $85,676.00 | $85,676.00 | $85,676.00 | $85,676.00 | $85,676.00 |
| Rent | 14,400.00 | 14,400.00 | 14,400.00 | 14,400.00 | 14,400.00 | 14,400.00 |
| Advertising | 9,000.00 | 9,000.00 | 9,000.00 | 9,000.00 | 9,000.00 | 9,000.00 |
| Maintenance | 1,500.00 | 1,500.00 | 1,500.00 | 1,500.00 | 1,500.00 | 1,500.00 |
| Administration | 2,250.00 | 2,250.00 | 2,250.00 | 2,400.00 | 2,400.00 | 2,400.00 |
| Supplies | 2,250.00 | 2,250.00 | 2,250.00 | 2,400.00 | 2,400.00 | 2,400.00 |
| Insurance | 4,000.00 | 4,000.00 | 4,000.00 | 4,000.00 | 4,000.00 | 4,000.00 |
| Utilities | 3,750.00 | 3,750.00 | 3,750.00 | 3,750.00 | 3,750.00 | 3,750.00 |
| Depreciation | 6,833.33 | 6,833.33 | 6,833.33 | 6,833.33 | 6,833.33 | 6,833.33 |
| Loan Interest | 5,756.85 | 5,756.85 | 5,756.85 | 5,756.85 | 5,756.85 | 5,756.85 |
| Outside Services | 6,000.00 | 6,000.00 | 6,000.00 | 6,000.00 | 6,000.00 | 6,000.00 |
| Total Expenses | $141,416.18 | $141,416.18 | $141,416.18 | $141,716.18 | $141,716.18 | $141,716.18 |
| **NET PROFIT (LOSS)** | **$48,208.82** | **$50,833.82** | **$82,458.82** | **$58,783.82** | **$61,408.82** | **$64,033.82** |

**Pro Forma Monthly Cash Flow for Professional Fitness for Month 31 to Month 36**

| | 31 | 32 | 33 | 34 | 35 | 36 |
|---|---|---|---|---|---|---|
| **REVENUES** | | | | | | |
| Initiation Fees | $78,000.00 | $52,000.00 | $52,000.00 | $52,000.00 | $52,000.00 | $52,000.00 |
| Monthly Dues | 159,375.00 | 162,000.00 | 164,625.00 | 167,250.00 | 169,875.00 | 172,500.00 |
| Total Revenues | $237,375.00 | $214,000.00 | $216,625.00 | $219,250.00 | $221,875.00 | $224,500.00 |
| **EXPENSES** | | | | | | |
| Salaries | $95,356.00 | $95,356.00 | $95,356.00 | $95,356.00 | $95,356.00 | $95,356.00 |
| Rent | 14,400.00 | 14,400.00 | 14,400.00 | 14,400.00 | 14,400.00 | 14,400.00 |
| Advertising | 9,000.00 | 9,000.00 | 9,000.00 | 9,000.00 | 9,000.00 | 9,000.00 |
| Maintenance | 1,500.00 | 1,500.00 | 1,500.00 | 1,500.00 | 1,500.00 | 1,500.00 |
| Administration | 2,400.00 | 2,400.00 | 2,400.00 | 2,400.00 | 2,400.00 | 2,400.00 |
| Supplies | 2,400.00 | 2,400.00 | 2,400.00 | 2,400.00 | 2,400.00 | 2,400.00 |
| Insurance | 4,000.00 | 4,000.00 | 4,000.00 | 4,000.00 | 4,000.00 | 4,000.00 |
| Utilities | 3,900.00 | 3,900.00 | 3,900.00 | 3,900.00 | 3,900.00 | 3,900.00 |
| Depreciation | 6,833.33 | 6,833.33 | 6,833.33 | 6,833.33 | 6,833.33 | 6,833.33 |
| Loan Interest | 5,756.85 | 5,756.85 | 5,756.85 | 5,756.85 | 5,756.85 | 5,756.85 |
| Outside Services | 6,000.00 | 6,000.00 | 6,000.00 | 6,000.00 | 6,000.00 | 6,000.00 |
| Total Expenses | $151,546.18 | $151,546.18 | $151,546.18 | $151,546.18 | $151,546.18 | $151,546.18 |
| **NET PROFIT (LOSS)** | **$85,828.82** | **$62,453.82** | **$65,078.82** | **$67,703.82** | **$70,328.82** | **$72,953.82** |

## D.    Pro Forma Income Statements

Pro forma income statements have also been prepared for the period of three years. The interest income reported on this statement is calculated based on two equal deposits into a 90-day money market fund paying an interest of 5 percent APR. The deposits are made in the beginning of the second period—month 4, and on day 1 of the fourth period in year 1—month 10. It is assumed that the interest income is paid on October 31 of each year.

In summary, the pro forma income statement shows a net income after taxes of:

- $192,848.97 for Year 1.
- $290,249.37 for Year 2.
- $421,829.95 for Year 3.

### Pro Forma Income Statement for Professional Fitness for Year 1 Ended October 31, 199X

**REVENUES**

| | |
|---|---|
| Initiation Fees | $780,000.00 |
| Monthly Dues | 588,750.00 |
| Interest Income | 2,290.31 |
| **Total Revenues** | **$1,371,040.31** |

**EXPENSES**

| | |
|---|---|
| Salaries | $443,340.00 |
| Payroll Taxes (10%) | 44,334.00 |
| Rent | 129,600.00 |
| Advertising | 108,000.00 |
| Maintenance | 18,000.00 |
| Administration | 15,000.00 |
| Supplies | 15,000.00 |
| Insurance | 36,000.00 |
| Utilities | 33,750.00 |
| Depreciation | 81,999.96 |
| Loan Interest | 64,601.40 |
| Outside Services | 60,000.00 |
| **Total Expenses** | **$1,049,625.36** |
| Profit Before Taxes | $321,414.95 |
| Taxes (40%) | 128,565.98 |
| **NET INCOME** | **$192,848.97** |

**Pro Forma Income Statement for Professional Fitness for
Year 2 Ended October 31, 199X**

### REVENUES

| | |
|---|---|
| Initiation Fees | $624,000.00 |
| Monthly Dues | 1,379,250.00 |
| Interest Income | 9,119.91 |
| **Total Revenues** | **$2,012,369.91** |

### EXPENSES

| | |
|---|---|
| Salaries | $799,308.00 |
| Payroll Taxes (10%) | 79,930.80 |
| Rent | 172,800.00 |
| Advertising | 108,000.00 |
| Maintenance | 18,000.00 |
| Administration | 25,500.00 |
| Supplies | 25,500.00 |
| Insurance | 42,000.00 |
| Utilities | 40,500.00 |
| Depreciation | 81,999.96 |
| Loan Interest | 69,082.20 |
| Outside Services | 66,000.00 |
| **Total Expenses** | **$1,528,620.96** |
| **Profit Before Taxes** | **$483,748.95** |
| Taxes (40%) | 193,499.58 |
| **NET INCOME** | **$290,249.37** |

**Pro Forma Income Statement for Professional Fitness for Year 3 Ended October 31, 199X**

### REVENUES

| | |
|---|---|
| Initiation Fees | $676,000.00 |
| Monthly Dues | 1,872,750.00 |
| Interest Income | 21,593.27 |
| | |
| Total Revenues | $2,570,343.27 |

### EXPENSES

| | |
|---|---|
| Salaries | $1,086,192.00 |
| Payroll Taxes (10%) | 108,619.20 |
| Rent | 172,800.00 |
| Advertising | 108,000.00 |
| Maintenance | 18,000.00 |
| Administration | 28,350.00 |
| Supplies | 28,350.00 |
| Insurance | 48,000.00 |
| Utilities | 45,900.00 |
| Depreciation | 81,999.96 |
| Loan Interest | 69,082.20 |
| Outside Services | 72,000.00 |
| | |
| Total Expenses | $1,867,293.36 |
| | |
| Profit Before Taxes | $703,049.91 |
| Taxes (40%) | 281,219.96 |
| | |
| **NET INCOME** | **$421,829.95** |

## E.    Return on Investment (ROI)

The return on investment—ROI—can be calculated from the income statements. The fixed assets cost $1,274.055. Thus from the income statements, it can be seen that:

- ROI in Year 1 = $192,848.97/$1,274,055 = 15.1%.
- ROI in Year 2 = $290,249.37/$1,274,055 = 22.8%.
- ROI in Year 3 = $421,829.95/$1,274,055 = 33.1%.

## F. Pro Forma Balance Sheets

The pro forma balance sheets for Professional Fitness follow. The depreciation on fitness and office equipment was calculated using the straight-line method over a period of five years. The estimated total assets of the club during its first three years of operation are:

- Year 1: $1,015,474.78.
- Year 2: $1,047,390.29.
- Year 3: $1,159,708.53.

**Pro Forma Balance Sheet for Professional Fitness for Year 1—October 31, 199X**

### ASSETS

**CURRENT ASSETS**

| | | |
|---|---:|---:|
| Cash | $ 15,000.00 | |
| Short-term Investments | 122,474.78 | |
| Merchandise Inventory | 5,000.00 | |
| Office Supplies | 5,000.00 | |
| Total Current Assets | | $147,474.78 |

**BUILDING & EQUIPMENT**

| | | | |
|---|---:|---:|---:|
| Building | $675,000.00 | | |
| Less Accumulated Depreciation | 135,000.00 | $540,000.00 | |
| Fitness Equipment | $400,000.00 | | |
| Less Accumulated Depreciation | 80,000.00 | 320,000.00 | |
| Office Equipment | $ 10,000.00 | | |
| Less Accumulated Depreciation | 2,000.00 | 8,000.00 | |
| Total Building & Equipment | | | 868,000.00 |
| **Total Assets** | | | **$1,015,474.78** |

### LIABILITIES

**CURRENT LIABILITIES**

| | | | |
|---|---:|---:|---:|
| Salaries Payable | $ 45,240.00 | | |
| Account Payable | 3,000.00 | | |
| Total Current Liabilities | | 48,240.00 | |
| Total Liabilities | | | $48,240.00 |

### PARTNERS' EQUITY

**CONTRIBUTED CAPITAL**

| | | | |
|---|---:|---:|---:|
| 6 Partnership units at $150,000 per unit | $900,000.00 | | |
| Total Contributed Capital | | $900,000.00 | |
| **RETAINED EARNINGS** | | 67,234.78 | |
| Total Partners' Equity | | | 967,234.78 |
| **Total Liabilities and Partners' Equity** | | | **$1,015,474.78** |

**Pro Forma Balance Sheet for Professional Fitness for Year 2—October 31, 199X**

## ASSETS

### CURRENT ASSETS

| | | | |
|---|---|---|---|
| Cash | | $ 25,000.00 | |
| Short-term Investments | | 361,390.29 | |
| Merchandise Inventory | | 5,000.00 | |
| Office Supplies | | 5,000.00 | |
| Total Current Assets | | | $396,390.29 |

### BUILDING & EQUIPMENT

| | | | |
|---|---|---|---|
| Building | $675,000.00 | | |
| Less Accumulated Depreciation | 270,000.00 | $405,000.00 | |
| Fitness Equipment | $400,000.00 | | |
| Less Accumulated Depreciation | 160,000.00 | 240,000.00 | |
| Office Equipment | $10,000.00 | | |
| Less Accumulated Depreciation | 4,000.00 | 6,000.00 | |
| Total Building & Equipment | | | 651,000.00 |
| **Total Assets** | | | **$1,047,390.29** |

## LIABILITIES

### CURRENT LIABILITIES

| | | | |
|---|---|---|---|
| Salaries Payable | $75,696.00 | | |
| Account Payable | 3,500.00 | | |
| Total Current Liabilities | | 79,196.00 | |
| Total Liabilities | | | $79,196.00 |

## PARTNERS' EQUITY

### CONTRIBUTED CAPITAL

| | | | |
|---|---|---|---|
| 6 Partnership units at $150,000 per unit | $900,000.00 | | |
| Total Contributed Capital | | $900,000.00 | |

### RETAINED EARNINGS

| | | | |
|---|---|---|---|
| RETAINED EARNINGS | | 68,194.29 | |
| Total Partners' Equity | | | 968,194.29 |
| **Total Liabilities and Partners' Equity** | | | **$1,047,390.29** |

**Pro Forma Balance Sheet for Professional Fitness for Year 3—October 31, 199X**

## ASSETS

### CURRENT ASSETS

| | | |
|---|---|---|
| Cash | $ 35,000.00 | |
| Short-term Investments | 680,708.53 | |
| Merchandise Inventory | 5,000.00 | |
| Office Supplies | 5,000.00 | |
| Total Current Assets | | $725,708.53 |

### BUILDING & EQUIPMENT

| | | | |
|---|---|---|---|
| Building | $675,000.00 | | |
| Less Accumulated Depreciation | 405,000.00 | $270,000.00 | |
| Fitness Equipment | $400,000.00 | | |
| Less Accumulated Depreciation | 240,000.00 | 160,000.00 | |
| Office Equipment | $10,000.00 | | |
| Less Accumulated Depreciation | 6,000.00 | 4,000.00 | |
| Total Building & Equipment | | | 434,000.00 |
| **Total Assets** | | | **$1,159,708.53** |

## LIABILITIES

### CURRENT LIABILITIES

| | | |
|---|---|---|
| Salaries Payable | $95,356.00 | |
| Account Payable | 3,900.00 | |
| Total Current Liabilities | | 99,256.00 |
| Total Liabilities | | $99,256.00 |

## PARTNERS' EQUITY

### CONTRIBUTED CAPITAL

| | | |
|---|---|---|
| 6 Partnership units at $150,000 per unit | $900,000.00 | |
| Total Contributed Capital | | $900,000.00 |
| **RETAINED EARNINGS** | | 160,452.53 |
| Total Partners' Equity | | 1,060,452.53 |
| **Total Liabilities and Partners' Equity** | | **$1,159,708.53** |

## IX.  SUMMARY

Professional Fitness is to be located in the city of San Marino, California. It will be the first up-scale weight training and aerobic facility in the city. The club will cater to the over-40 age group and will pride itself in offering an exceptional level of personal service to its members. This will be complemented by the offering of state-of-the-art fitness equipment. Equipment to be offered include high-end weight resistance machines, exercise bicycles, stair climbers, treadmills, cross-country ski machines, a soundproofed aerobic room with a custom-designed, spring-loaded aerobic mat, satin-finished dumbbells and barbells, and a sauna in both the male and female locker rooms. The club will provide child-care facilities for members while they work out, and house a health bar, pro shop and an upscale members' lounge.

The total start-up costs will be $1,274.055. Members will be charged an initiation fee of $675 and monthly dues of $75. At this price, the club will break even with 1,096 members. The club expects conservatively to attract 1,200 members in its first year, 1,800 in the second year, and 2,300 in the third year of operation. A 15.1 percent return on investment can be expected in the first year, 22.8 percent in the second, and 33.1 percent in the third. A positive monthly cash flow is obtained every month for the first three years of operation. Promotional expenses amount to $9,000 per month for the first three years of operation. This expense is to be viewed by the club as an investment for the future.

Professional Fitness will succeed due to the following differential advantages:

- None of the club's three major competitors are presently specifically targeting the over-40 market.

- There are currently no upscale weight training and aerobic clubs in San Marino.

- The level of service that will be offered by the club will be unmatched by any of its competitors.

- The aging of the American population will ensure that the potential market for Professional Fitness will increase in the future.

- Fees will be acceptable because of the relatively inelastic price sensitivities of upscale fitness consumers in the trading zone of the club.

- The increased emphasis on improving the quality of life for older people and the widely publicized benefits of weight training programs for seniors will also ensure the success of the club.

## BIBLIOGRAPHY

"American Service Finance Renewal Study (1989)." *National Health Club Association*, 1991 (reprinted with permission).

Branch, Eleanor. "Making Your Fitness Their Business." *Black Enterprise*, Sep. 1991: 83–90.

Broadwell, Laura. "Girls Just Wanna Work Out." *Women's Sports & Fitness*, Sep. 1990: 45–48.

Brownstein, Vivian. "Consumers Will Help the Economy Stay in Shape Next Year." *Fortune*, Oct. 23, 1989: 31–32.

Cooper, James C., and Madigan, Kathleen. "Cross Your Fingers, Knock Wood: That May Be a Recovery Out There." *Business Week*, Mar. 16, 1992: 31.

Cooper, Kenneth H., M.D. "Fighting Back Against Bone Loss." *The Saturday Evening Post*, Mar. 1991: 32–36.

Engel, Margaret. "Beware of Fitness Club Contracts." *Glamour*, Aug. 1987: 92.

"Health Clubs Cool Down." *Club Industry*, Mar. 1991: 17–18.

"Health Clubs Look Beyond the Baby Boomers." *Changing Times*, Feb. 1990: 95.

Horowitz, Janice M. "From Workouts to Wellness." *Time,* July 30, 1990: 64.

"Is Your Health Club Healthy?" *Changing Times,* Sep. 1989: 116–118.

Konrad, Walecia. "Health Clubs: Exercise Caution." *Business Week,* June 6, 1988: 142–143.

Kotler, Philip. *Marketing Management* (Englewood Cliffs, NJ: Prentice Hall, 1991), 7th ed., pp. 171–173, 395–396.

Loro, Laura. "Health Clubs Stretch Markets." *Advertising Age,* May 16, 1988: 28.

Los Angeles County City Ordinance, Article III—C-1 Commercial Zone, Sect. 23.14 (C), p. 220.

Mandel, Michael J. "Bummed-Out in America." *Business Week,* Mar. 16, 1992: 34–35.

Mozoomdar, Iain. "A Study to Determine the Effectiveness of World Gym, Pasadena" (unpublished). Nov. 1991.

O'Reily, Brian. "New Truths about Staying Healthy." *Fortune,* Sep. 25, 1989: 57–66.

Reddick, Marshall E. *Entrepreneurship* (Los Angeles: California State University, Los Angeles, 1990), p. 143.

Rodkin, Dennis. "Health Clubs Sweat the Details in Ads." *Advertising Age,* Dec. 3, 1989: 38–39.

Rubenstein, Carin. "Here's to Your Health." *New Choices for the Best Years,* Jan. 1990: 35–39.

Schefer, Dorothy. "The New Body Building." *Vogue,* May 1989: 368.

Sussman, Vic. "Muscle Bound." *U.S. News and World Report,* May 20, 1991: 85–88.

Waldrop, Judith. "Feeling Good." *American Demographics,* May 1990: 6.

Zarrow, Susan. "The New Diet Priorities." *Prevention,* Sep. 1991: 33–36, 118–120.

# APPENDIX

# Questionnaire

A study is being conducted to help us run the gym more effectively. Please answer the questions honestly as we would like to know how you guys/gals *REALLY* feel! Thank you for your help.

1. Sex: _____ Male _____ Female

2. Age: a. Under 21   b. 21–25   c. 26–30   d. 31–35   e. 36–40   f. Over 40 HANG IN THERE!

3. I have to travel _____ to get to the gym.

   a. 0–3 miles   b. 4–6 miles   c. 7–10 miles   d. 11–15 miles   e. 16–20 miles   f. Over 20 miles

4. I joined this gym because: (Check ALL that apply)

   a. the equipment is great!

   b. I want to get buffed! (or more attractive, for you gals/guys out there!)

   c. it is close to where I live or work.

   d. my friends joined and encouraged me to join too.

   e. of the abundance of attractive men/women! AT LEAST YOU WERE HONEST!

   f. the hours are very convenient.

   g. the training atmosphere is great!

   h. the membership fee was cheap/reasonable.

   i. Other: _____

5. I feel that the membership fee as compared to other similarly equipped gyms is:

   a. Cheap   b. A bargain!   c. Reasonable   d. Expensive   e. Exorbitant

6. I usually train (per week): a. 1–2X   b. 3X   c. 4X   d. 5X   e. 6–7X ANIMAL!!!

7. I usually train: a. Before 8 a.m.   b. 9–Noon   c. 1–3 p.m.   d. 4–7 p.m.   e. After 7 p.m.

8. I find the informational and teaching capabilities of the gym instructors to be:

   a. Excellent!   b. Good   c. Average   d. Poor   e. Ineffective   f. Never needed one!

9. I use the following equipment: (*Check # of times per week* for EACH equipment) THANKS!

|  | 1X | 2X | 3X | 4X | 5–7X | Never (0X) |
|---|---|---|---|---|---|---|
| a. Bench presses (Flat or Incline) | ____ | ____ | ____ | ____ | ____ | _____ |
| b. Squat rack or leg press machine | ____ | ____ | ____ | ____ | ____ | _____ |
| c. Leg extension or curl machines | ____ | ____ | ____ | ____ | ____ | _____ |
| d. Weight stations/Assisted chin-up | ____ | ____ | ____ | ____ | ____ | _____ |
| e. Lower abs machine/Crunch board | ____ | ____ | ____ | ____ | ____ | _____ |
| f. Stairmaster | ____ | ____ | ____ | ____ | ____ | _____ |
| g. Lifecycle | ____ | ____ | ____ | ____ | ____ | _____ |
| h. Treadmill | ____ | ____ | ____ | ____ | ____ | _____ |

10. For my purposes, the quantity and poundages of the free weights are:

    a. Sufficient   b. Insufficient   c. Don't use free weights so don't care!

11. I would like to see the following equipment added in the future:

    (Check *ALL* that apply! - Better more than less!)

    a. _____ Additional squat rack/free weights/benches/bars (any type)  Specify: _____

    b. _____ Other machines   Specify: _____

    c. _____ There is NO NEED for more equipment. *Are you serious? Really?*

12. I feel that the shower facilities are:

    a. Excellent!   b. Above average   c. Average   d. Below average   e. Venice Beach
                                                                           is cleaner!!

# 6

# BUSINESS PLAN FOR CALL HOME FOR LUNCH

*Developed by*
**Carole A. Lane**

# Executive Summary

"Home" recognizes the importance of conserving the business and professional person's most valuable asset, time, while providing a lunch that is enjoyable, affordable, and healthful. We will meet these needs in several professional complexes by combining ease of ordering with delivery of our home-style lunches.

Our menu of delicious sandwiches and accompanying salad combined with a service that is unique to the area will bring us back time and again. While there are restaurants and fast-food services in the general area, pizza is the only food that is offered for delivery. Delivery will provide us a competitive edge which will make our product irresistible: quality food, competitive prices, and delivery all wrapped into one. Our slogan will be "Call Home for Your Lunch."

Professional and business complexes not having a food service establishment on the premises have been identified in the mid-Wilshire area of Los Angeles. The potential clientele base for the initial phase is 26,520 professional and office personnel. Operations have been designed to accommodate an extremely small percentage (.18%) of that base resulting in a potential growth opportunity of 550%. With such tremendous growth potential, Home will be able to plan for and control its growth.

After development of contacts in these areas, expansion of our services is planned to other professional complexes. Expansion to an individual building is planned within four to six years and will include catering of business meetings and other group functions.

# Table of Contents

## I. BACKGROUND OF THE FOOD SERVICE INDUSTRY

The food service industry was designed for the purpose of planning, preparing, and serving food outside the home and in large volume. Quantity food production and service characterized the monasteries, abbeys, and colleges of the Middle Ages. World Wars I and II fostered advances in mass feeding technology; World War I saw the introduction of cafeteria service to replace less efficient table service. World War II saw the spread of vending machines and other quick service equipment.

Food service systems are comparable in many ways to conventional manufacturing industries. Both acquire goods in various states of processing, convert the individual items into a product, sell and deliver the product at a cost compatible with the objectives of the institution. The basic end product of the food system is the meal or individual items that form the meal.

The food service industry can be categorized into four segments: institutional (e.g., hospitals and the military), conventional restaurants, quick service, and specialty shops. What differentiates these segments is not only the provision of nutritional, palatable meals but the service provided in each type of establishment. As the third largest industry in the United States, the food service industry provides not only a variety of products but also a level of services which can fill the needs of anyone.

"Home" will help fill the demand for specialty shops that cater to the professional businessperson.

## II. DESCRIPTION OF THE INDUSTRY PRODUCT LINE

### A. Products

There is an endless supply of products to satisfy each individual's particular tastes. Fast-food establishments generally concentrate on one particular type of food. The four basic categories are hamburgers, chicken, pizza, and fish. Specialty shops also concentrate on providing one type of food while the conventional restaurant fills all other needs. Each of these market segments can be found in areas in which we intend to establish a clientele.

Home will fill the niche between these two categories with a variety of products that are healthful as well as tasteful.

### B. Services

A variety of services is also available in the food service industry. These services range from fast food and cafeteria style to those provided by elegant establishments which anticipate each individual's wants. Home's ordering and delivery service will provide a combination of these extremes thus filling a gap not widely serviced by the industry.

In addition to home-style lunches, Home will offer a catering service for business meetings.

## III. DESCRIPTION OF MARKET SEGMENT

Home is designed to appeal to business and professional people who are on tight schedules and cannot afford the time for a restaurant meal. Our delivery service will accentuate the clientele's need for consideration of one of their most valuable assets: time.

The majority of our clientele will be from the surrounding professional complexes in which there is no on-site food service establishment. Professional and business complexes meeting this criterion have been identified in the mid-Wilshire area of Los Angeles. These are within a one-hour drive from Home's base.

A study conducted by the National Restaurant Association indicated that there is a steady progressive increase in the percentage of food expenditures made away from home as income rises. This percentage averages 35.4% where annual earnings are above $25,000. However, there is a trend in workers over 54 to decrease their away-from-home food expenditures. A U.S. Bureau of the Census report estimates away-from-home food expenditures to decline to anywhere between 19.8% and 24.1% of total food expenses in workers 55 and older.

The typical customer will work in a professional office, be between the ages of 22 and 55 and have an average family income greater than $25,000 per year.

## IV.  CHANGES IN THE ECONOMICS OF THE INDUSTRY

Employment and the number of food-service establishments have grown as the population has grown. All forecasters agree that our population will continue to grow in the years ahead assuring a growing and healthy food service industry. With higher incomes, people consistently "eat out" more frequently. Again, forecasters agree that personal income will continue to rise. All of this spells continued growth for the food industry.

Consumers are spending a growing proportion of their food dollars away from home. Food service industry sales have more than tripled in the 1970s, rising from $42.7 billion in 1970 to $133.1 billion in 1982. The percentage of lunches eaten out is much higher than for any other meal. During weekdays, 13% of lunches are consumed in public eating places while only 3% of breakfasts and 8% of dinners are eaten at such establishments.

Technological advances in the past have made an impact on the food service industry and undoubtedly will continue to do so in the future. Dishwashers, convenience foods and microwave ovens have helped cut kitchen preparation time and labor costs.

The food service industry is the third largest industry in America and has one of the largest growth rates. Approximately 559,000 food service operations exist in the United States. Of these, about 380,000 are for-profit establishments open to the public. Currently, the food service industry prepares one-fifth of all food produced in the United States (40 billion pounds with total industry sales in excess of $200 billion in 1990).

One measurement of the growth of the industry is employment growth. According to the Bureau of Labor Statistics, employment growth in the food service industry outpaced that of most other industries during the 1980s. The forecasted increase from 5.6 million employees in 1978 to 7.8 million employees in 1990 represents a 39.5% growth. The total

industry had sales in excess of $70 billion in 1978. In 1990, sales exceeded $200 billion.

Specialty shops have shown an increasing amount of acceptance compared to the restaurant scene. Specialization of services (i.e., catering) and foods alike have an appeal which has spurred development in these areas.

## V.  DESCRIPTION OF THE COMPETITIVE STRUCTURE OF THE INDUSTRY

Competitors in this industry can come from many sources including other food service operations, supermarkets and the home. As stated earlier, people with higher incomes consistently eat out more often. Since our product is designed to be comparable to home-prepared cold lunches at a competitive cost with the associated convenience of delivery and is directed at that portion of the market segment with higher incomes, it is anticipatd that there will be a reduction in competition from the home.

Supermarkets and other food service industries which offer convenience and quick service (i.e., fast food) are centered around a limited menu: hamburgers, pizza, chicken, and fish. We plan to capture the market segment which has become bored with the same menu and is looking for a change. Since our emphasis is on ease of order combined with delivery of service which these other establishments will be unable to provide, we expect to create a new market segment in which there is virtually no competition. A survey of business and professional people indicated that one out of five respondents would buy more from a delivery service food establishment than any other food service establishment.

A complete survey of consumer preferences was conducted on a sample of heavy (more than 8 times per month) use of fast-food establishments. Four of the top five complaints were: restaurant is too crowded during meal times; you can't get a table during busy periods of the day; it takes too long to get your order; and you don't get good value for your money. Based on our system of operations, the first two complaints are not a factor in satisfying our customers. Since orders will be delivered prior to required times, the third complaint also should not enter into the relationship between Home and its customers. Elimination of these major problem areas should compel our customers to have more satisfaction with our services. Since we plan to have quality sandwiches, we will not scrimp on the contents or the grade of our fillings.

## VI.  MARKETING PLAN

### A.  Market Segment

Home will cater its service to the business and professional workforce in the mid-Wilshire area of Los Angeles. Within a four-square-block area, there is approximately 1,326,000 square feet of office space. The average occupancy rate is 80%. Using a liberal standard of 400 square feet per employee, there is a potential clientele base of 26,520 professional and office personnel. Once established, we feel that we will be able to expand to other professional areas in Los Angeles.

Building a relationship of confidence in the quality of our product combined with efficient, courteous service will provide excellent contacts for expansion to our catering service.

### B.  Position

Home's positioning is to provide a service to those business and professional persons who must maintain tight schedules but still want the luxury of having their lunches prepared for them at a reasonable price. Our slogan will be indicative of the value of our clientele to us as well as the quality of our menu: Call Home for Your Lunch. Since a key role is played by secretarial staff in the professional complex, we will endeavor to prioritize the secretary's importance in reaching our goals by offering discounts and other incentives.

### C.  Distribution

Distribution of our product is to be made by private automobile. Our drivers will be familiar with each area since recruitment will be from the college campuses adjacent to these complexes. There is easy access to the freeway system from Home's base.

Each automobile will be equipped with large ice chests to ensure freshness of food upon delivery. College students will be recruited through the job placement centers at CSULA and Los Angeles City College. Orders will be separated by geographic area to ensure the most efficient use of personnel as well as individual service. Utilizing dependable staff, we will be recognized by our clientele as we approach each office.

### D.  Pricing

A limited selection of quality food will be the key to maintaining our competitive price range. With limited choices, food costs can be more easily monitored and controlled. All sandwiches will include a side dish salad (e.g., macaroni, potato, pasta). An assortment of breads, meats, and cheeses will provide a wider range of variety. The average charge for a sandwich will be in the $3.50 to $4.50 range, exclusive of beverage.

### E.  Promotional Support

The first year's promotion and advertising budget of Home will be geared toward individual contact with potential clientele. Prospective clients will be given a "hook," such as a coupon, which will help to determine the effectiveness of the presentation during this initial contact.

Initial contact will also be made through the distribution of flyers containing menu items and prices. With the accent on delivery and ease of ordering, customers who call before 9:30 A.M. will be given a 10% discount.

The utilization of a marketing manager will enable continuous feedback on quality of food and service.

## VII.  PRODUCTION PLAN

Foods requiring cooking will be cooked one day in advance. Final preparation of meats and cheeses will be accomplished in the morning (i.e., slicing). Since we will institute portion control procedures to ensure a consistent and ample quantity of sandwich fillings, meats and cheeses will also be separated into portions during this time to eliminate costly errors. Separation of fillings into portions will also reduce the time needed to fill orders. Salads will be prepared one day in advance to allow the most flavorful blend of ingredients prior to distribution. On the morning of the distribution, salads will be portioned into individual serving containers for ease of completing full orders.

Rather than implement an assembly-line process as is generally utilized by the fast food chains, we will concentrate on individual orders. This will reduce the inherent risks of impersonalized service. By keeping the customer first in our minds during preparation of the order, we will foster the concept of customer satisfaction. The kitchen will be organized to maximize space and convenience to produce the most efficient use of manpower and available equipment. Shelves will be installed above each counter area to minimize wasted time and energy in restocking supplies. A diagram of the kitchen layout is provided in this section.

Rather than lease expensive commercial property, the operation will be based initially

**Kitchen Setup**

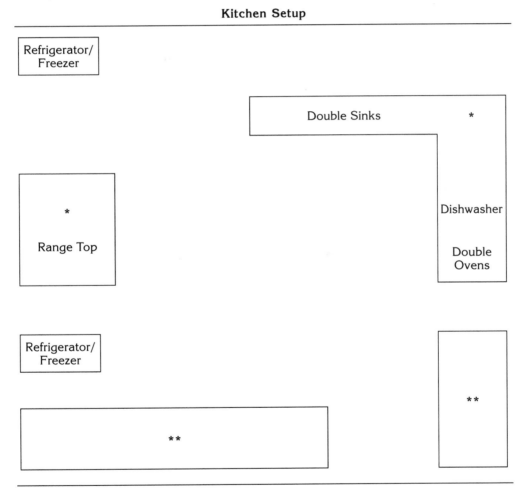

*Existing counter workspace.
**Projected additional counter workspace.

Note: Each counter area will have an additional counter shelf one-third the depth of the counter workspace. This shelf will be utilized for additional stocking of ingredients during our production period and eliminate unnecessary steps for restocking.

in a private home. This will permit a more rapid growth due to the reinvestment of profits into the business.

To accomplish our goal of high quality fresh food, we will require a minimum amount of equipment for processing our product: refrigerator, freezer, slicing machine, cooking utensils, and a stove with an oven. Because of the high relative cost of renting a refrigerator and the low cost of purchasing, the refrigerator will be purchased. Since the required cooking times will occur in the afternoon, not interfering with personal meal preparation, we will utilize the oven currently on the premises.

Food products are available through various food distributors in the area. Catering equipment needs will be supplied on a rental basis from Mayhew Catering in Riverside.

## VIII.   FINANCIAL PLAN

### A.   Fixed Assets

A minimal amount of capital expenditure will be required due to the use of the on-the-premises equipment. Since the business will operate from a private home, it will be possible to utilize the existing ovens, dishwasher, stove and food processor. A refrigerator/freezer and food slicer remain the only fixed asset expenditures. Expansion to an individual building will provide the opportunity for determination of the best capital structure for Home (leasing versus purchasing).

### B.   Working Capital

Personal savings are to be used for start-up costs and the first six months of operation. Several investors have indicated their interest in funding Home's expansion after a developed stable market has been proven, at the end of the first six months of operation. In addition, provision of personal financial statements to financial institutions has yielded an avenue of financing available for growth. Upon expansion to an individual building, equity financing will be utilized. Equity financing will enable Home to receive an increased amount of cash at a time when it will be most necessary.

### C.   Expansion

Utilization of current available space will allow expansion of our market segment significantly prior to requiring additional space or equipment. Rental of catering equipment, linens, and utensils is available through a competitor out of the area.

Expansion will be to an individual, currently existing building that has easy access to the freeway system for distribution. This growth requirement will occur within four to six years after start-up at which time adequate funds will be available for initial down payments on leased and purchased equipment. Equity financing will be available based on the growth potential and stability of the organization.

### D.   Capital Structure

Home's capital structure will consist of 20% capital stock, 70% long-term notes, and 10% short-term financing (through accounts payable). Home's entrance into the market will be accomplished with $2,000 cash and $7,000 long-term notes provided by myself. The long-term notes will permit a tax advantage for the investment since the payments will not represent capital gains while providing an expense for the business.

Home will enter the marketplace as a sole proprietorship thus enabling an increased value to be attached to capital stock that is required for financing future growth.

### E.   Cash Flow

Delivery staff will be given a petty cash fund of $25 each to be used for making change. They will be responsible for replenishing coins used from bills received. To enhance the cash flow of Home, delivery staff will also be required to make daily deposits of monies collected upon delivery to branch offices of Home's bank. These deposit slips will be returned to Home's base of operations on subsequent days following each deposit.

There will be no monthly rental charge for Home's base so that an expense can be used as a personal business deduction.

The following schedules summarize the projected revenues and expenses for Home for the first four years of operation:

## IX.  ORGANIZATIONAL PLAN

Although inventory control is a key to profitability, people are the key to generating sales in the food service industry. "Home" will staff its operation with homemakers and college men and women. These employees will be friendly, energetic, and intelligent.

The homemakers will be the initial contact for our clientele. They will initiate telephone contact with prospective clients and request orders. Additional homemakers will prepare the side dishes which will accompany each sandwich order and fill individual orders as they are received. The college students will provide the delivery service of these filled orders.

All employees will be part-time, with the exception of management. As part-time employees, they will not receive benefits such as medical insurance or vacation pay. In addition, there will be no overtime costs associated with

### Schedule 1    Start-Up Costs Sources and Uses of Cash

| | | |
|---|---:|---:|
| Sources of Funds | | |
| Accounts payable financing | $1,000 | |
| Long-term financing | 7,000 | |
| Equity financing | 2,000 | |
| Total Sources | | $10,000 |
| | | |
| Uses of Funds | | |
| Kitchen equipment | $  900 | |
| Delivery equipment | 200 | |
| Supplies | 400 | |
| Food inventory | 1,500 | |
| Beverage inventory | 500 | |
| Total Uses | | $ 3,500 |
| | | |
| Available Working Capital to Begin Operations | | $ 6,500 |

### Schedule 2    Sales Forecast

| | Monday | Tuesday | Wednesday | Thursday | Friday |
|---|---|---|---|---|---|
| Average # expected orders | 45 | 53 | 57 | 50 | 58 |
| Average cost | × $4 | × $4 | × $4 | × $4 | × $4 |
| Daily sales | $180 | $212 | $228 | $200 | $232 |

| | |
|---|---:|
| Monday | $    180 |
| Tuesday | 212 |
| Wednesday | 228 |
| Thursday | 200 |
| Friday | 232 |
| Expected weekly sales | $ 1,052 |
| Number of weeks open | × 52 |
| Expected annual sales | $54,704 |

Schedule 3    Expense Schedule

|  | Cost | % Expense | % Total Sales |
|---|---|---|---|
| Payroll |  |  |  |
| Telephone | $ 7,932 | 30.6 |  |
| Preparation | 7,932 | 30.6 |  |
| Delivery | 9,274 | 38.8 |  |
| Total | $23,860 | 100.0 | 43.6 |
| Advertising/Promotion |  |  |  |
| Coupons | $   200 | 50.0 |  |
| Flyers | 200 | 50.0 |  |
| Total | $   400 | 100.0 | .7 |
| Direct Operating Expenses |  |  |  |
| Travel reimbursement | $ 3,640 | 62.4 |  |
| Cleaning supplies | 100 | 1.7 |  |
| Packaging supplies | 1,690 | 29.0 |  |
| Menus | 400 | 6.9 |  |
| Total | $ 5,831 | 100.0 | 10.7 |
| Utilities | $   600 | 100.0 | 1.1 |
| General/Administrative |  |  |  |
| Long-term note | $   360 | 10.4 |  |
| Interest | 840 | 24.4 |  |
| Office supplies | 250 | 7.2 |  |
| Insurance | 2,000 | 58.0 |  |
| Total | $ 3,450 | 100.0 | 6.3 |
| Repairs/Maintenance | $   200 | 100.0 | .4 |

part-time employment. Part-time employees will be paid minimum wage. Part-time drivers receive mileage reimbursement at the rate of 25 cents per mile in addition to the minimum wage commencing at arrival to Home's base for order pick-ups. The general manager will work on a commission of 5% for the first year of operation. Thereafter, salary will be commensurate with assumed responsibility and Home's growth. The marketing manager will work on a commission-draw basis. A weekly salary of $300 plus expenses accompanied by a bimonthly bonus commission of 10% for the first three months of patronage by new clientele will be given. This bonus will encourage follow-up visits by the marketing manager and resolution of problems as they arise.

Initially, Home will be staffed by two telephone solicitors, two delivery persons, and the general manager. The telephone solicitors are being recruited to permit continuity of the initial contact. The cooks and counter help will be recruited from friends and neighbors. In lieu of a salary, they will be paid by Home's catering a

function for them. In order to prevent any misunderstandings, records will be kept of time worked and the value of this time deducted from the cost of the catering. The general manager will assume all other responsibilities associated with the enterprise. The kitchen manager will be paid a weekly salary of $300 which will be adjusted as supervisory responsibilities increase.

Telephone solicitors will be paid solely on a commission basis. As sales increase, their salaries will increase. The chart (on page 6·14) illustrates the organization structure of Home upon opening as well as expected growth requirements. The job descriptions which follow the chart delineate each section's responsibilities.

Job Descriptions

1. *General Manager.* Administration of management functions, which includes:
   Hiring/firing of personnel.
   Bookkeeping.
   Ensuring compliance with industry regulations.

Schedule 4 Pro Forma Income Statement Monthly for the Year Ending June 30, 1994

| | Year Ending 06/30/94 | July | Aug | Sept | Oct | Nov | Dec | Jan | Feb | March | April | May | June |
|---|---|---|---|---|---|---|---|---|---|---|---|---|---|
| Sales | | | | | | | | | | | | | |
| Food | $46,400 | $3,580 | $3,580 | $4,092 | $4,092 | $4,092 | $3,580 | $3,580 | $4,045 | $4,092 | $4,092 | $4,092 | $3,580 |
| Beverage | 8,205 | 632 | 632 | 722 | 722 | 722 | 632 | 632 | 715 | 722 | 722 | 722 | 632 |
| Total Sales | $54,704 | $4,212 | $4,212 | $4,814 | $4,814 | $4,814 | $4,212 | $4,212 | $4,760 | $4,814 | $4,814 | $4,814 | $4,212 |
| Cost of sales | | | | | | | | | | | | | |
| Food | $12,876 | $1,053 | $1,053 | $1,204 | $1,204 | $1,204 | $1,053 | $1,053 | $1,187 | $1,204 | $1,204 | $1,204 | $1,053 |
| Beverage | 684 | 53 | 53 | 60 | 60 | 60 | 53 | 53 | 59 | 60 | 60 | 60 | 53 |
| Total Cost of Sales | $14,360 | $1,106 | $1,106 | $1,264 | $1,264 | $1,264 | $1,106 | $1,106 | $1,246 | $1,264 | $1,264 | $1,264 | $1,106 |
| Gross Profit | $40,344 | $3,106 | $3,106 | $3,550 | $3,550 | $3,550 | $3,106 | $3,106 | $3,514 | $3,550 | $3,550 | $3,550 | $3,106 |
| Controllable expenses | | | | | | | | | | | | | |
| Payroll | $23,860 | $1,837 | $1,837 | $2,100 | $2,100 | $2,100 | $1,837 | $1,837 | $2,076 | $2,100 | $2,100 | $2,100 | $1,837 |
| Advertising/ promotion | 400 | 30 | 30 | 35 | 35 | 35 | 30 | 30 | 40 | 35 | 35 | 35 | 30 |
| Direct operating | 5,831 | 443 | 443 | 513 | 513 | 513 | 443 | 443 | 507 | 513 | 513 | 513 | 443 |
| Utilities | 600 | 50 | 50 | 50 | 50 | 50 | 50 | 50 | 50 | 50 | 50 | 50 | 50 |
| General and administrative | 3,450 | 288 | 288 | 288 | 288 | 288 | 288 | 288 | 282 | 288 | 288 | 288 | 288 |
| Repairs/maintenance | 200 | 200 | 0 | 0 | 0 | 0 | 0 | 200 | 0 | 0 | 0 | 0 | 0 |
| Total Expenses | $34,431 | $2,848 | $2,648 | $2,986 | $2,986 | $2,986 | $2,648 | $2,848 | $2,955 | $2,986 | $2,986 | $2,986 | $2,648 |
| Income before Taxes | $ 6,003 | $ 258 | $ 458 | $ 564 | $ 564 | $ 564 | $ 458 | $ 458 | $ 501 | $ 564 | $ 564 | $ 564 | $ 458 |

## Schedule 5  Pretax Cash Budget for Six Months Ended December 31, 1993

| | July | Aug | Sept | Oct | Nov | Dec | Jan | Feb | March | April | May | June |
|---|---|---|---|---|---|---|---|---|---|---|---|---|
| **Sources of Cash** | | | | | | | | | | | | |
| Profits | $ 258 | $ 458 | $ 564 | $ 564 | $ 564 | $ 458 | $ 458 | $ 541 | $ 564 | $ 564 | $ 564 | $ 458 |
| Depreciation | 31 | 31 | 31 | 31 | 31 | 31 | 31 | 31 | 31 | 31 | 31 | 31 |
| Net Cash Flow | $ 289 | $ 489 | $ 595 | $ 595 | $ 595 | $ 489 | $ 489 | $ 572 | $ 595 | $ 595 | $ 595 | $ 489 |
| Beginning cash balance | 6,500 | 6,789 | 7,278 | 7,873 | 8,468 | 9,063 | 9,552 | 10,041 | 10,613 | 11,208 | 11,803 | 12,398 |
| Ending Cash Balance | $6,789 | $7,278 | $7,873 | $8,468 | $9,063 | $9,552 | $10,041 | $10,613 | $11,208 | $11,883 | $12,398 | $12,887 |

### Schedule 6    Balance Sheet Year Ended June 30, 1994

| | | |
|---|---:|---:|
| **Assets** | | |
| Cash | $12,887 | |
| Food inventory | 1,500 | |
| Beverage inventory | 500 | |
| Supplies | 400 | |
| Kitchen equipment | 900 | |
| less accumulated depreciation | (300) | |
| Delivery equipment | 200 | |
| less accumulated depreciation | (67) | |
| Total Assets | | $16,020 |
| | | |
| **Liabilities** | | |
| Accounts payable | $1,000 | |
| Notes payable | 6,640 | |
| Total Liabilities | $7,640 | |
| | | |
| **Stockholders Equity** | | |
| Common stock | $5,447 | |
| Retained earnings | 2,933 | |
| Total Equity | $8,380 | |
| | | |
| Total Liabilities and Equity | | $16,020 |

### Schedule 7    Pro Forma Income Statement
### Years Ending June 30, 1994, 1995, 1996, and 1997
### Assuming 10% Annual Growth in Sales for Initial Unit

| | *1994* | *1995* | *1996* | *1997* |
|---|---:|---:|---:|---:|
| **Sales** | | | | |
| Food | $51,149 | $56,264 | $61,890 | $68,079 |
| Beverage | 9,026 | 9,928 | 10,921 | 12,013 |
| Total | $60,175 | $66,192 | $72,811 | $80,092 |
| | | | | |
| **Cost of sales** | | | | |
| Food | $15,044 | $16,548 | $18,203 | $20,023 |
| Beverage | 752 | 828 | 910 | 1,001 |
| Total | $15,796 | $17,376 | $19,113 | $21,024 |
| Gross Profit | $44,379 | $48,816 | $53,698 | $59,068 |
| | | | | |
| **Controllable expenses** | | | | |
| Payroll | $26,246 | $28,871 | $31,758 | $34,933 |
| Advertising/promotion | 440 | 484 | 532 | 586 |
| Direct operating expenses | 6,414 | 7,056 | 7,761 | 8,537 |
| Utilities | 660 | 726 | 799 | 878 |
| General and administrative | 3,795 | 4,175 | 4,592 | 5,051 |
| Repairs/maintenance | 220 | 242 | 266 | 293 |
| Total | $37,775 | $41,554 | $45,708 | $50,278 |
| | | | | |
| Income before Taxes | $ 6,604 | $ 7,262 | $ 7,990 | $ 8,790 |

**Home Organization Chart**

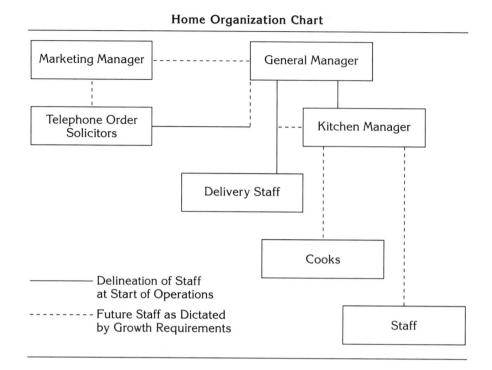

Coordinating various departments.
Planning and developing menu.
Purchasing.

2. *Marketing Manager.* Assists in menu planning designs, advertising, and creating new ideas to help attract clientele; initial contact with professionals to develop relationship of confidence and a need of our services; provides feedback to telephone order solicitors on continual basis regarding new contacts and potential improvements in skills; and learns of clientele's satisfaction or complaints so that we can improve future performance, if possible.

3. *Kitchen Manager.* Has charge of all food preparation. Must have knowledge of food preparation and appreciation of good food standards. Must be proficient in cost control. Supervises kitchen staff so must know how to work with and direct people. Plans meals, supervises, and coordinates work of order taking with cooks and other kitchen staff, seeing that food preparation is economically and technically correct; requisitions food supplies; is responsible for profitable operation of the food preparation department, schedules work hours and recommends salary adjustments.

4. *Telephone Order Solicitor.* Provides continual contacts with customers to obtain orders; receives feedback from marketing manager so that customers are contacted at convenient times; suggests specials of the day; processes orders to kitchen manager for coordination of preparation. Must work quickly and get orders accurately; must possess poise and self-control and get along with other people.

5. *Cook.* Prepares and portions meat and salads; coordinates with kitchen manager on menus, preparation, and portion sizes; participates in meetings forecasting weekly food and beverage business.

6. *Staff.* Prepares individual orders, identifies customer delivery information and order amounts.

7. *Delivery Staff.* Responsible for picking up individual orders and delivering orders in a timely manner.

# 7

# BUSINESS PLAN FOR EAST-BOUND TRADERS

*Developed by*
**Lydia Bilynsky**

# Executive Summary

This is a proposal for East-Bound Traders, a new export management company to be located in Woodland Hills, California. The company will provide a package of export services. The company will serve as an export intermediary for Los Angeles area manufacturers.

The product mix will be limited to industrial equipment and supplies. International scope will focus on Eastern and Central Europe, particularly Ukraine. The owners' established contacts in Ukraine, as well as their knowledge of the Ukrainian language and culture will be their competitive advantage.

The project will require an initial investment of $20,000. The owners will provide capital from their personal funds to cover the initial investment. It is projected that the company can capture 15% of the total export volume passing through the Los Angeles Customs District within four years. A 100% return on investment is anticipated during the second full year of operation.

Transaction volume is expected to increase at a yearly rate of 15%. Transaction volume is projected at $7,604,375 for the fourth year of operations. This is expected to result in a 37% gross profit margin, and a 26% net profit margin at the end of four full years of operation.

# Table of Contents

## I.  INTRODUCTION

East-Bound Traders will be a new private export management and trading company located in Los Angeles. The company will initially be set up as strictly an export management company (EMC). Long-range goals are for East-Bound Traders to eventually evolve into a full-fledged export trading company (ETC). This marketing plan will focus on the formation of the company as an EMC.

East-Bound Traders will serve as an export intermediary for small Los Angeles area manufacturers. It will act as the export department for these firms providing the following services: (1) export consulting, (2) market research, (3) contact facilitation with foreign buyers, (4) legal and documentation assistance, and (5) distribution and freight forwarding assistance. The company will not take title to goods. It will charge customers on a commission fee basis.

The company will constrain its activities to a product mix of light industrial equipment and supplies. International scope will focus on markets in Eastern and Central Europe, particularly Ukraine.

The United States trade deficit indicates the imbalance in the domestic market. Imports are rising faster than exports and competition for U.S. market share is more fierce than ever. Domestic market growth opportunities are declining for U.S. manufacturers. However, virtually untapped new markets have emerged in Eastern and Central Europe as a result of the collapse of communism and the Soviet Union. These markets, closed to Western goods for almost 50 years, present a variety of export opportunities for U.S. manufacturers.

Small firms, classified as those with fewer than 100 employees, account for approximately 26% of all exporting firms in the United States. However, smaller firms are less likely to engage in international business, considering that only about 8.5% of all firms classified as small are engaged in exporting.[1] Most small firms lack the management knowledge, financial resources, and manpower to organize direct in-house exporting departments. This is where the export intermediary steps in. East-Bound Traders will function as the export department of these firms providing the necessary knowledge and manpower, without requiring the large financial outlay needed to start an in-house export department.

## II.  SITUATION ANALYSIS

### 1.  Situation Environ

#### Business and Economic Conditions

California is the nation's top exporting state. California exports account for approximately 15% of the total U.S. export sales.[2] Industrial products, including computers, are the number one industry exports totaling over $13.5 billion.[3] Much of the focus on international trade has been on the Pacific Rim countries.

Exports through the Los Angeles Customs District have increased at an average of 14.64% per year over the past 15 years.[4] Pacific Rim nations are the major trading

[1] Albert G. Holzinger, "Reach New Markets," *Nation's Business,* Vol. 78, No. 12, December 1990, p. 19.
[2] Scott Ellsworth, "State Export Profiles," *Business America,* Vol. 113, No. 5, March 9, 1992, p. 19.
[3] Ellsworth, p. 18.
[4] Los Angeles Area Chamber of Commerce, *Dimensions of a World Class Market,* 1990.

partners for the Los Angeles Customs District. The Los Angeles area Chamber of Commerce estimates that direct employment in international trade has increased on an average of 8.7%, accounting for 6.5% of the county's nonagricultural employment.

No data were available for the volume of exports to Eastern and Central Europe through the Los Angeles Customs District. However, national statistics include Eastern Europe and the Commonwealth of Independent States (CIS). In 1991, total exports to the CIS grew by 8% exceeding $5 billion, with exports of manufactured goods increasing by 35%.[5] The CIS is ranked 24th as a market for U.S. products, and the International Trade Administration (ITA) predicts that exports to Eastern Europe and the CIS combined will exceed $25 billion over the next 8 years.[6]

The service industry is growing in California and nationwide. EMCs fall under the standard industrial classification 8742, management consulting services. Demand for services is expected to increase at a rate of 5% over the next year, and national employment in services is forecast to increase by 2%.[7] Business services is also the second largest growth industry in Los Angeles County with the highest employment gains over the past 10 years.

### Demand Trends

Current U.S. economic and market conditions have increased the demand for export services. Manufacturers are faced with declining market opportunities with many products in the maturity or decline stage of the product life cycle. However, certain products considered technologically obsolete in the domestic market often represent high technology in the markets of Eastern and Central Europe. Foreign sales can help small manufacturers achieve economies of scale by increasing production and reducing per unit production costs resulting in higher profitability overall. The fall in the value of the dollar has also made U.S. exports more competitive. U.S. products are relatively cheaper when compared with similar foreign goods.

The opening of Eastern and Central European markets has prompted a high demand for Western products, especially U.S. goods. There is also interest on the part of manufacturers to export to Eastern and Central Europe.

A trade poll conducted by *Nation's Business* in September 1990 found that 17% of the survey participants responded that Eastern Europe and the former Soviet Union have major sales potential for their products. However, 48% of the respondents were not engaged in any import or export activity.

Additional trade poll results indicating demand for export services are presented in Tables 1 and 2. Percentages refer to multiple responses by participants.

**Table 1 Factors That Deter a Company from International Trade**

| | |
|---|---|
| 26% | Shortage of financing |
| 30% | Lack of sales leads |
| 25% | Difficulties in finding agents |
| 27% | Costs and complexity |

[5] John Jelacic, "The U.S. Trade Outlook in 1992," *Business America,* Vol. 113, No. 7, April 6, 1992, p. 2.
[6] Victor Bailey, Ray Converse, and Richard Humbert, "Untapped Markets Are Opening Throughout the Region," *Business America,* Vol. 113, No. 7, April 6, 1992, p. 6.
[7] U.S. Department of Commerce, International Trade Administration, *U.S. Industrial Outlook,* January 1993, p. 54-4.

**Table 2   Services That Companies Would Like Greater Access To**

| | |
|---|---|
| 42% | Specific sales leads |
| 33% | Introduction to agents/distributors |
| 16% | Assessment of trade potential |
| 16% | Consulting |

Overall, firms are interested in transaction-creating services. Lack of financial resources, contacts, and knowledge is what deters companies from exporting. East-Bound Traders will be a solution to the problems these companies face and fill an obvious market need.

## 2.  Neutral Environ

### Financial Environment

The U.S. Export-Import Bank (Eximbank) is the principal government agency that sponsors various programs to aid exporters. Eximbank gives top priority to small business and export intermediaries.

Under the conditions of the Export Trading Company Act of 1982, Eximbank set up the Working Capital Guarantee Program. This is a financing program that guarantees loans to EMCs and ETCs, amongst others.

Eximbank also provides direct loans to foreign buyers of U.S. goods, and intermediary loans to fund export middlemen who extend loans to foreign buyers. Export credit insurance is also available from the Foreign Credit Insurance Association (FCIA), an agent of Eximbank.

### Government Environment

The ITA, part of the U.S. Department of Commerce, announced in March 1993 that expanding exports is their top priority. The department is actively promoting a customer service focus in its relationships with U.S. business. The Commerce Department has taken an active role in promoting trade in Eastern and Central Europe as a means of strengthening democracy in these nations. They also provide and publish contact facilitation services and material such as the *Export Yellow Pages* which are available free of charge.

The Small Business Administration (SBA) also has programs for export intermediaries. Regional offices sponsor matchmaker conferences and offer export counseling. The SBA in conjunction with the State of California and the Export Managers Association of California has established the first small business center focused exclusively on export counseling in Los Angeles.

### Special Interest Environment

Numerous national and local organizations exist that sponsor various educational and business seminars, and help with contact facilitation. Some of these organizations include (1) National Association of Export Management Companies, (2) American Association of Exporters and Importers, (3) Foreign Trade Association of Southern California, and (4) The San Fernando Valley International Trade Association.

## 3.  Competitor Environ

There are numerous export management, trading, and consulting firms in Southern California. Many firms can be characterized as general traders, that is, they export all products to many countries. EMCs are characteristically small employing 2 to 50 people. These are mostly private family-owned businesses, though some are subsidiaries of larger corporations. Three direct competitors have been identified in the Los Angeles and Orange County areas.

Crown Pacific International
18001 S. Mitchel St.
Irvine, CA 92714

This firm was established in 1978, employs 13, and generates revenues between $1 and $5 million. The firm is basically a general trader, importing and exporting a variety of products. The firm has started to use barter to conduct some business in the CIS.

Asnata Akselrod Inc.
467 S. Arnaz Dr.
Los Angeles, CA 90048

This is a female-owned business established in 1987. The owner is the single employee and the company generates under $1 million in revenues per year. The primary international focus is trade with Russia. The company also imports collectibles.

Robert Slater Company
P.O. Box 8415
Newport Beach, CA 92660

This is a well-established firm, in business since 1946. The company employs 12 people and generates yearly revenues of $5–10 million. Primary international focus is on Eastern Europe, the former Soviet Union, and the Pacific Rim.

## 4.  Company Environ

East-Bound Traders will be a small family-owned business located in Woodland Hills, CA. Initially, it will employ three people: Lydia Bilynsky, president; Oleh Bilynsky, vice-president; and one assistant.

The product mix will be limited to light industrial equipment and industrial supplies. International focus will be on Eastern and Central Europe, initially primarily on Ukraine. Initial capital outlays will come from personal funds.

The owners will use their contacts in Ukraine, as well as their knowledge of the Ukrainian language and culture as a competitive resource. This will be the competitive advantage. Oleh Bilynsky also is fluent in several other Eastern and Central European languages, and has experience buying industrial equipment.

East-Bound Traders will start out as an EMC, with eventual plans for it to evolve into a full service ETC. Services that will be provided include (1) export consulting, (2) market research, (3) contact facilitation with foreign buyers, (4) legal and documentation assistance, and (5) distribution and freight forwarding assistance. East-Bound Traders will provide additional services if requested, or refer the party to a qualified source. The company will contract out for legal, accounting, and research services when necessary.

## III.  TARGET MARKET

## 1.  Segmentation

East-Bound Traders will target small private manufacturers of industrial products in Los Angeles County. According to the Department of Commerce, these are the firms that are most likely to benefit from and employ the services of an EMC. As East-Bound Traders will be a new establishment, it will focus on the local area to keep down resource costs and provide personal service. The distribution of these firms is presented in Table 3.

**Table 3   Los Angeles County
Industrial Products Manufacturers**

| No. of Employees | No. of Firms | Revenues |
|---|---|---|
| 1–19 | 2,213 | < $5 million |
| 20–99 | 527 | < $15 million |
| | 2,740  Total Firms | |

## 2.  Buyers and Decision Makers

The decision maker is the company president, usually the president is also the owner. Often the owner will confer with family members, personal legal counsel, and accountant for advice before making a major business decision.

## 3.  Buyers' Perceptions

Decision makers in small firms often have an "attitudinal barrier" when it comes to employing an EMC or any other type of export intermediary.[8] Many feel international business is extremely complex and best left to the multinational corporations.

There is also the view that exporting is unnecessary because of the perception that the domestic market contains unlimited growth opportunities. However, many firms are simply unaware of the export potential for their products.

Psychological factors also play a role in the perceptions of small business decision makers. Small firm owners

> are often depicted as independent, achievement-oriented individuals. One key characteristic of such individuals is their need to assume that their outcomes result from their own efforts and are not left to influences beyond their control. They prefer situations where they can control and direct decisions affecting their operations.[9]

These perceptions must be taken into consideration by the marketer.

[8] Charles R. Stoner and Rajinder S. Arora, "What Export Trading Companies Mean to Small Business," *American Journal of Small Business*, Vol. 7, No. 4, April–June 1984, p. 59.
[9] Stoner and Arora, p. 60.

## 4. Needs

Overall, small firms employing an EMC are seeking marketing oriented services. A 1989 study also showed that small firms have a need for the key mechanics in exporting including funds transfer, documentation, and general market information.[10]

A study by De Noble and Belch (1988) showed that Southern California firms seek transaction-creating services. These services include (1) the ability to discover new markets, (2) establishment of contacts with potential foreign buyers, and (3) knowledge of foreign markets and competitive conditions.

## IV. PROBLEMS, THREATS, AND OPPORTUNITIES

### 1. Problems

Eastern and Central European nations are currently facing hard currency shortages which could present an obstacle to U.S. export sales. This problem will be dealt with by arranging for barter, buyback, and countertrade agreements.

### 2. Threats

The political and economic situation in Eastern and Central Europe still remains volatile. The current conditions can change at any time making these markets inaccessible. The company would have to consider markets in other regions that are more stable if a problem arises.

### 3. Opportunities

Barter, buyback, and countertrade opportunities exist. Contact could be developed with Ukraine Trading House Company in Kiev, Ukraine. This company represents clients throughout Europe and handles barter activities. The company could serve as a useful partner in the countertrade process.

## V. BUSINESS OBJECTIVES AND GOALS

Strategies and plans are based on the following financial and marketing objectives. It is important to note that an EMC does not take title to goods and therefore does not consider cost of goods sold in earnings and profit calculations. This results in slightly elevated figures.

1. To obtain a transaction volume of $7,604,375, capturing a 15% market share of total exports through the Los Angeles Customs District in a period of four years.
2. To increase transaction volume by 15% each year for the first four years of operation.

---

[10] Alex F. De Noble, Richard M. Castaldi, and Donald M. Moliver, "Export Intermediaries: Small Business Perceptions of Services and Performance," *Journal of Small Business Management*, Vol. 27, No. 2, April 1989, p. 36.

3. Obtain a gross profit margin of 27% by the end of the fourth year of operation.
4. Obtain an overall net profit margin of 26% at the end of the fourth year of operation.
5. To achieve a 100% return on investment within the first two years of operation.

## VI.  MARKETING STRATEGY

East-Bound Traders will be an early entrant into the market. It will be one of the first firms to specialize in trading specifically with Eastern and Central European countries. Early entry will guarantee significant market growth opportunities.

The company will use a specialty-market niching strategy to establish its position in the market. East-Bound Traders will focus on the following roles to support its niching strategy: (1) customer size specialist, (2) geographic specialist, and (3) product line specialist.

A triple benefit positioning strategy will therefore also be employed. The company will position itself as the leading authority on industrial products trade to Eastern and Central Europe for small manufacturers. This differentiation along with a customer service focus will also be used as a market expansion strategy.

Firms that used to do business with the former Soviet Union may respond by claiming to be specialists in the new Eastern and Central European markets. East-Bound Traders plans to face the competition head-on by using a meet-the-competition pricing strategy. This is supported by the differentiation strategy and the firm's competitive advantage. That is, the owners will use their established contacts in Ukraine as well as knowledge of the Ukrainian culture and language as a competitive resource and advantage.

## VII.  MARKETING TACTICS

### 1.  Product

1. Set up an information channel with overseas contacts to have the most current market information possible.
2. Provide pretransaction assessment and posttransaction follow-up to generate repeat volume.
3. Tailor all services to individual customer needs.
4. Register with the California Association of Export Managers and the San Fernando Valley International Trade Association to gain credibility.

### 2.  Price

The price will be set as a fixed commission fee. The charge will be 3% of the dollar volume of the transaction generated through the company.

### 3.  Place

1. The company will service its customers directly.
2. The company will locate transportation intermediaries for clients directly.
3. Market research will be contracted out to research companies operating out of Kiev, Ukraine.

### 4.  Promotion

1. Promotion will be through trade show participation. The firm will participate in a minimum of six trade shows in the Los Angeles area.
2. The owners will attend all local matchmaker conferences sponsored by the Small Business Administration.
3. The company will list with the Department of Commerce's *Export Yellow Pages,* as well as other publications such as the *Southern California International Trade Register* and the yearly *Directory of U.S. Exporters.*

## VIII.  ORGANIZATION, EVALUATION, CONTROL, AND IMPLEMENTATION

Figures and calculations used in this section are all estimates. The cash flow and profit and loss statements are estimated on a yearly basis. This procedure is based on the "Trade Stream Model" developed by United States Department of Commerce. This was the method suggested in their *Export Trading Company Handbook* that is applicable to small firms focusing on specific regions and/or products.

**Organization Chart
for Project East-Bound Traders**

### 1.  Project Development/Schedule of Estimated Costs and Expenses

**Table 4    Initial Investment Schedule**

| Item | Unit Cost | Cost |
| --- | --- | --- |
| (3) Computers | $2,000 | $ 6,000 |
| (1) Fax machine | 1,200 | 1,200 |
| (3) Telephones | 75 | 300 |
| (1) Telex | 1,000 | 1,000 |
| Office furniture | — | 6,000 |
| (1) Laser printer | 3,000 | 3,000 |
| Miscellaneous |  | 2,500 |
| Total |  | $20,000 |

Cost Estimates

1. Assistant's Salary: $23,000, yearly increase 3%
2. Social Security/Benefits: 20% of wages
3. Promotion: 6 trade shows @ $1,000
4. Travel: $4,000 monthly
5. Rent: $1,200 per month
6. Telephone/Fax/Telex: $350 per month
7. Utility: $150 per month
8. Office Supplies: $300 per month
9. Legal/Accounting Fees: $1,250 per month
10. Automobile: $500 per month
11. Depreciation: Assume straight line over 4 years

## 2.   Break-Even Analysis

Estimated average sale: $750,000

$$5,000,000/750,000 = 6.66 \text{ or } 7 \text{ sales in the first year}$$

Fee @ 3%: $22,500 per average sale
Variable costs per sale:

$$114,200/7 = 16,314 \text{ per sale}$$

Break-even:

$$0 = F/P - V$$
$$0 = 16,900/22,500 - 16,314$$
$$\text{Breakeven} = 2.73 \text{ sales}$$

**Yearly Cash Flow**

| | Start-Up | Year 1 | Year 2 | Year 3 | Year 4 |
|---|---|---|---|---|---|
| Cash on hand | $30,000 | $ 10,000 | $ 28,900 | $ 58,630 | $ 70,546 |
| Receipts | | 150,000 | 172,500 | 19,375 | 228,131 |
| Total Cash | | $160,000 | $201,400 | $257,005 | $294,177 |
| Expenses | | −86,600 | −88,600 | −88,600 | −86,600 |
| Wages | | −27,600 | −28,428 | −29,280 | −30,158 |
| Overhead | | −16,900 | −16,900 | −16,900 | −16,900 |
| Equipment | 20,000 | 0 | 0 | 0 | 0 |
| Cash to owners | | 0 | 0 | −35,000 | −86,473 |
| Taxes | | 0 | −8,842 | −16,679 | −25,942 |
| Total Excess Cash | $10,000 | $ 28,900 | $ 58,630 | $ 70,546 | $ 43,604 |

## Profit and Loss Statement

| Year | 1 | 2 | 3 | 4 |
|---|---|---|---|---|
| Volume | 5,000,000 | 6,612,500 | 6,612,500 | 7,604,375 |
| *Revenue* | | | | |
| Fees | $150,000 | $172,500 | $198,375 | $228,131 |
| Start-up cost | 20,000 | | | |
| Gross Profit | $130,000 | $172,500 | $198,375 | $228,131 |
| *Controlled Expenses* | | | | |
| Salary | $ 23,000 | $ 23,690 | $ 24,400 | $ 25,132 |
| SS/benefits | 4,600 | 4,738 | 4,880 | 5,026 |
| Promotion | 6,000 | 6,000 | 6,000 | 6,000 |
| Travel | 48,000 | 50,000 | 50,000 | 48,000 |
| Automobile | 6,000 | 6,000 | 6,000 | 6,000 |
| Dues/subscriptions | 2,000 | 2,000 | 2,000 | 2,000 |
| Legal/accounting | 15,000 | 15,000 | 15,000 | 15,000 |
| Office supplies | 3,600 | 3,600 | 3,600 | 3,600 |
| Telephone/fax/telex | 4,200 | 4,200 | 4,200 | 4,200 |
| Utilities | 1,800 | 1,800 | 1,800 | 1,800 |
| Total Controllable | $114,200 | $117,028 | $117,880 | $116,758 |
| *Uncontrollable Expenses* | | | | |
| Depreciation | 0 | 3,500 | 3,500 | 3,500 |
| Insurance | 5,000 | 5,000 | 5,000 | 5,000 |
| Rent | 14,400 | 14,400 | 14,400 | 14,400 |
| Licenses | 2,000 | 2,000 | 2,000 | 2,000 |
| Total Fixed | $ 16,900 | $ 16,900 | $ 16,900 | $ 16,900 |
| Total Expenses | $131,100 | $141,928 | $142,780 | $141,658 |
| Net Profit/Loss before Taxes | $ −1,100 | $ 30,572 | $ 55,595 | $ 86,473 |

## Balance Sheet

| | Year 1 | Year 2 |
|---|---|---|
| *Current Assets* | | |
| Cash | $28,900 | $58,630 |
| *Fixed Assets* | | |
| Equipment | 20,000 | 16,500 |
| Total Assets | $48,900 | $91,130 |
| | | |
| *Liabilities* | | |
| Taxes owed | 0 | 8,842 |
| Net Worth | $48,900 | $82,288 |

## IX.  SUMMARY

East-Bound Traders will be a new private export management company located in Woodland Hills, California. The company will provide a package of export-related services to small firms in the Los Angeles area.

The company will limit its product mix to industrial equipment and supplies. The scope of international coverage will focus on Central and Eastern European markets, particularly Ukraine. The owners will use their established contacts in Ukraine, as well as their knowledge of the Ukrainian language and culture as a competitive advantage over any competitors.

The company will benefit small manufacturers who do not have the managerial knowledge, manpower, or financial resources to get involved in direct exporting. Currently, exporting is more important than ever with the fierce import competition for domestic market share. The company will serve as the export intermediary for these firms, charging a commission fee of 3% on only the transaction volume generated.

The new venture will require an initial investment of $20,000. The owners are prepared to finance the project all in cash from their personal funds. The anticipated 100% return on investment is expected during the second year of operation.

The company projects that it will capture 15% share of the export volume passing through the Los Angeles Customs District. Transaction volume is expected to increase 15% yearly and reach a level of $7,604,375 in the fourth year of operation. This would generate a gross profit margin of 37%, and a net profit margin of 26% at the end of the fourth full year of operation.

The company will use a differentiation and niching strategy to compete in the marketplace. As the markets of Eastern and Central Europe are just emerging, East-Bound Traders will be an early entrant in the market. This will guarantee market growth opportunities for the firm.

## X.  BIBLIOGRAPHY

Bailey, Victor, Ray Converse, and Richard Humbert. "Untapped Markets Are Opening Throughout the Region." *Business America,* Vol. 113, No. 7, April 6, 1992, pp. 6–8.

Barovick, Richard, and Patricia Anderson. "EMCs/ETCs: What They Are, How They Work." *Business America,* Vol. 113, No. 14, July 13, 1992, pp. 2–5.

Becker, Don, Ed. *Directory of United States Exporters.* New York: Journal of Commerce, Inc., 1992.

"Building Business Ties with Russia/NIS/Eastern Europe." *Business America,* Vol. 114, No. 6, March 22, 1993, pp. 2–7.

Darnay, Arsen J., Ed. *Service Industries USA.* Detroit: Gale Research, Inc., 1992.

Delphos International. "Eximbank Provides Financing for U.S. Export Trading and Management Companies." *Business America,* Vol. 113, No. 5, March 9, 1992, pp. 21–22.

De Noble, Alex F., Richard M. Castaldi, and Donald M. Moliver. "Export Intermediaries: Small Business Perceptions of Services and Performance." *Journal of Small Business Management,* Vol. 27, No. 2, April 1989, pp. 33–41.

Ellsworth, Scott. "State Export Profiles." *Business America,* Vol. 113, No. 5, March 9, 1992, p. 18.

Holzinger, Albert G. "Reach New Markets." *Nation's Business,* Vol. 78, No. 12, December 1990, pp. 18–25.

Jelacic, John. "The U.S. Trade Outlook in 1992." *Business America,* Vol. 113, No. 7, April 6, 1992, pp. 2–5.

Los Angeles Area Chamber of Commerce. *The Los Angeles Area: Dimensions of a World Class Market,* 1990.

"Secretary Brown: Expanding Exports 'Dramatically' Is Priority for the U.S. Department of Commerce." *Business America,* Vol. 114, No. 7, April 5, 1993, pp. 6–7.

Smith, Timothy J. "Collapse of the Soviet Union Opens Opportunities in Independent States." *Business America,* Vol. 113, No. 7, April 6, 1992, pp. 16–18.

*Southern California Business Directory and Buyers Guide.* Database Publishing Co., 1993.

Stoner, Charles, and Rajinder S. Arora. "What Export Trading Companies Mean to Small Business." *American Journal of Small Business,* Vol. 8, No. 4, April–June 1984, pp. 56–62.

"The ABCs of Exporting." *Business America,* Vol. 113, No. 9, World Trade Week, 1992, pp. 2–34.

U.S. Department of Commerce, International Trade Administration. *Contact Facilitation Service Directory.* Washington DC, June 1984.

U.S. Department of Commerce, International Trade Administration. *The Export Trading Company Guidebook.* Price Waterhouse and the Council for Export Trading Companies, February 1984.

U.S. Department of Commerce, International Trade Administration. *U.S. Industrial Outlook.* January 1993.

"U.S. Government Programs for Export Intermediaries." *Business America,* Vol. 113, No. 4, July 13, 1992, p. 6.

# 8

# BUSINESS PLAN FOR CARTRIDGE RECYCLING SERVICES, INC.

*Developed by*
**Luanne Tadian**

# TABLE OF CONTENTS

# LIST OF TABLES AND FIGURES

# EXECUTIVE SUMMARY

Cartridge Recycling Services, Inc. (CRSI) performed economic, industry, market, and risk analysis to determine the viability of entering the toner cartridge recycling market in Southern California. This information was then used to develop a business and strategic plan.

The company will function in all capacities as a two-owner partnership, employing two individuals, and will be centrally located in Alhambra, CA.

Like many small businesses, CRSI is most vulnerable to financial risk, specifically, undercapitalization and insufficient reserves. Consequently, each partner will invest $10,000 up front with additional sources of capital in the form of savings, home mortgage, or bank loan for $5,765. The company expects to break even from operations in month 4 and recoup the initial investment by month 5.

Initially, CRSI will offer only toner cartridge recycling products and services. Research shows that 28.45 million cartridges will be sold in 1993—recycled cartridges account for 30% of this figure. Of the outstanding recycled market, CRSI will attempt to capture .04% through mass mailing, direct sales, and promotional campaigns. The marketing budget is set at $1,750.

Sales performance will be based on unit volume, while customer satisfaction will be based on biannual surveys.

The company will obtain initial supplies and inventory from LCSI and will continue to use LCSI as a supplier of spent cartridges, drums, and fuser wands. Additional cartridges will be obtained from consumer buybacks.

CRSI will differentiate itself from other companies through capacity fill and quality toner. The company will use these tools to position itself as number 1 in quantity/quality print and service excellence.

Detailed information concerning the introduction of CRSI into the toner recycling market can be found throughout this plan and in the Appendix.

## INTRODUCTION

As people have become more environmentally aware and have tried to conserve resources and reduce waste, the recycling industry has boomed. Many entrepreneurs are identifying new products to recycle and creating new markets and industries.

A by-product of this new awareness is the toner recharging industry. Post Script and other laser printers are fast becoming a major industry. As a result of the decline in price of these machines, they are also becoming routine office fixtures for big and small companies alike. The most popular laser printers use laser engines made by Canon and Hewlett-Packard (HP). These engines are intended to accept a throwaway plug-in toner cartridge. The cost of new toner cartridges, good for 3,000 to 4,000 pages, is $90–$120 each.[1]

Most factory-built cartridges are only filled to 50 percent capacity and when the toner runs out, the cartridge is disposed of. So far, most of these cartridges end up as landfill and as of yet are not biodegradable.[2]

Although recycled cartridges currently make up a small part of the market, many government agencies and businesses are recognizing the cost-effectiveness and the inherent benefits to the environment that this industry provides.

For about half the cost of a new cartridge, companies such as Laser Cartridge Services, Inc. (LCSI), take apart and clean used cartridges, replace old parts, and refill the toner bin. LCSI is a small minority-owned business that offers new and recharged toner cartridges; laser printers, copiers, fax supplies, enhanced cartridge drums, and quality graphics toner. Service and maintenance on copier machines and printers are also offered. LCSI is based out of Gainesville, Virginia. The company has been incorporated for three years and has been offering its services for 26 months with a staff of 17. In addition to the services offered in Virginia, LCSI has five in-house contracts with firms in the Los Angeles (LA) area. LCSI plans to phase out these clients by June 1, 1993.

The focus of this business plan is the purchase of the LA clients from LCSI and the start-up of a new business in the LA area.

### Present Status

Research indicates that by the close of 1993, 28.45 million laser cartridges will be used each year in the United States.[3] The number of businesses in Southern California using laser printers is tremendous and successfully tapping into this market could prove to be extremely lucrative. Cartridge Recycling Services Inc. (CRSI) will purchase the existing LA client base from LCSI and will function in all capacities as a two-owner partnership. CRSI will incorporate under Subchapter S to enable the company to have the liability protection of a corporation and be taxed as a partnership. To begin operations, CRSI will only sell toner cartridges—new and remanufactured. In an effort to minimize start-up expenses, CRSI will employ only two individuals to help with general office duties and production. The company hopes to begin operations June 1, 1993.

---

[1] Lu, Cary, "On the Cheap: Toning Down Laser Printing Costs," *Inc*, December 1990.
[2] "Consumer Watch," *PC World*, January 1992, p. 43.
[3] "Toner Cartridges Focus of Recycle Drive," *PC Week*, July 22, 1991, p. 22.

## Strategic Opportunities

Our intentions on this project were to determine where the market was heading in terms of recharging; whether a significant difference existed between those knowledgeable about the service and those that were not; and what barriers, if any, would limit the successful entrance into the market.

A survey of 100 businesses in the San Gabriel Valley area was conducted through direct and telephone interviews. Of those surveyed, 95% use laser printers and/or copy machines that require cartridges. About 75% of the businesses purchase new cartridges, while 1% use recycled and 2% use both. In addition, 15% were unaware of the service, but were interested in learning more about it. For detailed results, a sample survey, and a list of business categories tested, see Appendix.

In addition to the survey, an economic analysis was performed. The analysis evaluated the viability of such a business based on the state of the economy at the national, state, and local levels as forecasted for IVQ 1992 and 1993.

Overall, CRSI believes that the market is acceptable to our service and prices. CRSI believes that there is an opportunity for the company to earn a high profit margin on production at lower costs in a rapidly growing market. Also, with increasing technological changes, home users will enter the customer profile.

## Company Thrust

CRSI wants to earn substantial profits by building a reliable reputation within the local business community and focusing on future growth potential. CRSI takes pride in our aesthetic values and will remain socially and environmentally aware. Not only are we providing a service that helps reduce waste going into landfills, but we will donate a percentage of profits to local charities and foundations. CRSI will help our business customers cut costs by reducing overhead, enhancing print quality, and improving their business image.

## Business Strategies

Initially, CRSI will attempt to capture those consumers that are directly associated with the product, especially businesses that are interested in cutting overhead costs. In an attempt to gain exposure, CRSI will use a mass mailing and direct sales campaign to meet its sales goals in the first year. We will always promote the reduction in overhead costs and the inherent benefits to the environment. In addition, whether a business purchases our product, CRSI will promote its buyback of spent cartridges.

Once the business is established within the local business community, CRSI will focus on contracting companies such as government agencies and large corporations. We will begin implementation of the high-volume, self-sustaining in-house contract options.

## Resource Requirements

To begin operations, each partner will invest $10,000. CRSI expects to break even from operations in the fourth month. However, the time needed to recoup our investment would be five months. For the first three months that CRSI will be losing money, the company would need to borrow $5,765 (see Cash Flow Statement).

CRSI will employ two individuals to help with general office duties and production. In order to capitalize on each individual owner's experience and expertise in the field, one partner will handle sales and promotion while the other handles production and distribution. The employees will be hired on a part-time basis. A breakdown of the expected start-up costs follows:

**Start-Up Costs**

|  | One-Time | Periodic |
|---|---|---|
| Equipment Needed for Rebuilding: | | |
| 1. Two IBM-compatible 386 computers with 3.5"/5.25" floppy drives, 2 meg RAM, 40 megabyte hard disk drive with super color VGA monitor | $ 3,000 | |
| 2. One Canon Series II laser printer | 1,500 | |
| 3. One Hewlett-Packard Series III laser printer | 2,500 | |
| 4. Two vacuum sealers @ $35 each | 70 | |
| 5. Two specialized vacuums @ $250 each | 500 | |
| 6. Four screwdriver sets @ $10 each | 40 | |
| 7. Initial supplies for remanufacture | 1,000 | |
| Total Equipment Cost | $ 8,610 | |
| Equipment Needed for Selling Service: | | |
| 1. Space rent (1,000 sq. ft. @ $1.66/sq. ft.) | | $1,665 |
| 2. One 1985 Ford AeroStar Van | 5,000 | |
| 3. Salary ( 2 employees @ 2,000/mo.) | | 4,000 |
| 4. Furniture | 1,000 | |
| 5. Telephone equipment | 250 | |
| 6. Office supplies | | 100 |
| 7. Insurance (van @ $100/business @ $75) | | 175 |
| 8. Advertising expense | | 1,750 |
| 9. Utilities | | 250 |
| 10. Telephone bill | | 400 |
| Total Selling/Service Costs | $14,590 | |
| Total One-Time Costs | $14,860 | |
| Total Periodic Costs | | $8,340 |

## Performance Measures and Milestones

Because a good reputation is built on superior service and quality products, CRSI will survey clients on a biannual basis. The survey will help determine in which areas upgrades need to be made and what problems need to be resolved.

Sales performance will be based on unit volume rather than dollar volume. Each quarter, CRSI will post the unit milestone for that quarter's sales. If the standard is not met, then action will be taken to ensure that it is met in following quarters.

For more detailed information on these topics, see the Table of Contents.

# COMPANY ANALYSIS

### Location Analysis

CRSI realizes that economic conditions for Southern California are very weak. However, CRSI also realizes that it is cheaper to start or expand a business when times are tough.

With the ever-increasing vacancy rates, building owners wage competitive battle to win tenants in an overbuilt market by offering half or free rent. In addition, tenants can still negotiate lower rents before leases expire. Because CRSI wants to keep start-up costs at a minimum, a review of office rents will help determine the best location for operations.

Average office rent in downtown Los Angeles fell to $25.51 (per square foot) in 1992:IIIQ. In the mid-Wilshire area, average rents fell to $20.83, and in the Tri-City area to $23.55. The San Gabriel Valley reported average rents of $19.97 in 1992:IIIQ.[4]

In addition to rental costs, the company also considered income and property taxes, security, and freeway access. Because of the characteristics of the service, location is only relevant in terms of service calls. Most of the business is carried out away from the office, as are promotional strategies. Thus freeway access is important in determining service time guarantees. The office provides production facilities and telephone/reception space. Because of the value of the equipment used in production, security for the area was also a determining factor.

After careful review of the preceding factors, CRSI determined that location of the office should be in Alhambra, California. This location would allow the company quick access to three main freeways into and out of Los Angeles (the 60, 10, and 710). These routes also connect to other important highways—the 101, and 210. In addition to the easy freeway access, the company would be able to take advantage of the low rental rates in the San Gabriel Valley. Alhambra's police department is located close to the downtown area, which would ensure quick response by police authorities should the need arise.

## Product

Toner cartridges are single, self-contained, replaceable units. Inside the cartridge is a source of toner, a photosensitive drum, and a spent-toner holding tank. Most toners are basically a mixture of ferric oxides, polyethylene, and lubricants.

Fundamentally, toner starts out in the cartridge's fresh toner tank where a magnetized roller picks up a layer of the toner. Meanwhile, the photosensitive drum gets flooded with light and is electrostatically charged, and then selectively discharged by a laser beam so that a charged pattern remains on the drum.

As the drum rotates, toner gravitates to the charged pattern. As the drum rotates further, toner particles transfer to a highly charged piece of paper. The paper then goes on to a fusion roller assembly where with heat and pressure, the toner is forced onto the paper for a final hard copy.[5]

The toner remaining on the drum gets scraped off by wiper pads and is routed to the spent-toner holding tank. This process continues for each page until the toner in the cartridge runs out. Most factory-built cartridges are only filled to 50% capacity and when the toner runs out, the cartridge is discarded.

---

[4] "Data Bank," *Los Angeles Business Journal,* various issues for October and November 1992.
[5] Lancaster, Don, "Hardware Hacker-Toner Cartridge Reloading," *Radio Electronics,* May 1991, p. 65.

CRSI will offer new and recharged toner cartridges, enhanced cartridge drums, and graphics quality toner. Other services administered by CRSI's professional staff will include quick response to service calls, free pickup and delivery of supplies, weekend service calls, and free preventive maintenance. Most importantly, CRSI plans to offer a 100% unconditional guarantee on supplies and services.

## Market

Potential clients consist of any users of laser printers. This encompasses many industries and most markets. However, CRSI wants to start small and perfect the product/service before expanding into other areas. For this reason, CRSI will, initially, target those small businesses that are directly associated with the product and are interested in cutting overhead costs.

## Technology Position

There are basically two methods used in the remanufacturing of toner cartridges. Each company within the industry uses one or a combination of these techniques. In addition, some companies alter the process to meet their production needs.[6] In order to avoid disclosing any valuable trade secrets, CRSI will discuss the technical process it plans to use only fundamentally.

Before we begin, note that the photosensitive drums must *never* be exposed to strong light, or to any light at all over any long period of time. It is also important never to get fingerprints on the drum—cotton gloves should be worn. And lastly, care should be taken as toner, in theory, can explode a vacuum cleaner.[7] A mask should be worn during the entire process.

The first method, called "drill and fill" or "punch-and-go," dates back to 1985—a year after Hewlett-Packard Company introduced the first LaserJet. Two holes are drilled into the cartridge on the first reload. After drilling the holes, the spent toner is shaken or vacuumed out. The hole is then resealed using plain old Scotch tape or a nickel Caplug. The fresh-toner hole is used to accept a bottle of new toner and then resealed.[8] This method is not used by CRSI because it does not take into account the wear on the scraper blades and photoconductor drums. Refilled cartridges by this method produce lower-quality output than new cartridges, have shorter life spans, and may expose the printers to damage.

The other method, the one used by CRSI, is to simply take the cartridge completely apart. Internal parts are examined for damage or wear, and damaged parts are replaced including the drum. New toner is added and the cartridge is put back together. This method allows the cartridge to be refilled up to 3 times; 6 times if the drum is replaced.[9] This process produces print quality equal to that of a new cartridge. By using graphics quality toner, the cartridge produces sharper, darker, crisper prints; and less toner is used. Using less toner per page means lower costs per print.

---

[6] C'DeBaca, Charles, President, *Laser Cartridge Services, Inc.* Gainesville, VA: August 5–21, 1991. Training Seminar.
[7] *Radio-Electronics*, p. 66.
[8] Thomas, Susan G., "New Lamps for Old: Are Recycled Cartridges Finally Worth Considering?" *PC Magazine*, November 26, 1991, p. 214.
[9] *Inc.*, December 1, 1990.

## Technological Rigidities

Once the cartridge has been rebuilt, it is necessary to test and verify that the toner spreads evenly, there is no residual dust on inner components, and there are no scratches. In order to combat the possibility of equipment malfunction, CRSI will purchase two IBM Compatible Computers and two Laser Printers from LCSI.

Another possible rigidity could happen if the company were to underestimate demand for the product/services. Because of this possibility, CRSI is going to work at less than capacity during the first year so as not to build inventories unrealistically or underproduce. Producing at less than capacity will allow CRSI time to expand its clientele without increasing its overhead and training costs.

## Operational Resources

Because of the characteristics of the service—most of the business is carried out away from the office—the office only provides production facilities and telephone/reception space. In addition, the units are compact, easy to handle, and require limited storage space. For these reasons, CRSI has determined that the company will lease a 1,000-square-foot office. As the operation grows, the company can either expand the facilities or relocate.

On average, it takes approximately 15 minutes to rebuild and clean a cartridge. Without going through detailed calculations, one individual working full time (6 hours with 2 hours allotted for lunch and breaks) should be able to produce 480 cartridges a month.

Major equipment needed for rebuilding include the computer, printer, vacuum, vacuum sealer, screwdrivers, and miscellaneous items. Other equipment is needed for delivery and Administrative functions associated with sales and service. A list of these requirements is shown in the analysis of start-up costs.

## Strengths and Weaknesses

As seen in Table 1, CRSI believes that the experience and expertise in marketing is a strength. This will serve to strengthen the company, quality, and service reputation that it intends to build. The owners' experience will increase the promotion effectiveness and sales force effectiveness in future years. By centrally locating in San Gabriel, CRSI believes that it will have adequate geographic coverage of the San Gabriel Valley area. The importance of the marketing function is high because all sales will be based on the marketing ability of the sales force.

The financial performance of the company is marked "average" because the cost/availability of capital is dependent on the approval of funds from the bank. The profitability of the

**Table 1    Company Strengths and Weaknesses**

| | Performance | | | Importance | | |
| Functions | Strong | Average | Weak | High | Medium | Low |
|---|---|---|---|---|---|---|
| Marketing | X | | | X | | |
| Finance | | X | | X | | |
| Manufacturing | X | | | | X | |
| Organization | X | | | X | | |
| Competition | | X | | | | X |

company is not a concern because the product has a high profit margin. The high profit margin is seen as the key to the company's financial stability. Initially, CRSI plans to focus its attention on access to capital.

CRSI believes that the manufacturing aspect of the company is very strong. Facilities are adequate for the intended production capacities that are planned. The workforce is seen as dedicated and able not only to perform the skills necessary of them but also to ensure that delivery is made on time. The technical manufacturing skills are not difficult and are easy to master. For this reason, CRSI feels that efforts on this function should just maintain the status quo.

The organization is seen as strong. The background of each of the owners serves as testimonial to their leadership abilities. These abilities will help in the control and motivation of the employees. The leadership style will promote tight control when deadlines need to be met but will allow for flexibility and responsiveness to meet employee needs.

Competitive performance is marked as average because (1) the company has not begun operations and has no record to evaluate; and (2) it is important for the company to determine at what level it will choose to compete. Competition has low importance. Although CRSI will remain acutely aware of the competition, it will focus more on continually improving its product and services.

## Bases of Competition

Clients of the remanufactured cartridges base their purchase on price, quality, and quantity output. CRSI will address each of these characteristics differently.

The price of most remanufactured cartridges falls within the $35–$65 price range. In addition, it is standard for recycling companies to purchase spent cartridges.

Quality refers to the print. The quality of the print is determined by the quality of the toner placed into the cartridge. Like most products, toners have varying degrees of quality. The best quality toner is graphics quality.

Quantity output refers to the number of pages that the cartridge can print before it is spent. New Original Equipment Manufacture (OEM) cartridges are good for approximately 3,000 copies because they are only filled to 50% capacity. Rebuilt cartridges are good for up to 5,000 copies because they are filled to 80% capacity. Overfill of a cartridge can damage the print quality.

## Key Success Factors

Competition in this emerging field can be intense because of the comrade shared by many of the companies. This interdependence is reflected in the similarity of prices offered both locally and across the country. Companies within the industry are acutely aware of the competition and little is gained through price cuts. A firm can raise its prices, hoping its competitors will follow suit, but, when a company cuts its price to gain a competitive edge, other firms are likely to do the same.[10]

Because pricing is not a means to compete effectively, CRSI will try to differentiate itself from other companies by the amount and quality of toner used, maintenance services offered, and the 100% unconditional guarantee.

When CRSI reconditions a cartridge, that cartridge will be taken completely apart for examination. All parts will be cleaned and inspected. Every part not meeting our exacting standards

---

[10] Doan, David, Vice-President *Laser Cartridge Network*. Anaheim, CA: August 7, 1992. Telephone Interview.

will be replaced. Cartridges will then be filled with Graphics Quality Toner to 80% capacity. The cartridge will then be tested, vacuum-sealed, packaged, and returned to the customer.

In addition to free pickup and delivery, CRSI will offer a free preventive maintenance program which extends the life of the machine. All products and services will be unconditionally guaranteed.

CRSI will continually train their employees in customer relations and product quality with cutting-edge technology. CRSI believes that by providing a quality product and service, we will be able to maintain strong customer loyalty and low turnover rates.

## Competitive Position

CRSI will attempt to position itself as number 1 in quantity and quality print. The company will continually strive for excellence in service.

# INDUSTRY ANALYSIS

## History/Economic Factors

The recycling or remanufacturing of laser-printer toner cartridges dates back to 1985, a year after H-P Co. introduced the first LaserJet. Holes were drilled into the cartridge, spent toner was drained and replaced with a fresh batch, and the cartridge was resold. This drill-and-fill technique did not take into account the wear on the scraper blades and photosensitive drum. The cartridges produced lower than quality output, had shorter life spans, and exposed the printers to damage.

By 1987, recyclers became more sophisticated. They disassembled the cartridges, and cleaned and inspected every part before adding toner.

By 1990, replacement parts (photoconductor drums) became available, and refillers became manufacturers. Parts were replaced instead of refurbished. Additionally, the recycled cartridges yield more copies and higher quality than new OEM cartridges.[11]

Although there are no barriers to entry, with the exception of initial capital and technological know-how, there are few firms offering these services. There are about 5,000 firms that recycle used cartridges across the country.[12]

Economic factors that affect the industry include inflation and interest rates. Inflation during 1992:IIIQ rose at an annual rate of 2.4%. Some slight acceleration to a range of 3% to 3.5% is expected in the latter half of 1993. Interest rates are at all-time lows and due to the economic uncertainty, consumers and businesses continued to pay down debt.[13]

The weak economy serves as an incentive for companies to downsize, restructure, and cut costs. Recharging offers these companies a way to cut costs without cutting the quality of their output.

On one hand, the expected containment of inflation is bad news. An increase in inflation helps the industry by allowing companies to raise their prices without fear of losing customers. Customers are more likely to accept higher prices in an inflationary environment than when prices are more stable.

[11] Ambrosio, Johanna, "Data Centers Do Good by Recycling Well," *Computerworld*, May 25, 1992, p. 65.
[12] Welch, Mary, "Recycling Pays Off 'a Lot,'" *Atlanta Business Chronicle*, January 14, 1991.
[13] Economic Consultants, "Economic Forecast: The Nation, California, and Southern California," June 1, 1992, p. 1.

On the other hand, the low rate of inflation has led to low interest rates. With the decline in interest rates, more companies are able to pass the Positive Net Present Value test and increase their level of investment. Companies that remanufacture cartridges can increase their purchases of industrial equipment durable goods. These purchases enhance productivity, leading companies to hire more workers—increasing income and consumption. Taken in context, this enhances the economic recovery of the nation.

## The Players

It is a thin line that separates America's top rechargers from a list of some 5,000 companies in the United States. The largest of these companies are rebuilding between 20,000 and 35,000 cartridges per month (cpm). Table 2 names nine such companies. The smaller companies may be running less than 5,000 cpm.

## The Recharging and Recycling (R&R) Market

An estimate of the laser printer population in the United States is shown in Figure 1. Here, Canon LBP engines comprise about 79.2% of the U.S. market. Because of its speed, resolution, and low cost, the street price is now $1,200 to $1,300.

The pie chart in Figure 2 illustrates the structure of the U.S. replacement cartridge market for all printer and copier engines. Please note that rechargers account for 31.7% of the market with the *smaller* firms selling more cartridges than the top and middle sectors combined.

An expanded breakdown of the American recharging industry is shown in Figure 3. This chart reflects that the small mom-and-pop firms make up roughly 42% of the market.

## Cartridges

The line graph in Figure 4 shows the growth and expected growth in demand for toner cartridges. It estimates that by 1994, 31.2 million cartridges will be used in the United States. It is expected that once more companies become educated to the merits of using recycled cartridges—it saves money, helps the ecology, and creates jobs—the industry will continue its rapid growth. As seen in Figure 3, U.S. rechargers are expected to capture roughly 50% of the market for replacement cartridges.

**Table 2   America's Top Cartridge Rechargers**

| | | |
|---|---|---|
| Cartridge Connection<br>Indianapolis, Indiana | Lasertek<br>Las Vegas, Nevada | Qume Corporation<br>Milpitas, California |
| Future Graphics<br>Chatsworth, California | Nashua Cartridge Products<br>Exeter, New Hampshire | Spring Point<br>New York, New York |
| Dataproducts<br>Simi, California | PM Company<br>Cincinnati, Ohio | West Point Products<br>Valley Grove, West Virginia |

**Figure 1    U.S. Laser Printer Population
(1 to 10 Pages Per Minute)**

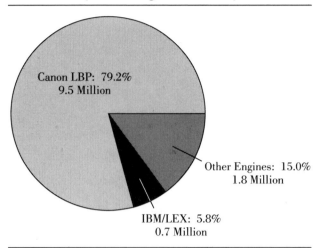

*Note:* 1992—12 million machines (estimated).

*Source:* Diamond Research Corporation.

**Figure 2    U.S. Replacement Cartridge Market**

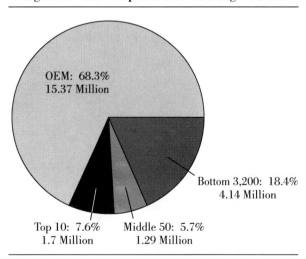

*Note:* 1992—22.5 million cartridges.

*Source:* Diamond Research Corporation.

**Figure 3   U.S. Recharging Industry 1992 Structure**

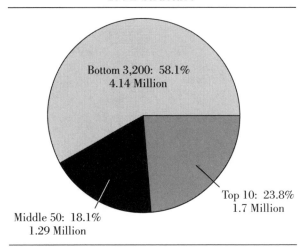

*Note:* 7.13 million printer and copier cartridges.

*Source:* Diamond Research Corporation.

**Figure 4   Printer and Copier Cartridge Growth Forecast**

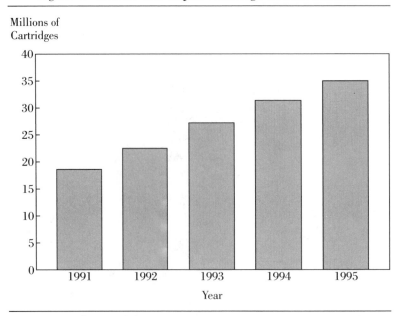

*Source:* Diamond Research Corporation.

## New Jobs

As stated earlier, the recharging industry creates jobs at three levels—top rechargers (2,000–40,000 cpm), mid-sized rechargers (200–2,000 cpm), and the small, mom-and-pop establishments (50–200 cpm). Figure 5 illustrates that expansion in the industry is expected to bring employment to approximately 16,300 American workers by 1995. If you work out the calculations, this number breaks down to 6 or 7 jobs per 1,000 cpm for the smaller one- and two-person firms. This number should only be used as a yardstick because operating hours for firms vary from firm to firm. Some businesses operate around the clock, seven days a week. This is done to reduce the number of office, clerical, and managerial workers needed. Other rechargers are highly diversified with employees engaged in selling and servicing of other products.

## New Distribution Channels

Because rechargers build solid, personal relationships with local, state, and national accounts, they represent a new channel of distribution for office products. As competition grows, and profits shrink, rechargers become more diversified. They can begin offering transparencies, ink jet films, mailing labels, and color toners.

## Equipment Service and Maintenance

Having developed a knowledge of the electrophotographic process, rechargers can expand into copiers, fax machines, and related office equipment. This expansion should be natural.

**Figure 5    Estimated Jobs Recharging and Recycling Industry**

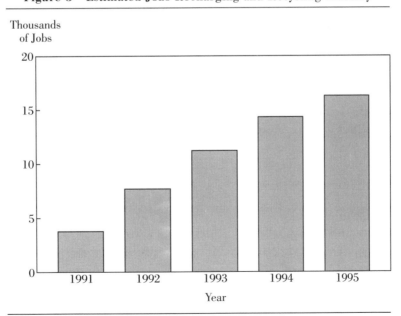

*Source:* Diamond Research Corporation.

## Future Outlook

An important factor in the projected growth of the toner cartridge recharging industry is the landmark Supreme Court decision handed down on June 8, 1992. In the case of *Kodak v. Image Technical Services,* the court ruled against monopolistic practices by OEMs. This decision will reach across many industries. OEMs will no longer be able to control service by tying the sale of parts to the sale of service contracts, fees, and purchase of supplies.

The future outlook for the R&R industry is phenomenal as more end users are driven by what the industry calls the 3 E's—Ecology, Economy, and Employment. Every purchasing agent should derive satisfaction from the knowledge that by purchasing recharged toner cartridges, they have taken a direct action to save money for their company, protect the environment for mankind, and create jobs for their fellow citizens.

# MARKET ANALYSIS

## Market Scope/Segmentation

CRSI will be centrally located in the San Gabriel Valley with operations in Alhambra, CA. Travel of any kind is extremely rough on toner cartridges, therefore, CRSI will initially serve a 15–20 mile radius. This will ensure the guarantee of 2-hour response time.

Initially, CRSI will focus on small businesses whose focus is to reduce overhead. These businesses will have earnings less than $1,000,000 annually and are high-volume users of the product. We will attempt to focus on the following professions: attorneys, printers, graphic artists, and doctors.

## Customer Characteristics

CRSI believes that businesses in its target market share the following characteristics: (1) they are directly associated with the product; (2) they are professional and image oriented; (3) like most businesses, they are interested in cutting overhead costs without sacrificing quality or quantity; and (4) they are responsive to social and environmental issues.

Once the company has established itself within the business community, it will begin focusing on expansion by bidding on contracts with government agencies and large corporations. Also, CRSI will begin offering self-sustaining, in-house contract options.

CRSI placed its potential customers into four categories: innovators, early adopters, early majority, and late majority. The innovators and early adopters, it is estimated, will account for 75% of sales. Approximately 15%–20% of sales will come from the early majority while the late majority will account for only 5% of sales. These last two groups have limited knowledge about the product. Therefore, CRSI will concentrate its sales efforts on the latter two groups.

Duplicating services, print and copy shops, served as innovators for the toner recharging industry as they are closely associated with the product. Credibility has been built because these firms have used the product and cut costs while maintaining production levels.

The early adopters of our service are those primarily concerned with image and cost savings. CRSI has placed attorneys and government agencies into this category. An attorney's image is projected in the person's ability as well as document appearance. Other early adopters would include government agencies, the film industry, and medical professions. These consumers are looking to maintain budgets by cutting expenditures.

Small businesses and universities started using recycled cartridges after the industry built a positive reputation and the product proved to be cost-effective. These consumers only capitalize on a sure thing and are adamantly against high-risk ventures because monetary flexibility has not been obtained (they have no money to lose). This group is the early majority.

The late majority opens up the market to home users due to the decrease in price and improved reliability of the product over time. All the kinks have been removed and usage is easy.

## Sales Tactics

The sales tactics used by CRSI are threefold. The object of these tactics is to contact 6,000 companies within the first year. The company is striving for a 4% rate of return/250 companies—2% from flyers, 1% from newspapers, and 1% from direct sales. If each company purchases two cartridges per month, CRSI will meet its desired goal.

Initially, CRSI will send out a packet which contains an introduction to the company, a flyer, and a memo from the president. Each page will include telephone number and address (see Appendix). Approximately four to six weeks later, CRSI will send out a follow-up letter reminding the companies of our services and products.

CRSI's second strategy to increase sales is to use personal selling. Concurrent with the follow-up letters, the company will initiate our program of *Reach out and Call Someone.* Our market survey indicates that two hours of cold calling can produce 10 leads. Leads are persons who are interested in our products and services. Four hours of cold calling, twice a week, can produce 2,000 highly qualified prospects per year. Due to the experience and expertise in sales, it is expected that a large percentage of these prospects will become customers.

The third strategy concerns sales training and motivation. CRSI proposes to spend a portion of its advertising budget on training for its partners and employees. The training will include sales and marketing classes, tapes for motivation, selling, and self-improvement. In addition, CRSI will offer paid attendance at symposiums, seminars, and lectures on customer relation skills, selling, and new products.

We believe that success is dependent on its people. A high level of ongoing training and motivation will ensure the company's success today and in the future.

For those customers not interested in purchasing the product, CRSI will offer to buy their spent cartridges. It is believed that most companies will accept this offer if they are not already involved in a recycling program. By throwing the cartridge into the trash, they hurt the environment and add to the nation's landfill problem. By selling CRSI the cartridge, they earn $8.00 and increase supplies for the company.

## Distribution Channels

CRSI is planning to purchase supplies from LCSI at reduced cost. In addition to these supplies, the company will get a portion of its cartridges from consumer buybacks. The cartridges will then be recharged and resold to clients. Staples, an office outlet store, buys spent cartridges from customers of their systems and supplies them to rebuilders for a higher price. The cost to CRSI would be $10.00. Thus, the company's first efforts on buybacks will be to purchase them from consumers for $8.00—generating a $2.00 savings per cartridge. As the company grows, CRSI will look for additional suppliers. Initially, our expected channels of distribution are depicted below.

## Pricing

Remanufactured cartridges typically sell for $35–$65 each with the exchange of an old cartridge. Even at these low prices, there are excess profits to be earned yielding expectations of rapid growth in the life cycle.

The survey CRSI conducted showed that 62.5% of businesses that purchase recycled cartridges in the San Gabriel Valley are paying between $30 and $60 for each cartridge. Because CRSI has chosen a price-skimming strategy, we feel that the starting price for these cartridges should be set at $59.95 each—which we will reduce over time. At this sales price, CRSI expects monthly operations to break-even when gross sales equal 185 units/month. This figure is determined from the following equation:

$$\text{Gross sales} = \text{Variable cost (VC)} + \text{Fixed cost (FC)} + \text{Profit}$$
$$59.95X = 15X + 8{,}340 + 0$$
$$X = 186 \text{ Units/Mo}$$

See the Appendix for the Price Schedule and Break-Even graph.

## Promotion and Advertising

CRSI has decided to limit its media campaign to the Alhambra, Rosemead, San Gabriel cities at this time. We do not wish to say no to anyone just because they are not in our target area; however, we want to reserve our potential customers for expansion in the future.

CRSI is holding in reserve a strategy of introductory pricing and giveaway schemes. Implementation of these programs will be dependent on actual sales after four months of operation. If sales are over projections, the program will be kept in reserve; however, if sales are under projections, we will launch the following programs:

1. **Tell a Friend for Four Grand.** A free cartridge for existing customers who provide us a qualified lead.
2. **Try It, You May Like It.** We will offer a free trial period of 3 days' unlimited use. If a new customer likes it, they can recycle their cartridge and keep the trial one.
3. **The More the Merrier.** For every fifth cartridge recycled, the customer gets one free.
4. **Empowerment.** This is a commission program offered to employees. The employee will earn 6% of selling price in addition to their regular salary.

All of these programs will have an open termination date. Review of the progress will be made on a monthly basis. Adjustments will be made on an as-needed basis.

As presented earlier, the sources of promotion will include direct mailing, flyers, and business cards. Upon expansion, computing trade shows will be added to this list. The medias of promotion will be limited to the *Los Angeles Times* and the *San Gabriel Valley Journal*. Upon expansion, the company will list itself with *Recharge*, the industry magazine. Also, it will begin to take advantage of other magazines: *MACWEEK, Home Office Computing,* and *Radio-Electronics.* CRSI has determined that it will budget $1,750 per month for promotions and advertising. The consumer expected media of promotion are detailed in the Appendix.

## Major Competitors

As stated earlier, most of the toner recharging companies are small mom-and-pop shops that operate within distinct boundaries. Competition from these firms will be limited outside their boundaries. However, there are larger firms that operate at state and national levels. These firms are considered CRSI major competitors. These competitors are (but not limited to):

### Qume Corporation

Qume Corporation located in Milpitas, California, remanufactures their cartridges for resale. They pay up to $10 for every returned cartridge. Also, for each cartridge returned, Qume donates $5 to the participating firms' designated charity or to a fund in the name of the corporation set aside for employee education and recreation programs.[14] Qume coats the photoconductor drum by using a direct image polymer process, which protects the drum from toner wear and tear. This process means that the cartridges have a longer life and improved quality. In addition, these cartridges can then be recycled between 10 and 15 times. Once the parts are no longer recyclable, they are shredded and melted down for other uses. Qume cartridges are resold to dealers or users for $89.95.[15]

### Dataproducts Corporation

Dataproducts Corporation, located in Woodland Hills, California, also remanufactures its cartridges for resale. This company isn't convinced that drums can withstand multiple lives, so it replaces the photoconductor drums with new drums and remanufactures the other wearable parts.[16] The Dataproducts Imaging Supplies Division participates in a fund-raising program in which Seattle businesses give their used cartridges to a nonprofit group that feeds the hungry. Dataproducts pays the organization $10 for each cartridge.[17] Dataproducts toner cartridges sell for $79 and can be recycled between five and seven times. Like Qume, once the cartridge is no longer recyclable, the company shreds and melts them down for other uses.[18]

### Lexmark International

Lexmark International of Lexington, Kentucky, also has a nationwide cartridge recycling program. Its program covers six IBM LaserPrinter models in its 4019 and 4029 series. Upon request, Lexmark sends customers a postage-paid container for the return of spent cartridges. These cartridges are then given to a workshop for handicapped adults, who make money by selling the parts to recyclers.[19]

In an effort to discourage third-party recycling and hold on to the laser-cartridge business, Canon and Hewlett-Packard have started their own "recycling" programs. These companies are quick to assert that their programs are an effort to keep cartridges (which are not biodegradable) out of landfills.

### Canon

Canon has a nationwide recycling program that applies to all of its copiers, fax machines, and printers that use a disposable all-in-one cartridge. Canon will send users a prepaid UPS shipping

---

[14] *PC World*, p. 43.
[15] *PC Week*, p. 22.
[16] *PC Magazine*, p. 214.
[17] *PC World*, p. 43.
[18] *PC Week*, p. 22.
[19] *PC World*, p. 43.

label for cartridges to be returned. These cartridges are then disassembled, melted down, and used as raw material. For each cartridge returned, Canon will donate $.50 to the National Wildlife Federation and the Nature Conservancy.[20]

### Hewlett-Packard

Hewlett-Packard Company (HP) of Palo Alto, California, has expanded its program to encourage users to recycle empty toner cartridges. The program encourages users to return the cartridges to HP. The company disassembles the cartridges. Some of the parts are reused while others are melted down and used as raw materials. Like Canon, HP provides users with prepaid UPS shipping labels. In addition, HP will donate $1 to the National Wildlife Federation or the Nature Conservancy for each returned cartridge.[21]

CRSI will counter these efforts by making firms aware that even if they do nothing else, they can sell their empty cartridges to recyclers for $5–$10 each. The company can then donate as much of the proceeds as they want to the environmental groups of *their* choice.

### Market Share and Sales

As stated earlier, by the close of 1993, 28.45 million laser cartridges will be purchased in the United States. BIS Strategic Decisions in Norwell, Massachusetts, states that 70%–80% of those cartridges will still be thrown away.[22] Assuming that this figure is 70%, then the other 30% is expected to be the remanufactured market. Thus the recycled market will account for 8.535 million cartridges.

Of the outstanding cartridge recycling market, CRSI will attempt to capture .04 percent. This figure was obtained by the following formula:

$$\frac{\text{Expected sales in units}}{\text{Total recycled market}} = \frac{3030}{8.535 \text{ million}}$$

Without going through detailed calculations, if CRSI spent six hours a day rebuilding cartridges, the company could produce 5,760 cartridges a year. It can be noted that expected sales for the first year fall short of potential production abilities because:

1. CRSI is assuming that in the first months of operation, setting up and getting into routines will occur.
2. It is unrealistic to think that the company will have the exposure in the business community to make large sales.
3. During this breaking-in period, the partners will not be able to devote their full energies to sales.

As time progresses and all kinks are worked out, CRSI can concentrate more on sales and expect sales to increase. However, it is not reasonable to assume that sales will continue to grow at the same rate the entire year. CRSI is constrained the first year by the geographic boundaries it has set. The company believes that it will take six months to saturate the specified customer

---

[20] Ibid.
[21] "HP Printer-Cartridge Recycling Program Goes National," *MacWeek*, January 8, 1991.
[22] *PC Week*, p. 22.

base, at which time a leveling off of sales will occur. During this time, CRSI will determine the viability of entering new markets and market segments as a means to increase sales and/or market share. The company will also look into expanding its service area.

# STRATEGIC PLANNING

## Long-Term Goals

### *Sales*

CRSI's goal is to sustain annual growth rates of at least 10%. The company plans to expand facilities to meet the desired growth rate, and will also expand the geographic area it plans to service as well.

### *Employment*

In order to meet desired sales and service levels, CRSI plans on adding one individual to the staff at least every six months for the first three years. In order to ensure that the company does not become overstaffed or understaffed, CRSI will evaluate the necessity of each increase. If the company is operating at less than capacity, then the addition will not be made. If the company is operating at or near capacity and sales are expected to increase, then the addition will be made.

### *Product*

During the second year of operations, CRSI will implement fax and copy services. In addition, the company will offer repair services for printers, fax machines, and copy equipment. During the third year, the company will begin bidding on large government and corporate contracts.

## Key Performance Indicators

Like most companies, CRSI will look at its profit margin, production abilities, and asset value as indicators of its performance in the industry. CRSI would like to parallel the industry performance levels with these factors. These indicators are useful in the short run.

However, the *key* performance indicator will be the level of customer satisfaction with the quality of the product and its upgrades. This is viewed as a long-term indicator of customer loyalty and turnover. CRSI will continuously poll its client base for comments and suggestions. CRSI believes that happy customers not only give the company a good reputation in the local environment but can aid in the sales tactics employed by the firm. The company recognizes that some of the best referrals come from the customers themselves.

## Plan Assumptions

CRSI has made certain assumptions concerning the following areas in the execution of this plan.

### *Economy*

Despite the costs associated with opening a business in California (regulations, taxes, labor, and real estate costs), the national and local economy make the prospect of operations amenable to CRSI. The economic potential lies in expectations of (1) stable inflation and lower interest rates; (2) lower rental rates; and (3) more management skill on the streets due to layoffs by other firms.

### Industry

A recession usually means that more businesses are failing than succeeding and that markets are contracting overall. But like the bold investor who buys stocks when everyone else is selling, the toner recharging industry sees opportunity where most others see disaster. As seen in the Industry Analysis, this is a rapidly growing industry. It is assumed that (1) the industry will continue to grow at the same rate over time; and (2) with advancements in technology, there will continue to be high profit margins on production.

### Market

With the preceding assumptions in mind, CRSI is assuming that (1) the San Gabriel Valley is receptive to the services offered; (2) the small size of the company will add to the expected high profit margins on production; and (3) the company will achieve customer loyalty through increased toner fill capacity and lower overhead costs.

## Risk Analysis

Risks are conditions that may prevent the company from achieving its objectives. In an effort to determine what risks should be minimized, CRSI developed Table 3. Across from each element, and marked with an "X" is the level of risk associated with that element. The overall level of risk is assigned to the column in which most of the elements fall. This determines the level of risk associated with the company achieving its desired objectives.

Like many small businesses, CRSI is most vulnerable to financial risk. Specific problems the company will try to avoid include undercapitalization, inefficient collection practices, and insufficient reserves to cover emergencies.

Most firms within the industry are small mom-and-pop shops that started out in a garage with initial capital in the form of home mortgages, savings, and notes payable. The partners of CRSI plan on investing $10,000 initially. If necessary, the partners will take out a home mortgage for additional capital. However, the first two options include a loan from the Small Business Administration (SBA) or bank. This also accounts for the possibility of insufficient reserves.

CRSI will try to avoid inefficient collection practices by requesting payment for cartridges upon receipt. Companies that cannot pay up front will be put on a 30-day payment plan. CRSI is not expecting this to be a big problem because most of the companies we will be dealing with will be accustomed to paying twice the cost for the same product. Thus payment to us should be easier.

**Table 3   Risk Analysis**

| | | Rating | |
| Element | Low | Medium | High |
|---|---|---|---|
| Industry | X | | |
| Market | | X | |
| Competitive position | X | | |
| Strategy | | X | |
| Assumptions | X | | |
| Financial performance | | | X |
| Management performance | X | | |
| Future performance | | X | |
| Others | X | | |
| Overall risk | X | | |

This market is a medium risk because it depends on the reception of CRSI and its services to the segment. Future performance is then based on the reputation and credibility the company earns. Strategy can make or break a company. It is our goal to achieve a low risk factor in these areas by concentrating on meeting the product and service needs of the client. This awareness will also help in the formulation of strategies for increased sales and market share.

The elements marked as "low" risk are based on the experience and expertise the partners will bring to the firm. As can be seen in Table 3, most of the elements fall in the "low" risk rating group. The low risk elements will serve as a foundation for the business and will aid in the minimization of high risk elements. Also, the overall risk rating of low supports the proposal to open operations in the San Gabriel Valley.

## Business Strategies

### Market Strategy

In order to make as many people and businesses aware of our products and services as quickly as possible, CRSI will initially use a mass mailing and direct selling campaign.

### Product-Line Strategy

Initially, the company will only sell toner cartridges—new and remanufactured. The company will focus its efforts on toner fill capacity and quality.

### Technology Strategy

The company will research and implement cutting-edge technology into the production process.

### Operations Strategy

The strategy used to keep operations running smoothly is continuous Education and Training opportunities.

### Financial Strategy

Savings, home mortgage, SBA and bank loans will be potential sources of funds.

**Milestone Schedule (Expected Cost)**

| Strategy | Year 1 | Year 2 | Year 3 | Strategy Cost |
|---|---|---|---|---|
| Geographic expansion | $0 | $ 100 | $ 0 | $ 100 |
| Production/service expansion | 0 | 2,000 | 0 | 2,000 |
| Government contracts | 0 | Time | Time | 0 |
| Contract bidding | 0 | Time | Time | 0 |
| Manpower expansion | 0 | 24,000 | 24,000 | 48,000 |
| Total Cost | $0 | $26,100 | $24,000 | $50,100 |

**Strategy Plan**

| Task | Month | | | | | | | | | | | |
|---|---|---|---|---|---|---|---|---|---|---|---|---|
| | 1 | 2 | 3 | 4 | 5 | 6 | 7 | 8 | 9 | 10 | 11 | 12 |
| Operators/tax license | █ | | | | | | | | | | | |
| Purchase L.A. clients | █ | | | | | | | | | | | |
| Bank loan | | | █ | █ | | | | | | | | |
| Suppliers | █ | | | | | | | | | | | |
| Facilities | █ | | | | | | | | | | | |
| Equipment | █ | | | | | | | | | | | |
| Inventory/supplies | █ | | | | | | | | | | | |
| Hire employees | | █ | | | | | | | | | | |
| Product training | | █ | █ | | | | | | | | | |
| Direct mail campaign | | █ | █ | █ | | | | | | | | |
| Follow-up letters | | | | | | | █ | █ | █ | | | |
| Promotion program | | | | | █ | | | █ | | | | |
| Telemarketing | █ | █ | █ | █ | █ | █ | █ | █ | █ | █ | █ | █ |
| Client survey | | █ | | █ | | | | | █ | █ | | |
| Sales/motivation training | | █ | █ | | | | █ | | | █ | | █ |
| Recharge listing | | | █ | | | | | | | | | |

# MANAGEMENT TEAM

## Key Personnel/Responsibilities

*Luanne Tadian.* BS in Psychology/Biology; MBA in Management; four years' experience in the toner recharging industry. Two of these years were spent as the Vice-President in charge of Research/Sales/and Marketing for LCSI. Luanne, co-partner of CRSI, will be in charge of Sales, Marketing and General Office Management.

*Ernie C'DeBaca.* BS in Business, one year of experience in the production of cartridges for computer, fax, and copy machines. Three years' experience in the production and development of Computer Systems. Ernie, also co-partner, will handle production and distribution functions of the company.

*Angela C'DeBaca.* Five years' experience as a secretary/receptionist of a million-dollar software developer/vendor. Eighteen months' experience as an administrative secretary. Angela will function as a secretary/receptionist for CRSI.

*John or Jane Doe.* Position has yet to be filled. This individual will be hired to perform production and general office duties.

**CRSI Organizational Chart**

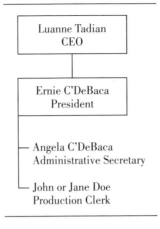

## Manpower Milestones

The milestones in manpower are depicted in Table 4. As stated earlier, all hiring will be based on a review of the company and its ability to meet the demand and service needs of the clients. The increase in personnel depicted in Table 4 is based on the assumption that CRSI expands geographically, and increases its product and service base during years 2 and 3.

**Table 4    Manpower Milestones**

| *Function* | *Year 1* | *Year 2* | *Year 3* |
|---|---|---|---|
| General and administrative | 1 | 2 | 2 |
| Marketing | 1 | 1 | 2 |
| Research/engineering | 1 | 1 | 1 |
| Production | 1 | 2 | 2 |
| Other personnel | 0 | 0 | 1 |
| Total | 4 | 6 | 8 |

# FINANCIAL ANALYSIS

The Financial Analysis appears on pages 8·28–8·29.

**PROJECTION OF FINANCIAL STATEMENTS**

SUBMITTED BY  Luanne Tadian

| | | ACTUAL | PROJECTIONS → | | | | | |
|---|---|---|---|---|---|---|---|---|
| SPREAD IN HUNDREDS ■ DATE | | 6/30/93 | 7/31/93 | 8/31/93 | 9/30/93 | 10/3/93 | | 11/30/93 |
| SPREAD IN THOUSANDS □ PERIOD | | MONTH | MONTH | MONTH | MONTH | MONTH | | MONTH |
| **P R O F I T and L O S S** | 1 NET SALES | 21 00 | 42 00 | 63 00 | 105 00 | 197 00 | 1 | 180 00 |
| | 2 | | | | | | 2 | |
| | 3 | | | | | | 3 | |
| | 4 Less: Materials Used | | | | | | 4 | |
| | 5   COST OF GOODS SOLD | 5 25 | 10 51 | 15 75 | 26 25 | 36 75 | 5 | 45 00 |
| | 6 GROSS PROFIT | 15 75 | 31 49 | 47 25 | 78 75 | 110 25 | 6 | 135 00 |
| | 7 Less: Sales Expense | (186 10) | (37 50) | (37 50) | (37 50) | (37 50) | 7 | (37 50) |
| | 8   General & Administrative Expense | (45 90) | (45 90) | (45 90) | (45 90) | (45 90) | 8 | (45 90) |
| | 9   Depreciation | | | | | | 9 | |
| | 10 | | | | | | 10 | |
| | 11 OPERATING PROFIT | (216 25) | (51 91) | (36 15) | (4 65) | 26 85 | 11 | 51 60 |
| | 12 Less: Other Expense | | | | | | 12 | |
| | 13 Add: Other Income | 200 00 | | | | | 13 | |
| | 14 PRE-TAX PROFIT | (16 25) | (51 91) | (36 15) | (4 65) | 26 85 | 14 | 51 60 |
| | 15 Income Tax Provision | | | | | | 15 | |
| | 16 NET PROFIT | (16 25) | (51 91) | (36 15) | (4 65) | 26 85 | 16 | 51 60 |
| **C A S H   P R O J E C T I O N** | 17 CASH BALANCE (Opening) | — | (11 85) | (45 25) | (57 65) | (28 05) | 17 | 43 55 |
| | 18 Add: Receipts: Cash Sales & Other Income | 21 00 | 42 00 | 63 00 | 105 00 | 147 00 | 18 | 180 00 |
| | 19   Cash Sales Plus Receivable Collections | | | | | | 19 | |
| | 20   Investment | 200 00 | | | | | 20 | |
| | 21 | | | | | | 21 | |
| | 22   Bank Loan Proceeds | | | | | | 22 | |
| | 23   Other Loan Proceeds | | | | | | 23 | |
| | 24   TOTAL CASH AND RECEIPTS | 221 00 | 42 00 | 63 00 | 105 00 | 147 00 | 24 | 180 00 |
| | 25   Less: Disbursements: Trade Payables | | | | | | 25 | |
| | 26     Direct Labor | | | | | | 26 | |
| | 27 OPERATING & OTHER EXPENSES | (84 25) | (75 40) | (75 40) | (75 40) | (75 40) | 27 | (75 40) |
| | 28 | | | | | | 28 | |
| | 29   Capital Expenditures | (148 60) | | | | | 29 | |
| | 30   Income Taxes | | | | | | 30 | |
| | 31   Dividends or Withdrawals | | | | | | 31 | |
| | 32   Bank Loan Repayment | | | | | | 32 | |
| | 33   Other Loan Repayment | | | | | | 33 | |
| | 34 TOTAL CASH DISBURSEMENTS | (232 85) | (75 40) | (75 40) | (75 40) | (75 40) | 34 | (75 40) |
| | 35 CASH BALANCE (Closing) | (11 85) | (45 25) | (57 65) | (28 05) | 43 55 | 35 | 148 15 |
| **B A L A N C E   S H E E T** | 36 ASSETS: Cash and Equivalents | | | | | | 36 | |
| | 37   Receivables | | | | | | 37 | |
| | 38   Inventory (Net) | | | | | | 38 | |
| | 39 | | | | | | 39 | |
| | 40 CURRENT ASSETS | | | | | | 40 | |
| | 41   Fixed Assets (Net) | | | | | | 41 | |
| | 42   Prepaid Expenses | | | | | | 42 | |
| | 43   Other | | | | | | 43 | |
| | 44 | | | | | | 44 | |
| | 45 TOTAL ASSETS | | | | | | 45 | |
| | 46 LIABILITIES: Notes Payable-Banks | | | | | | 46 | |
| | 47   Notes Payable-Others | | | | | | 47 | |
| | 48   Trade Payables | | | | | | 48 | |
| | 49   Income Tax Payable | | | | | | 49 | |
| | 50   Current Portion L.T.D. | | | | | | 50 | |
| | 51 | | | | | | 51 | |
| | 52 CURRENT LIABILITIES | | | | | | 52 | |
| | 53   Long-Term Liabilities: | | | | | | 53 | |
| | 54 | | | | | | 54 | |
| | 55 | | | | | | 55 | |
| | 56 TOTAL LIABILITIES | | | | | | 56 | |
| | 57 NET WORTH: Capital Stock | | | | | | 57 | |
| | 58   Retained Earnings | | | | | | 58 | |
| | 59 | | | | | | 59 | |
| | 60 TOTAL LIABILITIES AND NET WORTH | | | | | | 60 | |

© 1984 Robert Morris Associates - Form C-117 Rev 8/84
ORDER FROM Bankers Systems, Inc. St. Cloud, MN 56302
Successor to Cadwallader & Johnson
These forms are intended for use in commercial lending transactions.
Where any other use is contemplated, it is suggested that a careful review
be made to ensure compliance with applicable laws and regulations.

| 12/31/93 MONTH | 1/31/94 MONTH | 2/28/94 MONTH | 3/31/94 MONTH | # | 4/30/94 MONTH | 5/31/94 MONTH | 6/30/94 YEAR | 6/30/95 YEAR | 6/30/96 YEAR | # |
|---|---|---|---|---|---|---|---|---|---|---|
| 210 00 | 210 00 | 210 00 | 210 00 | 1 | 210 00 | 210 00 | 1818 00 | 2399 80 | 2800 00 | 1 |
| | | | | 2 | | | | | | 2 |
| | | | | 3 | | | | | | 3 |
| | | | | 4 | | | | | | 4 |
| 52 50 | 52 50 | 52 50 | 52 50 | 5 | 52 50 | 52 50 | 454 51 | 599 94 | 770 00 | 5 |
| 157 50 | 157 50 | 157 50 | 157 50 | 6 | 157 50 | 157 50 | 1363 49 | 1799 86 | 2030 00 | 6 |
| (37 50) | (37 50) | (37 50) | (37 50) | 7 | (37 50) | (37 50) | (598 60) | (711 00) | (930 00) | 7 |
| (45 90) | (45 90) | (45 90) | (45 90) | 8 | (45 90) | (45 90) | (550 80) | (550 80) | (553 80) | 8 |
| | | | | 9 | | (20 00) | (20 00) | (20 00) | (20 00) | 9 |
| | | | | 10 | | | | | | 10 |
| 74 10 | 74 10 | 74 10 | 74 10 | 11 | 74 10 | 54 10 | 194 09 | 518 06 | 526 20 | 11 |
| | | | | 12 | | | | | | 12 |
| | | | | 13 | | | | | | 13 |
| 74 10 | 74 10 | 74 10 | 74 10 | 14 | 74 10 | 54 10 | 194 09 | 518 06 | 526 20 | 14 |
| | | | | 15 | | | | | | 15 |
| 74 10 | 74 10 | 74 10 | 74 10 | 16 | 74 10 | 54 10 | 194 09 | 518 06 | 526 20 | 16 |
| 148 15 | 282 75 | 417 35 | 551 95 | 17 | 686 55 | 821 15 | | | | 17 |
| 210 00 | 210 00 | 210 00 | 210 00 | 18 | 210 00 | 210 00 | 1818 00 | 2399 80 | 2800 00 | 18 |
| | | | | 19 | | | | | | 19 |
| | | | | 20 | | | 200 00 | | | 20 |
| | | | | 21 | | | | | | 21 |
| | | | | 22 | | | | | | 22 |
| | | | | 23 | | | | | | 23 |
| 210 00 | 210 00 | 210 00 | 210 00 | 24 | 210 00 | 210 00 | 2018 00 | 2399 80 | 2800 00 | 24 |
| | | | | 25 | | | | | | 25 |
| | | | | 26 | | | | | | 26 |
| (75 40) | (75 40) | (75 40) | (75 40) | 27 | (75 40) | (75 40) | (913 65) | (1281 80) | (1503 80) | 27 |
| | | | | 28 | | | | | | 28 |
| | | | | 29 | | | (148 60) | (20 00) | | 29 |
| | | | | 30 | | | | | | 30 |
| | | | | 31 | | | | | | 31 |
| | | | | 32 | | | | | | 32 |
| | | | | 33 | | | | | | 33 |
| (75 40) | (75 40) | (75 40) | (75 40) | 34 | (75 40) | (75 40) | (1062 25) | (1301 80) | (1503 80) | 34 |
| 282 75 | 417 35 | 551 95 | 686 55 | 35 | 821 15 | 955 75 | 955 75 | 1098 00 | 1296 20 | 35 |
| | | | | 36 | | | 134 60 | 282 71 | 318 96 | 36 |
| | | | | 37 | | | 62 89 | | 35 56 | 37 |
| | | | | 38 | | | 22 92 | 23 92 | 23 92 | 38 |
| | | | | 39 | | | | | | 39 |
| | | | | 40 | | | | | | 40 |
| | | | | 41 | | | 148 60 | 168 60 | 168 60 | 41 |
| | | | | 42 | | | 51 | 5 93 | | 42 |
| | | | | 43 | | | | 26 41 | 26 41 | 43 |
| | | | | 44 | | | | | | 44 |
| | | | | 45 | | | 306 49 | 570 46 | 573 45 | 45 |
| | | | | 46 | | | | | | 46 |
| | | | | 47 | | | 20 00 | | 20 00 | 47 |
| | | | | 48 | | | 40 00 | | 40 00 | 48 |
| | | | | 49 | | | | | | 49 |
| | | | | 50 | | | | | | 50 |
| | | | | 51 | | | | | | 51 |
| | | | | 52 | | | 60 00 | | 60 00 | 52 |
| | | | | 53 | | | | | | 53 |
| | | | | 54 | | | | | | 54 |
| | | | | 55 | | | | | | 55 |
| | | | | 56 | | | 60 00 | | 60 00 | 56 |
| | | | | 57 | | | 52 40 | 52 40 | 52 40 | 57 |
| | | | | 58 | | | 194 09 | 518 06 | 413 45 | 58 |
| | | | | 59 | | | | | | 59 |
| | | | | 60 | | | 306 49 | 570 46 | 573 45 | 60 |

## REFERENCES

1. Baumol, William J.; Blinder, Alan S. *Microeconomics.* New York: Harcourt Brace Jovanovich, 1991.

2. C'DeBaca, Charles, President *Laser Cartridge Services Inc.* Gainesville, VA: Training, 1989.

3. "Cartridges Offer easy Transfer of Images to Cloth, Wood, Leather." *MACWEEK,* December 18, 1990.

4. Chen, Steven C.M. "Printer Companies Turn a Little Green." *Home Office Computing* 8(10):10, October 1990.

5. "Consumer Watch: Recycling Toner Cartridges." *PC World,* January 1992, pp. 43–44.

6. "Data Centers Do Good by Recycling Well." *Computerworld,* May 25, 1992, pp. 65–66.

7. Diamond, Arthur S., "Recycling: The Right Track," *Recharger,* December 1992, pp. 38–86.

8. Doan, David, Vice-President *Laser Cartridge Network.* Anaheim, CA: August 7, 1992. Telephone Interview.

9. Dowling, Mark. "Aspen Imaging Plants Future in Toner." *The Denver Business Journal,* February 8, 1991.

10. *Economic Forecast: The Nation, California, and Southern California.* Economic Consultants, Inc., June 1, 1992.

11. "HP Printer-Cartridge Recycling Program Goes National." *MACWEEK,* January 8, 1991.

12. "Hardware Hacker—Toner Cartridge Reloading." *Radio-Electronics,* May 1991, pp. 65–71.

13. Koklanaris, Maria. *Washington Post,* Financial Section, January 28, 1991.

14. Leebe, Ken. Sales Representative *World Wide Computer Products,* Los Angeles, CA: August 7, 1992. Telephone Interview.

15. "New Lamps for Old: Are Recycled Cartridges Finally Worth Considering?" *PC Magazine,* November 26, 1991, p. 214.

16. "On the Cheap: Toning Down Laser Printing Cost." *Inc.,* December 1, 1990.

17. "Recycling Pays Off 'a Lot.'" *Atlanta Business Chronicle,* January 14, 1991.

18. "The Greening of the Toner Cartridge." *PC Magazine,* June 16, 1992, pp. 31–32.

19. "Toner Cartridges Focus of Recycle Drive." *PC Week,* July 22, 1991, p. 22.

# APPENDIX

# Questionnaire

The name of our company is Cartridge Recycling Services, Inc. We specialize in recycling and reconditioning toner cartridges for laser printers and copy machines at a cost that is less than replacing your old cartridges with new ones.

Type of Business _____

1. What is your immediate reaction to this service?

   | | |
   |---|---|
   | Great | .4419 |
   | Like it very much | .1395 |
   | Like it somewhat | .2093 |
   | Do not particularly like it | .1395 |
   | Do not like it at all | .0233 |
   | No response | .0465 |

2. Does your company use laser printers and or copy machines that require cartridges?

   Yes .9535          No .0465

   If you answered no to this question, please turn the questionnaire in—thank you for your time.
   If you answered yes, please continue.

3. Approximate number of copies made per week/month?

   Week 2046.42          Month 5015.38

4. Approximate number of cartridges your company purchases per month/year?

   Month 4.125          Year 12.26

5. What type of cartridges does your company purchase?

   New .79     Recycled .11     Both .023

6. How much do you pay for the cartridges you currently purchase?

   | | New | Recycled |
   |---|---|---|
   | $30 - 60 | .00 | .6250 |
   | $61 - 90 | .15 | .3750 |
   | $91 - 120+ | .84 | .0000 |

7. How do you feel about your current service?

   | | |
   |---|---|
   | Satisfied | .5588 |
   | Somewhat Satisfied | .0882 |
   | Not Satisfied | .0294 |

8. Cartridge Recycling Service will offer four levels of service.

    a) Full Service—$249.95. Includes recycling one cartridge plus 6 refills with a guarantee of 4,000 copies per refill.

    b) One-time service—$49.95 with exchange, 59.95 without exchange.

    c) A new OEM cartridge—$89.95

    d) Refill and cleaning of cartridges—$20.00

What are your comments regarding these services and prices?

| | |
|---|---|
| Very Cost Effective | .4168 |
| Environmentally useful | .3953 |
| Useful | .1163 |
| Budget Restraints | .0968 |

9. Based on your company's needs, how useful do you think the Cartridge Recycling Service would be to your company?

| | |
|---|---|
| Very Useful | .4872 |
| Useful | .2308 |
| Somewhat Useful | .1282 |
| Not very useful | .1282 |
| Not useful at all | .0256 |

10. How strongly do you feel about using this service if it were available to your company?

| | |
|---|---|
| Would definitely use it | .4419 |
| Would probably use it | .2791 |
| Would probably not use it | .2093 |
| Would definitely not use it | .0698 |

11. Where would you expect to see such a service advertised?

| | |
|---|---|
| Newspaper | .1304 |
| Magazine | .1014 |
| Catalogs | .2609 |
| Television | .0435 |
| Radio | .0000 |
| Direct Mail | .2754 |
| Telemarketing | .1594 |
| Other | .0290 |

Thank you, we appreciate your time and energy.

# Businesses That Responded to the Survey

1. Savings and loan.
2. 20th Century/Harper Films/Stargate.
3. Mortgage/realty.
4. Motorola.
5. Dentures/partials/dental.
6. CPA firms.
7. Health center/medical offices.
8. Service center.
9. Churches.
10. State preschool Headstart program.
11. Nonprofit organizations.
12. Consultant firms.
13. Newspaper.
14. Crafts and supplies.
15. Employment agency.
16. Printing service.
17. Facsimile transmission.
18. Travel companies.
19. Copy centers.
20. Law firms.
21. Postal agencies.

# Promotional Media

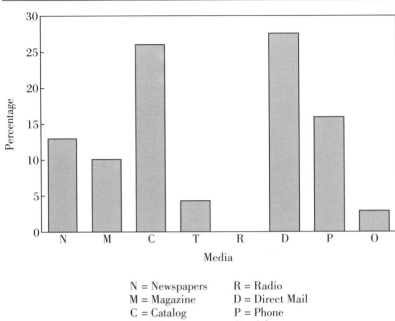

**Consumer Expected Media of Promotion**

N = Newspapers    R = Radio
M = Magazine      D = Direct Mail
C = Catalog       P = Phone
T = TV            O = Other

# Cartridge Output

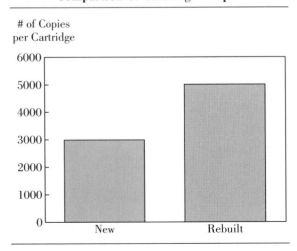

**Comparison of Cartridge Output**

# CRSI Flyer

---

## CARTRIDGE RECYCLING SERVICES INC.
## (818)284-CRSI

I would like to take this opportunity to introduce the products and services of Cartridge Recycling Services, Inc. (CRSI).  We are a small privately owned company  dedicated to helping you, the customer, cut costs, and protect the environment.

**CRSI offers the following products:**

* Both new and recharged toner cartridges.
* Enhanced cartridge drums.
* Only graphics quality toner is used, this is far superior to that used in the original cartridge.

**Other important services administered by CRSI's professional staff include:**

* Quick response to service calls.
* Free pick-up and delivery of supplies.
* Weekend service calls accepted.
* Free preventive maintenance on printer (s).

**Most importantly,** CRSI offers a **100% unconditional guarantee** on supplies and services.  Regardless of the reason, CRSI is committed to your satisfaction.  CRSI guarantees to meet or exceed the original manufacturer's specifications on all cartridges.

The enclosed material elaborates our committment.  CRSI will design a simple collection and replacement program that works easily for you.

We will gladly schedule an appointment to demonstrate our products.  For any questions, please feel free to call.

Sincerely,

Luanne F.B. Tadian
C.E.O.

---

# Memo from the President

## *Cartridge Recycling Services Inc.*

**MEMO:   FROM THE PRESIDENT**

### ABOUT OUR CARTRIDGES:

When we recondition a cartridge, that cartridge is taken completely apart for examination.  All parts are cleaned and inspected.  Every item not meeting our exacting standards is replaced.

We then fill the cartridge with our **Graphics Quality Toner**. This toner is richer & blacker than the toner in a "new" cartridge (OEM).  Plus, on average, we put **20% more toner** into the cartridge.  This means that your documents look crisper, the print is dark and professional, your graphics look sharper and you **use less toner**.

Finally, we again inspect and test the cartridge.  Those that pass this final inspection are vacuum-sealed (like new), packaged and returned to you.

**Don't want to save the empties for reconditioning?**  You don't have to have an empty to take advantage of the savings we offer. We can supply you with reconditioned cartridges at a slightly higher cost.

### ABOUT OUR SERVICE:

In addition to free pick up and delivery, we provide **Free Preventive Maintenance**. Most service companies charge an average of $25 per machine for this service.  We do it for free.

**Why not call and give us a try?**  You have absolutely nothing to lose.  Our products are the best in the market.  Your satisfaction is 100% unconditionally guaranteed!

## (818)284-CRSI

# Price Schedule

## Cartridge Recycling Services Inc.
### (818)284-CRSI

| | |
|---|---:|
| Rebuild/with Exchange | $49.95 |
| Rebuild/without Exchange | $59.95 |
| Rebuild/New Drum + 6 Refills | $249.95 |
| New OEM Cartridge | $89.00 |
| Fuser Cleaner Wands | $3.00 |
| CRSI Purchase of Spent Cartridges | $8.00 |
| Preventive Maintenance | $.00 |
| Pickup/Delivery | $.00 |

# Follow-Up Letter

---

## *CARTRIDGE RECYCLING SERVICES INC.*
## *(818)284-CRSI*

### ENHANCE YOUR IMAGE

Image. The who, what, why of the business world. You strive for it, you set it, you build it. Every printed word you create carries your image.

Now, improve the quality of every print you produce. How? By using the most technologically advanced, environmentally sensitive, and cost-effective method for toner cartridges - **REMANUFACTURING**.

### ADVANCED PERFORMANCE AND QUALITY

Our technical process is so good in every category - print quality, blacker solids, print volume and consistency - that cartridges remanufactured by CRSI outperform OEM cartridges. Whatever the application, you can count on our toner cartridges to deliver advanced performance.

Every cartridge remanufactured by CRSI is filled to capacity with our graphics quality toner. The result is a higher print yield. In fact, our cartridges average more prints than a "new" toner cartridge.

Sharper, richer blacks and superior solids are the mainstay of our product line. We pride ourselves on the appearance of your work.

### SUBSTANTIAL COST-SAVINGS

Cartridges remanufactured by CRSI cost less than 50% of the price charged for comparable OEM cartridges. That's a substantial cost savings on every toner cartridge you buy. The free preventive maintenance provided will increase your savings both now and in the future through fewer breakdowns and service calls.

### CONVENIENCE AND SERVICE

Our goal is to ensure your satisfaction. CRSI will custom design a program to service your company with no disruption or inconvenience to you. All products and services are 100% unconditionally guaranteed.

### A SMART CHOICE

In today's fast-paced business and professional world, keeping up your image can be an expensive proposition. Remanufacturing is a cost-effective way to improve your print quality and quantity while reducing overhead, leaving you with additional resources to spend or save.

We've helped many companies improve their print quality while trimming costs, we can do the same for you.

---

# Cost Savings Comparison Bar Chart

**Cartridge Recycling Services Cost Savings Comparison New versus Rebuild**

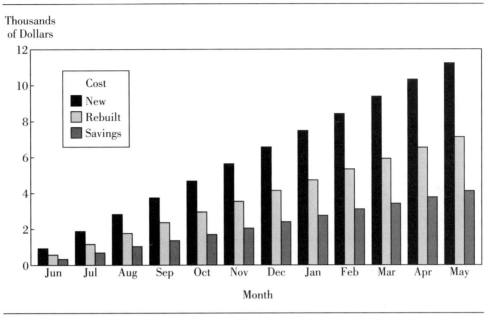

*Note:* Based on 10 cartridges per month. New cost $93.00 each. Rebuild cost $59.95 each.

# Break-Even Analysis

**Break-Even Graph**

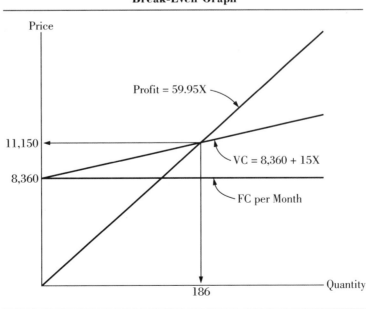

# 9

# BUSINESS PLAN FOR CANEVARI & CANEVARI

## An Accountancy Corporation

*Developed by*
**Mark L. Canevari**

# Executive Summary

Canevari & Canevari, An Accountancy Corporation ("the Corporation"), will be an income tax practice, small business management, and auditing firm located in the city of San Dimas, California. The Corporation will provide professional income tax planning and forms preparation to individuals and small businesses. Canevari & Canevari will also provide management for small businesses (defined as less than 20 employees), which will include preparation and maintenance of firms' financial records as well as performing operational reviews designed to reduce cost and increase efficiency. Finally, the Corporation will provide financial auditing services to selected municipalities located in the San Gabriel Valley who require independent compilations and/or reviews of their financial statements.

For individual income tax preparation, Canevari & Canevari, An Accountancy Corporation will target individuals and small businesses located in the communities of Covina, San Dimas, Chino, and Chino Hills. The decision to target these communities is made to capitalize on their proximity to the Corporation's office location in San Dimas, and to capitalize on the rapid population growth experienced by the Chino/Chino Hills area over the past ten (10) years. Additionally, small businesses and selected municipalities in the greater San Gabriel Valley are targeted, again due to their proximity to our office.

The distinct advantage offered by Canevari & Canevari is an unmatched level of professional service extended to our clients. The partners collectively have over twenty (20) years' experience preparing individual income tax returns and conducting systems and financial reviews for municipalities and small businesses. Canevari & Canevari will use state-of-art business application software for income tax and financial record-keeping preparation and retention. In addition, clients will gain a distinct advantage due to our active and constant participation in seminars and continuing education courses designed to provide the latest information on tax law and accounting procedural changes.

The start-up costs for Canevari & Canevari are estimated to be $45,340. Fees for services will be charged on an hourly basis for income tax preparation, a "retainer" fee basis (e.g., per month) for financial work performed for small business, and a negotiated, flat-fee basis for municipality audits. The expected return on investment will be approximately 2.27% in year one, 32.76% in year two, 46.64% in year three, and 94.76% in year four. The gross receipts from services provided during the first year of operation are estimated to be $146,800 and are expected to increase to $353,627 by the conclusion of year four.

# Table of Contents

# INTRODUCTION

## Statement of Purpose

The purpose of this business plan is to document the credibility and feasibility of operating Canevari & Canevari, An Accountancy Corporation, business venture in the city of San Dimas, California. Canevari & Canevari will provide professional income tax service, including tax planning and forms preparation. In addition, the Corporation will offer financial services to the small business owner, which will include bookkeeping, financial statement preparation, and income tax services. Finally, the Corporation will offer professional financial audit services to municipalities located in the greater San Gabriel Valley.

## Scope

This business plan will include an analysis of the situation, that is, neutral, competitor, and company environments; the target market to be reached; opportunities and threats; business objectives, strategy, and tactics; and financial implementation and controls.

## Limitations

The time constraint for completion of this business plan results in its content and detail being somewhat narrower in focus than if time were not a factor. However, this constraint offers the opportunity for the preparer to be specific and to the point when describing the entire business process and assessing whether or not the venture will be successful.

## Methods

This business plan consists of applied research since the strategies and tactics will be used by the owners of Canevari & Canevari to obtain a competitive edge over its competition. The data included in this plan are primarily the result of secondary research, with financial data based on a combination of actual cost figures and estimations.

## Assumptions

The preparer of this plan assumes that the economic environment of the area which Canevari & Canevari, An Accountancy Corporation, targets will remain constant; that is, small businesses will continue to operate, although perhaps not flourish due to the recession of the past several years. Additionally, this plan's preparer assumes that the demographics for the area will remain constant for at least the next four years.

# SITUATION ANALYSIS

This section is presented in the following manner:

A. Situation environment.
B. Neutral environment.
C. Competitor environment.
D. Company environment.

## The Situation Environment

The situational environment for Canevari & Canevari, An Accountancy Corporation, will be analyzed using the following categories:

1. Demographics.
2. Demand.
3. Economic and business conditions.
4. Laws and regulations.
5. Technology.

### Demographics

Demographics for San Dimas, Covina, Chino, and Chino Hills are shown in Table I; household demographics used to determine target for direct mail campaign are shown in Table II. These demographics will be used to determine the target market for the individual tax practice. In addition, business demographics to be used to target direct mailing for small businesses located in selected communities in the greater San Gabriel Valley are shown in Table III.

Table I   Population Demographics Growth

| City | 1990 Population | 1980 Population | Increase | % Increase |
|------|----------------|-----------------|----------|------------|
| Chino | 59,682 | 40,165 | 19,517 | 48.6% |
| Chino Hills | 27,068 | Not Incorporated | 27,068 | N/A |
| Total | 86,750 | 40,165 | 46,585 | 115.98 |
| Covina | 43,207 | 33,751 | 9,456 | 28.01 |
| San Dimas | 32,397 | 24,014 | 8,383 | 34.91 |
| Grand Total | 162,354 | 97,930 | 64,424 | 66.15 |

Source: U.S. Census Bureau, 1990/1980 Population and Housing Census.

Table II   Individual Tax Clients Household Demographics

| City | 1990 Number of Households |
|------|--------------------------|
| Chino | 8,510 |
| Chino Hills | 6,627 |
| Covina | 6,496 |
| San Dimas | 6,512 |
| Total | 28,145 |

Source: U.S. Census Bureau, 1990/1980 Population and Housing Census.

## Demand

There is one simple reason for the need to provide income tax service and assistance: filing tax returns is required by law. The demand for income tax services is directly related to supply and demand; as the demographics illustrate, the target communities (especially Chino and Chino Hills) have experienced rapid growth over the past 10 years.

## Economic and Business Conditions

The country has been gripped by an economic recession for the past three years. Especially hard hit has been the state of California. Many businesses have either discontinued operations or have relocated to other states in order to take advantage of less restrictive regulations (i.e., less costly pollution controls, etc.). As a result, Canevari & Canevari must be extremely competitive with its fee structure in order to attract and retain small business clientele. The Corporation's partners are fully aware of the current state of the economy and are prepared to offer quality services at competitive rates. (The competitive environment and pricing

Table III   Number of Businesses with Less Than 20 Employees

| City | Total # of Firms | # of Firms with < 20 Employees | Percentage |
|------|------------------|-------------------------------|------------|
| Arcadia | 1,774 | 1,583 | 89.2 |
| Azusa | 708 | 572 | 80.8 |
| Covina | 1,841 | 1,586 | 86.1 |
| Duarte | 381 | 307 | 80.6 |
| Glendora | 1,106 | 975 | 88.2 |
| La Verne | 484 | 410 | 84.7 |
| San Dimas | 891 | 780 | 87.5 |
| Sierra Madre | 242 | 222 | 91.0 |
| Temple City | 629 | 569 | 90.5 |
| Walnut | 873 | 755 | 86.5 |
| West Covina | 1,470 | 1,249 | 85.0 |
| Total | 10,399 | 9,008 | 86.6 |

Source: U.S. Census Bureau, 1990/1980 Population and Housing Census.

structure are discussed in the Competitor Environment and Billing Revenues sections, respectively.)

### Laws and Regulations

Canevari & Canevari, An Accountancy Corporation, must adhere to laws governing the preparation of income tax returns promulgated by the Internal Revenue Code.[1] The Corporation is also required to conduct financial and operational audits and reviews in accordance with generally accepted accounting principles set forth by the American Institute of Certified Public Accountants.[2] Finally, adherence to Governmental Auditing Standards as set forth by the Comptroller General of the United States is required for proper and thorough audits and reviews of governmental entities.[3]

### Technology

Each member of the Corporation will have the use of IBM Personal System 2 Model 55 SX computer with 4 megs of memory, WordPerfect 5.1 word processing software, Quicken software for bookkeeping preparation and retention, Turbo-Tax Professional Tax Software, Lotus 123, version 3.1 for spreadsheet preparation and financial statement presentation, and modems so that computers can be "tied into" client databases in order to provide enhanced financial services. Additionally, the Corporation will invest in a Hewlett Packard LaserJet series III printer.

## The Neutral Environment

This section will analyze the financial and governmental neutral environmental categories.

### Financial Environment

A small business loan is needed to start up Canevari & Canevari, An Accountancy Corporation. Funds will be sought from one of three banks located in the San Dimas area: Bank of America, Fidelity Federal Bank, or Wells Fargo. It has been determined that a $65,000 small business loan is needed. The loan will be secured by equity contained in the partners' rental property located in Highland Park (approximately $60,000) and in the partners' personal residence located in San Dimas (approximately $100,000). Rates quoted by these financial institutions noted a range from 8% to 8½% for a 30-year fixed rate. However, preliminary discussions with loan officers disclosed that rates are negotiable. As a result, a detailed business plan with clear and concise financial statements is needed in order to persuade lenders to provide the necessary funds at the most desirable rate.

### Government Environment

In order to contract with government agencies, certain guidelines must be met. Specifically, it is required that for any contract greater than $10,000, government entities will only contract with firms that meet the requirements of Minority/Women Owned Business Enterprises (M/WBE). Specifically, this guideline states that active ownership participation of the contractor entity must be composed of at least 15% of individuals who are either members of a minority race or women.[4] Canevari & Canevari meets this requirement since one of its two partners is a woman as well as a minority (see Company Environment for description of each of the owners).

## The Competitor Environment

### Individual Income Tax Preparation

Canevari & Canevari, An Accountancy Corporation, has many diverse and varied forms of competition. Regarding the preparation of income tax returns for individuals, the main competition comes from entrenched, well-known tax preparation firms such as H&R Block and Triple Checks. Both firms have a proliferation of offices within the target area of

---

[1] United States Department of Internal Revenue Services, Internal Revenue Tax Code, as of June 1, 1992.
[2] American Institute of Certified Public Accountants, *Generally Accepted Accounting Principles,* July 1992.
[3] Comptroller General of the United States, *Government Auditing Standards,* Superintendent of Documents, U.S. Government Printing Office: 1988.

[4] Office of General Services, State of California, *Procurement Guidelines,* May 1992.

Covina, San Dimas, the City of Chino, and Chino Hills; estimates are a combined 20–30 office locations. These firms target all individual taxpayers; however, their actual clientele is comprised for the most part of lower income bracket individuals. The expertise and training level of their tax preparers is limited to "basic" forms (i.e., long forms, personal itemized deductions; occasional small business returns, etc.). Average fee charged to each client is approximately $75.

Strengths of these firms are convenient operating business hours operations (i.e., 9 A.M. to 9 P.M. weekdays and 10 A.M. to 7 P.M. weekends). Weaknesses are the preparers' limited knowledge of the Tax Code; most preparers work on a part-time basis only during tax season; preparers who provide the tax service are usually not employed during nontax season and as such would be unavailable to accompany clients in the event of an IRS audit. As a result, services provided by these firms could be described as "assembly line-ish" and rather impersonal in nature.

Additionally, certified public accounting (CPA) and public accounting (PA) firms pose a material competitive threat. Specifically, over 200 CPAs and PAs are either listed and/or advertise in the target areas' yellow pages. These firms for the most part limit their target market to middle and upper-middle class clientele, and specialize in the preparation of more complex tax returns in addition to providing tax consultation services. As such, fees for services provided are higher; estimates range on average from $125 to $150 for basic services to several hundred dollars or more for more complex tax returns.

Their strengths are the public's perception of the expertise that is inherent with being a CPA or PA (i.e., continuing education required of its members; experience level of practitioners, etc.), reputation of high level of competency perceived by the general public, and the ability to provide wide and varying degrees of tax consulting and preparation services. However, weaknesses include billing rates that are considered by many consumers to be unaffordable, and an attitude that the average taxpayer would not receive the same level of service and consideration as that offered to

the more complex, and as a result, more expensive tax return.

Finally, competition is also inherent with taxpayers who prepare their own tax returns. Their strengths are that they are most familiar with their own financial situation and can expertly prepare their tax returns. Conversely, their most material weakness is that they may be preparing their returns in an incorrect manner and either not taking full advantage of provisions provided by the IRS Tax Code or creating errors and running the risk of audit and possibly paying additional taxes and penalties.

### Small Business Accounting Services

Competition for this target market is to a degree similar to that noted previously, with the exception that H&R Block and Triple Checks do not provide continuous accounting services. Small businesses either employ an individual to "maintain the books" and prepare monthly, quarterly, and/or yearly financial statements, or contract with accounting or CPA firms to perform these services. Strengths and weaknesses are similar to those noted within the Individual Income Tax Preparation section of this plan. However, an additional weakness is that small business owners may not be operating as efficiently as possible due to the belief that they cannot afford to allocate a portion of their operating budgets to professional accounting and operations analysis services.

### Contracted Government Services

All government entities and municipalities are required to undergo annual financial audits conducted by a certified public accountant as specified by the Single Audit Act of 1984.[5] As a result, competition for this target market will be other CPA firms, either local firms or those located out of the target area but whose specialty, expertise, and experience relate to governmental audits.

[5] Office of Management and Budget, "OMB Circular A-128, 'Audits of State and Local Governments,'" Single Audit Act of 1984.

## The Company Environment

Canevari & Canevari, An Accountancy Corporation, is owned and operated by Mark L. Canevari and Beulah S. Canevari. The following are brief biographies of each partner.

Mr. Canevari founded Mark L. Canevari, Tax Practitioner, Incorporated, in 1978. Mr. Canevari was also employed for over 11 years as a senior auditor for Los Angeles County's Auditor-Controller Department performing OMB A-128 audits of multimillion-dollar budgeted government entities and federally funded nonprofit agencies. In addition, Mr. Canevari has 2½ years of audit experience as lead auditor at a large local university, where he has acquired further expertise auditing federally funded grants and nonprofit entities. Mr. Canevari has controllership experience of a $12.5 million government entity. He was licensed by the state of California in 1985 to practice as a CPA. In addition, Mr. Canevari is a licensed Certified Internal Auditor and a Certified Fraud Examiner, and possesses an advanced degree in finance, further attesting to his level of commitment and expertise to provide quality accounting, auditing, and financial services.

Ms. Canevari has over 10 years' experience auditing a wide range of private companies and governmental entities. Her primary expertise is conducting economy and efficiency reviews designed to provide cost-effective enhancements to small business owners. In addition, Ms. Canevari has performed numerous financial audits and reviews for governmental entities. Her efforts have resulted in over $5 million in quantified savings realized by clients. Ms. Canevari is a Certified Public Accountant licensed to practice in California.

The Corporation will be financed by a long-term loan of $65,000 secured by equity in the partners' real estate assets. The partners are guaranteed a monthly salary of $3,000 each during year one; net income will be returned to the Corporation in the form of retained earnings to be used for future expansion.

The strengths of Canevari & Canevari include a high expertise level possessed by the partners, and a total commitment to providing quality accounting services. The weaknesses include the high degree of competition provided by tax preparation firms and other accounting firms, lack of existing clientele that would assist with obtaining additional clients through referrals, and the lack of a large support staff that would allow the Corporation to accept and work on multiple assignments at the same time.

## THE TARGET MARKET

Canevari & Canevari, An Accountancy Corporation, will locate their office in the city of San Dimas, California. The main reasons for choosing San Dimas are the proximity to the partners' residence and, more importantly, the rapid growth the immediate target area has experienced over the past 10 years. For example, as Table I of this plan illustrates, the population of Chino and Chino Hills has more than doubled during the past 10 years; in fact the City of Chino Hills did not exist 10 years ago! These figures clearly confirm that a definite need exists for quality individual income tax preparation. In addition, the ratio of households to CPAs who practice in the area (see Opportunities and Threats section later in this plan) further attests to this need.

It goes without saying that in this recessionary economy, small businesses need quality financial consultation in order to remain in business, let alone be competitive. As Table III indicates, 9,008 of the 10,339 businesses located in the target region are small businesses. Canevari & Canevari does not desire to "corner the market" and obtain a large number of small business clients; on the contrary, the Corporation's partners fully understand the need for personal, quality financial assistance. As a result, Canevari & Canevari plans to target no more than 1,000 small businesses through a direct mail campaign with an estimated rate of return of 1.5%.

Finally, selected municipalities are targeted for financial reviews and audits. The scope of these types of reviews is so broad, encompassing, and time-consuming (an average engagement is three months in duration) that no more than one or two audits can be conducted by Canevari & Canevari in any fiscal year. However, the expertise possessed by the partners guarantees to the user quality audits and financial reviews.

## OPPORTUNITIES AND THREATS

### Opportunities

Canevari & Canevari, An Accountancy Corporation, is presented with the following opportunities:

- Tax laws that require all individuals who are gainfully employed and earning salaries to file income tax returns.

- Rapid population growth within its tax preparation target area, highlighted by the 116% growth rate experienced by the Chino area over the past 10 years (see Table I).

- Lack of extensive advertising by major competitors. For example, a review of the yellow pages for the Pomona Valley (Chino and Chino Hills areas included) disclosed 140 CPA listings, of which *only 16* have a minimum ¹⁄₁₆-page ad.

- 86% (9,008) of all businesses within communities targeted for business accounting and auditing services employ less than 20 individuals (see Table III).

- All municipalities are required to have an annual audit of their statements of financial position.

First, the demographics regarding the number of households within the individual income tax preparation target area disclose ample opportunity for immediate penetration. Specifically, there are 39,685 households within the target area (see Table II). As a result, it can be reasonably inferred that at least one member of each of the households needs to file an income tax return.

Second, the rapid population growth experienced by the target area provides added opportunity for the Corporation. Particularly, the Chino and Chino Hills areas have experienced a growth rate that provides an opportunity to penetrate a market that does not have the tax preparation resources to support its demographics. Specifically, the ratio of households

to CPAs, 283.46:1 (39,685 households to 140 CPAs listed in the yellow pages for the entire Pomona Valley) concludes that there is a genuine need for quality income tax preparation services.

Third, the lack of advertising by competitors makes penetration into this market with effective advertising a viable possibility. Although it is unknown whether competitors are marketing their services using other forms of advertising such as direct mailings, Canevari & Canevari will undertake an extensive and effective campaign by using direct mailings and yellow pages advertisements.

Fourth, the number of small businesses included in the Corporation's target area makes for an ideal environment to penetrate the market and obtain clientele. As previously noted, the Corporation will undertake an extensive direct mailing campaign to penetrate and obtain a share of this lucrative market.

Finally, requirements that municipalities undergo financial scrutiny on an annual basis provide an opportunity for Canevari & Canevari to demonstrate its expertise in the governmental financial area. The Corporation will actively seek participation in the bidding process for these audits by submitting a detailed corporate profile to each municipality's contracting department, and providing proposals for audits and financial services as requested.

### Threats

Threats faced by Canevari & Canevari, An Accountancy Corporation, include the following:

- Continued economic recession.
- Lawsuits for malpractice.
- Entry of new competitors.

Primarily, the continued economic recession could have a detrimental effect upon the Corporation's penetration into the individual tax preparation and small business accounting markets. Management needs to remain keenly aware of the financial limitations inherent with the recession and ensure quality services at reasonable fees.

Next, malpractice lawsuits are a genuine concern given the current litigious environment. Canevari & Canevari will always strive to provide accounting and auditing services exercising due professional care while maintaining absolute independence in actions and deeds. To help guard against the disastrous results that could occur in the event of a successful lawsuit against the Corporation a $1,000,000 general malpractice liability insurance policy will be maintained at all times.

Finally, the entry of new competitors is a real and continuous threat. As a result, Canevari & Canevari will always strive to maintain the goodwill of its clients by providing quality professional tax and financial services at competitive fees. The Corporation dedicates itself to ensuring that each client is completely and thoroughly satisfied with the level of service provided.

## BUSINESS OBJECTIVES AND GOALS

### Mission Statement

Canevari & Canevari, An Accountancy Corporation, will always provide an exceptionally high quality level of professional financial services to our clients. The Corporation will ensure that the needs of each client are carefully determined and assessed, and that each engagement is performed exercising due professional care and undertaken with integrity and independence that is above reproach.

### Objectives of the Firm

- Establish a Subchapter S corporation under the laws of the state of California.
- Achieve a maximum 3% success rate with its direct mailing campaign to individual households and 1.5% to small business owners.
- Obtain the break-even point (i.e., recover start-up costs) by the end of year four.
- Achieve total revenues of at least $140,000 by the end of year one, and $350,000 by the end of year four.

## MARKETING STRATEGY

### Strategy

Canevari & Canevari, An Accountancy Corporation, will pursue a strategy that will focus on the narrow market segments of individual income tax return preparation, small business accounting and financial services, and governmental audits. As stated in the Company Environment section of this plan, both partners have extensive experience, expertise, and knowledge of the workings of each market segment and are ably suited to provide quality services. However, the partners realize that Canevari & Canevari now becomes a member of a strategic group comprised of many practitioners whose goals are similar. The challenge is to carry out the strategy in a manner that achieves the Corporation's objectives.

As a result, Canevari & Canevari needs to build and defend its market niche by providing quality services while employing a reasonable and equitable fee structure. Since income tax preparation and financial accounting and auditing services are in a mature stage whose only growth is tied into changing demographics of target areas, it cannot be stressed enough that the only manner in which to implement the Corporation's strategy is thoroughly dependent upon the quality of service provided to clients. An outstanding level of service coupled with a fair and equitable fee structure is crucial for the long-term survival of Canevari & Canevari.

### Feedback Measurement Controls

Recognizing the impact a successful strategy will have on the success of Canevari & Canevari, An Accountancy Corporation, has not escaped the partners. As a result, the partners have designed an intricate feedback networking system that will track the results of all direct mailing and advertising campaigns, as well as a quality control monitoring mechanism for the level of service provided to existing clientele. The feedback will be continuously assessed and improvements will be made, where needed, in order to help guarantee continued success and growth for the Corporation.

## MARKETING TACTICS

The business strategy of Canevari & Canevari, An Accountancy Corporation, will be implemented using the tactical variables:

- Product.
- Price.
- Promotion.
- Placement.

### Product

The product of Canevari & Canevari is financial accounting, auditing, and tax preparation services. The Corporation will use the most current accounting and word processing software applications on the market in order to provide clients with a product that possesses a professional appearance. As stated in the Company Environment section of this plan, the staff consists of highly capable and proficient professionals who are dedicated to providing a top-quality product.

The partners fully realize the importance of being available for the client at their convenience. As a result, business hours for Canevari & Canevari will be 12 noon to 9 P.M. weekdays and 10 A.M. to 7 P.M. weekends. In addition, the partners will maintain constant flexibility in regards to operating hours and will work with clients who have special needs or are under specific time constraints.

### Price

Canevari & Canevari has developed three billing rate schedules for clients. Revenue from tax clients as shown in the Income Statements is calculated on an average billing rate of $150 per client. This expected rate of return per client is based on the partners' past experience with tax preparation. Revenue from business clients is calculated on a per hour basis of $60. It is anticipated that 10 hours per month will be needed to service each business client. Finally, government contracts revenue is based on the size of the job and the amount successfully bid for the job. For further detail regarding pricing and its impact on expected revenue, please see the Implementation and Control section of this plan.

### Promotion

The promotion campaign that will be used to launch Canevari & Canevari, An Accountancy Corporation, is divided into two segments:

- Precommercialization phase.
- Regular promotion mix for the first four years of operation.

#### Precommercialization Phase

The precommercialization phase of the promotion will begin in July of the year preceding the first year of operation. The initial phase of the promotional campaign will consist of direct mailings to small business entities and the purchase of a ¼-page ad in the local yellow pages. Individuals will not be contacted by direct mailings in July since it is not during the traditional "tax season" and taxpayers in general are not contemplating tax effects or income tax preparation at this time. As a result, the partners conclude that a direct mail campaign conducted in July would be ineffective. Therefore, individual taxpayers will be targeted by a direct mail campaign conducted during December preceding the first year of operation, and January. Two examples of the direct mailings are included in the Appendix.

No form of direct mailing or advertising is planned to target governmental entities. As stated in the Opportunities and Threats section of this plan, contact with municipalities will be limited to submitting detailed profiles of the Corporation to each entity's contracting department. For each Request for Bid received by Canevari & Canevari, clear, concise, and detailed bids will be submitted, but only for proposals that the partners believe match their expertise.

No other form of promotion (i.e., newspapers, television, etc.) will be used. The image of the accounting profession is such that using these types of media is not perceived as professional, either by the public or its own members.

#### Regular Promotional Phase

Costs associated with this phase of promotion are expected to be $9,500 annually for years one through four. The direct mailing campaign will be conducted by concentrating the mailings during the first four months of each calendar year to target the individual income tax market, and the last three months of the calendar year to target small businesses who need year-end financial statement preparation.

The costs associated with both phases of the promotional campaign are detailed in the Implementation and Control section of this plan.

## Placement

The success of Canevari & Canevari is directly related to the quality of service provided to clients coupled with a fair and equitable fee structure. Therefore, as stated throughout this plan, the partners are keenly aware of the importance of providing a high quality, fairly priced product to the consumer. The partners of Canevari & Canevari are committed to this goal.

All net income derived from operations is to be reinvested into the Corporation as retained earnings. If target net income and retained earnings are achieved by the conclusion of year four, Canevari & Canevari will carefully assess the possibility of expansion and targeting other communities.

However, the Corporation will not lose sight of our level of expertise and *will not* venture into other business opportunities. The partners are dedicated to utilizing their expertise to provide the quality product which Canevari & Canevari is best suited to render.

## IMPLEMENTATION AND CONTROL

This section will describe in detail the financial implementation and control aspects of Canevari & Canevari, An Accountancy Corporation, as follows:

- Start-up costs.
- Break-even analysis.
- Detailed description of revenue and expense items.
- Pro forma income statements for years one through four.

- Pro forma cash flow statements for years one through four.
- Pro forma balance sheets for years one through four.

## Start-Up Costs

Start-up costs are detailed on the accompanying chart. Specifics include the following:

- A direct mail campaign consisting of 9,000 mailings to individual households and 1,000 mailings to small businesses.
- Approximately $26,000 incurred for office furniture, computers, and supplies.
- A $1,000,000 general liability insurance policy.

Total start-up costs approximate $45,000; Canevari & Canevari will obtain a $65,000 loan in order to cover the start-up costs. The remaining $20,000 will be deposited in a corporate bank account in order to protect Canevari & Canevari's liquidity.

## Break-Even Analysis

The method in which to determine the break-even point for Canevari & Canevari is simply to divide the amount of retained earnings at the end of each year by total start-up costs. As the break-even graph denotes, the Corporation will reach the break-even point during the fourth year of operation.

## Revenues and Expenses

Detailed pro forma income statements are included later in this section. Specifically, revenues sources for income shown on the first-year income statement are from tax clients and small businesses only. Due to the length of time it takes to develop, propose, and await awarding of contracts from governmental entities (i.e., six months to one year), a conservative approach the partners are taking is that no revenue will be generated from this source for the first year.

Individual tax client billings are based on a campaign of 9,000 direct mailings with a 3% success rate. Revenues are concentrated in the

**Canevari & Canevari, an Accountancy Corporation Start-Up Costs Statement**

| | | |
|---|---:|---:|
| Loan to Start Up Business | | $65,000 |
| Start-Up Costs | | |
| Articles of incorporation | $    500 | |
| Business license | 50 | |
| Fire/health/safety/city permits | 1,700 | |
| Rent deposit (1,000 sq. ft. @ $1.25 per sq. ft., 3 months prepaid, plus last month's rent, and one month security deposit) | 5,625 | |
| Utilities deposit | 350 | |
| Computers | 11,000 | |
| Software | 2,000 | |
| Office furniture | 10,000 | |
| Supplies | 1,000 | |
| Stationery | | |
|   Letterhead design | 45 | |
|   Business cards ($40 per 1,000) | 200 | |
|   Stationery for mail campaign ($62.50 per 1,000) | 900 | |
| Advertising campaign | | |
|   Bulk mailing permit | 70 | |
|   Postage for mail campaign | 3,150 | |
|   Yellow pages and trade journals | 5,000 | |
| Telephones (includes "800" number) | 750 | |
| Liability insurance ($1 million general liability coverage, 6 months prepaid) | 3,000 | |
| Total Start-Up Costs | | 45,340 |
| | | $20,000 |

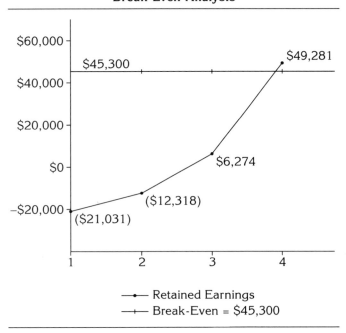

**Canevari & Canevari, an Accountancy Corporation Break-Even Analysis**

—•— Retained Earnings
—+— Break-Even = $45,300

first four months of each year because of what is referred to as the "tax season." The revenue for the remaining eight months is derived from tax client audits, providing additional tax services, and pro forma tax planning.

Business-generated revenue is based on a direct mail campaign of 1,000 mailings with a 1.5% success rate. Canevari & Canevari estimates that clients will require on average 10 hours of service each month. As a result, the Corporation will generate maximum gross revenue of $9,000 per month [1,000 × 1.5%] × [$60 per hour × 10 hours per month]. $90,000 in total revenue is expected from the first year of operation. Per month revenues are higher for the last eight months of each year due to our concentration on tax preparation during the first four months; as the tax season ends, this 'frees up" one of the partners to work on business audits as well as process residual tax client business.

The partners of Canevari & Canevari anticipate the awarding of one governmental contract for $50,000 in year two. As a result, an additional professional is added to the staff in order to conduct this review.

Expenses are estimated in the following manner:

- Costs are fixed for rent, advertising, insurance, utilities, depreciation, loan interest, and miscellaneous expenses.

- Office expense and travel, meals, and entertainment represent 5% of total revenue.
- Bad debt expense is based on 2% of total revenues.

## Return on Investment

The return on investment (ROI) for Canevari & Canevari, An Accountancy Corporation, is based on the net earnings at the end of each year divided by the amount of the original investment (i.e., start-up costs). Thus, ROI for each year is as follows:

ROI in Year 1    $(1,031)/$45,340 = (46.43%)
ROI in Year 2    $14,855/$45,340 = 32.76%
ROI in Year 3    $21,147/$45,340 = 46.64%
ROI in Year 4    $42,965/$45,340 = 94.76%

## SUMMARY

Canevari & Canevari, An Accountancy Corporation, is to be located in the city of San Dimas, California. The Corporation will specialize in income tax preparation, small business management, and governmental auditing. Canevari & Canevari will provide professional income tax planning and forms preparation to individuals and small businesses. Canevari & Canevari will also provide management for

### Canevari & Canevari, an Accountancy Corporation Pro Forma Monthly Income Statement for Month 1 through Month 12

| | 1 | 2 | 3 | 4 | 5 | 6 | 7 | 8 | 9 | 10 | 11 | 12 | TOTAL |
|---|---|---|---|---|---|---|---|---|---|---|---|---|---|
| **REVENUES:** | | | | | | | | | | | | | |
| Billings: | | | | | | | | | | | | | |
| Tax Clients | $6,000 | $13,000 | $13,000 | $13,000 | $1,000 | $1,000 | $1,000 | $1,000 | $1,000 | $2,000 | $2,000 | $2,000 | $56,000 |
| Business Clients | 3,000 | 4,000 | 5,000 | 6,000 | 9,000 | 9,000 | 9,000 | 9,000 | 9,000 | 9,000 | 9,000 | 9,000 | 90,000 |
| Interest Revenue | 46 | 43 | 56 | 71 | 86 | 83 | 80 | 76 | 72 | 68 | 65 | 62 | 808 |
| TOTAL REVENUES | $9,046 | $17,043 | $18,056 | $19,071 | $10,086 | $10,083 | $10,080 | $10,076 | $10,072 | $11,068 | $11,065 | $11,062 | $146,808 |
| | | | | | | | | | | | | | |
| **EXPENSES:** | | | | | | | | | | | | | |
| Salaries | $6,000 | $6,000 | $6,000 | $6,000 | $6,000 | $6,000 | $6,000 | $6,000 | $6,000 | $6,000 | $6,000 | $6,000 | $72,000 |
| Benefits(@ 30%) | 1,800 | 1,800 | 1,800 | 1,800 | 1,800 | 1,800 | 1,800 | 1,800 | 1,800 | 1,800 | 1,800 | 1,800 | 21,600 |
| Rent | 0 | 0 | 0 | 1,250 | 1,250 | 1,250 | 1,250 | 1,250 | 1,250 | 1,250 | 1,250 | 1,250 | 11,250 |
| Advertising | 1,000 | 1,000 | 1,000 | 1,000 | 500 | 500 | 500 | 500 | 500 | 1,000 | 1,000 | 1,000 | 9,500 |
| Office Expense | 452 | 852 | 903 | 954 | 504 | 504 | 504 | 504 | 504 | 553 | 553 | 553 | 7,340 |
| Travel, Meals, & Entertainment | 452 | 852 | 903 | 954 | 504 | 504 | 504 | 504 | 504 | 553 | 553 | 553 | 7,340 |
| Insurance | 0 | 0 | 0 | 0 | 0 | 0 | 500 | 500 | 500 | 500 | 500 | 500 | 3,000 |
| Utilities | 300 | 300 | 300 | 300 | 300 | 300 | 300 | 300 | 300 | 300 | 300 | 300 | 3,600 |
| Depreciation | 600 | 600 | 600 | 600 | 600 | 600 | 600 | 600 | 600 | 600 | 600 | 600 | 7,200 |
| Bad Debts From Billings | 181 | 341 | 361 | 381 | 202 | 202 | 202 | 202 | 201 | 221 | 221 | 221 | 2,936 |
| Loan Interest | 130 | 130 | 130 | 130 | 130 | 130 | 130 | 130 | 130 | 130 | 130 | 130 | 1,560 |
| Miscellaneous | 100 | 100 | 100 | 100 | 100 | 100 | 100 | 100 | 100 | 100 | 100 | 100 | 1,200 |
| Total Expenses | 11,016 | 11,975 | 12,097 | 13,469 | 11,890 | 11,890 | 12,390 | 12,389 | 12,389 | 13,008 | 13,008 | 13,007 | 148,527 |
| Profit Before Taxes | (1,970) | 5,068 | 5,959 | 5,602 | (1,804) | (1,807) | (2,310) | (2,313) | (2,317) | (1,940) | (1,943) | (1,945) | (1,719) |
| | | | | | | | | | | | | | |
| Taxes (40%) | | | | | | | | | | | | | (688) |
| | | | | | | | | | | | | | |
| NET INCOME | ($1,970) | $5,068 | $5,959 | $5,602 | ($1,804) | ($1,807) | ($2,310) | ($2,313) | ($2,317) | ($1,940) | ($1,943) | ($1,945) | ($1,031) |

### Canevari & Canevari, an Accountancy Corporation Pro Forma Monthly Income Statement for Month 13 through Month 24

| | 13 | 14 | 15 | 16 | 17 | 18 | 19 | 20 | 21 | 22 | 23 | 24 | TOTAL |
|---|---|---|---|---|---|---|---|---|---|---|---|---|---|
| **REVENUES:** | | | | | | | | | | | | | |
| Billings: | | | | | | | | | | | | | |
| Tax Clients | $6,600 | $14,300 | $14,300 | $14,300 | $1,100 | $1,100 | $1,100 | $1,100 | $1,100 | $2,200 | $2,200 | $2,200 | $61,600 |
| Business Clients | 3,600 | 4,800 | 6,000 | 7,200 | 10,800 | 10,800 | 10,800 | 10,800 | 10,800 | 10,800 | 10,800 | 10,800 | 108,600 |
| Government Contracts | 0 | 0 | 0 | 0 | 0 | 0 | 10,000 | 10,000 | 10,000 | 10,000 | 10,000 | 0 | 50,000 |
| Interest Revenue | 56 | 49 | 60 | 73 | 88 | 86 | 83 | 92 | 101 | 110 | 120 | 124 | 1,042 |
| TOTAL REVENUES | $10,256 | $19,149 | $20,360 | $21,573 | $11,988 | $11,986 | $21,983 | $21,992 | $22,001 | $23,110 | $23,120 | $13,124 | $220,642 |
| | | | | | | | | | | | | | |
| **EXPENSES:** | | | | | | | | | | | | | |
| Salaries | $6,600 | $6,600 | $6,600 | $6,600 | $6,600 | $6,600 | $9,600 | $9,600 | $9,600 | $9,600 | $9,600 | $9,600 | $97,200 |
| Benefits(@ 30%) | 1,980 | 1,980 | 1,980 | 1,980 | 1,980 | 1,980 | 2,880 | 2,880 | 2,880 | 2,880 | 2,880 | 2,880 | 29,160 |
| | | | | | | | | | | | | | |
| Rent | 1,250 | 1,250 | 1,250 | 1,250 | 1,250 | 1,250 | 1,250 | 1,250 | 1,250 | 1,250 | 1,250 | 1,250 | 15,000 |
| Advertising | 1,000 | 1,000 | 1,000 | 1,000 | 500 | 500 | 500 | 500 | 500 | 1,000 | 1,000 | 1,000 | 9,500 |
| Office Expense | 513 | 957 | 1,018 | 1,079 | 599 | 599 | 1,099 | 1,100 | 1,100 | 1,156 | 1,156 | 656 | 11,032 |
| Travel, Meals, & Entertainment | 513 | 957 | 1,018 | 1,079 | 599 | 599 | 1,099 | 1,100 | 1,100 | 1,156 | 1,156 | 656 | 11,032 |
| Insurance | 500 | 500 | 500 | 500 | 500 | 500 | 500 | 500 | 500 | 500 | 500 | 500 | 6,000 |
| Utilities | 300 | 300 | 300 | 300 | 300 | 300 | 300 | 300 | 300 | 300 | 300 | 300 | 3,600 |
| Depreciation | 600 | 600 | 600 | 600 | 600 | 600 | 600 | 600 | 600 | 600 | 600 | 600 | 7,200 |
| Bad Debts From Billings | 205 | 383 | 407 | 431 | 240 | 240 | 238 | 238 | 238 | 260 | 260 | 260 | 3,400 |
| Loan Interest | 130 | 130 | 130 | 130 | 130 | 130 | 130 | 130 | 130 | 130 | 130 | 130 | 1,560 |
| Miscellaneous | 100 | 100 | 100 | 100 | 100 | 100 | 100 | 100 | 100 | 100 | 100 | 100 | 1,200 |
| Total Expenses | 13,691 | 14,758 | 14,903 | 15,049 | 13,399 | 13,398 | 18,296 | 18,297 | 18,298 | 18,931 | 18,932 | 17,932 | 195,884 |
| Profit Before Taxes | (3,435) | 4,391 | 5,457 | 6,524 | (1,411) | (1,412) | 3,687 | 3,695 | 3,703 | 4,179 | 4,188 | (4,808) | 24,758 |
| | | | | | | | | | | | | | |
| Taxes (40%) | | | | | | | | | | | | | 9,903 |
| | | | | | | | | | | | | | |
| NET INCOME | ($3,435) | $4,391 | $5,457 | $6,524 | ($1,411) | ($1,412) | $3,687 | $3,695 | $3,703 | $4,179 | $4,188 | ($4,808) | $14,855 |

### Canevari & Canevari, an Accountancy Corporation Pro Forma Monthly Income Statement for Month 25 through Month 36

| | 25 | 26 | 27 | 28 | 29 | 30 | 31 | 32 | 33 | 34 | 35 | 36 | TOTAL |
|---|---|---|---|---|---|---|---|---|---|---|---|---|---|
| **REVENUES:** | | | | | | | | | | | | | |
| Billings: | | | | | | | | | | | | | |
| Tax Clients | $7,590 | $16,445 | $16,445 | $16,445 | $1,265 | $1,265 | $1,265 | $1,265 | $1,265 | $2,530 | $2,530 | $2,530 | $70,840 |
| Business Clients | 4,320 | 5,760 | 7,200 | 8,640 | 12,960 | 12,960 | 12,960 | 12,960 | 12,960 | 12,960 | 12,960 | 12,960 | 129,600 |
| Government Contracts | 10,000 | 10,000 | 10,000 | 10,000 | 10,000 | 10,000 | 10,000 | 10,000 | 10,000 | 10,000 | 10,000 | 0 | 110,000 |
| Interest Revenue | 97 | 96 | 115 | 137 | 163 | 167 | 172 | 176 | 181 | 186 | 193 | 199 | 1,882 |
| TOTAL REVENUES | $22,007 | $32,301 | $33,760 | $35,222 | $24,388 | $24,392 | $24,397 | $24,401 | $24,406 | $25,676 | $25,683 | $15,689 | $312,322 |
| | | | | | | | | | | | | | |
| **EXPENSES:** | | | | | | | | | | | | | |
| Salaries | $12,600 | $12,600 | $12,600 | $12,600 | $12,600 | $12,600 | $12,600 | $12,600 | $12,600 | $12,600 | $12,600 | $12,600 | $151,200 |
| Benefits(@ 30%) | 3,780 | 3,780 | 3,780 | 3,780 | 3,780 | 3,780 | 3,780 | 3,780 | 3,780 | 3,780 | 3,780 | 3,780 | 45,360 |
| | | | | | | | | | | | | | |
| Rent | 1,250 | 1,250 | 1,250 | 1,250 | 1,250 | 1,250 | 1,250 | 1,250 | 1,250 | 1,250 | 1,250 | 1,250 | 15,000 |
| Advertising | 1,000 | 1,000 | 1,000 | 1,000 | 500 | 500 | 500 | 500 | 500 | 1,000 | 1,000 | 1,000 | 9,500 |
| Office Expense | 1,100 | 1,615 | 1,688 | 1,761 | 1,219 | 1,220 | 1,220 | 1,220 | 1,220 | 1,284 | 1,284 | 784 | 15,616 |
| Travel, Meals, & Entertainment | 1,100 | 1,615 | 1,688 | 1,761 | 1,219 | 1,220 | 1,220 | 1,220 | 1,220 | 1,284 | 1,284 | 784 | 15,616 |
| Insurance | 500 | 500 | 500 | 500 | 500 | 500 | 500 | 500 | 500 | 500 | 500 | 500 | 6,000 |
| Utilities | 300 | 300 | 300 | 300 | 300 | 300 | 300 | 300 | 300 | 300 | 300 | 300 | 3,600 |
| Depreciation | 600 | 600 | 600 | 600 | 600 | 600 | 600 | 600 | 600 | 600 | 600 | 600 | 7,200 |
| Bad Debts From Billings | 440 | 646 | 675 | 704 | 488 | 488 | 285 | 285 | 285 | 310 | 310 | 310 | 5,224 |
| Loan Interest | 130 | 130 | 130 | 130 | 130 | 130 | 130 | 130 | 130 | 130 | 130 | 130 | 1,560 |
| Miscellaneous | 100 | 100 | 100 | 100 | 100 | 100 | 100 | 100 | 100 | 100 | 100 | 100 | 1,200 |
| Total Expenses | 22,901 | 24,136 | 24,311 | 24,487 | 22,687 | 22,687 | 22,484 | 22,485 | 22,485 | 23,137 | 23,138 | 22,139 | 277,077 |
| Profit Before Taxes | (894) | 8,165 | 9,449 | 10,735 | 1,701 | 1,705 | 1,913 | 1,916 | 1,921 | 2,539 | 2,545 | (6,450) | 35,246 |
| | | | | | | | | | | | | | |
| Taxes (40%) | | | | | | | | | | | | | 14,098 |
| | | | | | | | | | | | | | |
| NET INCOME | ($894) | $8,165 | $9,449 | $10,735 | $1,701 | $1,705 | $1,913 | $1,916 | $1,921 | $2,539 | $2,545 | ($6,450) | $21,147 |

## Canevari & Canevari, an Accountancy Corporation Pro Forma Monthly Income Statement for Month 37 through Month 48

| | 37 | 38 | 39 | 40 | 41 | 42 | 43 | 44 | 45 | 46 | 47 | 48 | TOTAL |
|---|---|---|---|---|---|---|---|---|---|---|---|---|---|
| **REVENUES:** | | | | | | | | | | | | | |
| **Billings:** | | | | | | | | | | | | | |
| Tax Clients | $9,108 | $19,734 | $19,734 | $19,734 | $1,518 | $1,518 | $1,518 | $1,518 | $1,518 | $3,036 | $3,036 | $3,036 | $85,008 |
| Business Clients | 5,184 | 6,912 | 8,640 | 10,368 | 15,552 | 15,552 | 15,552 | 15,552 | 15,552 | 15,552 | 15,552 | 15,552 | 155,520 |
| Government Contracts | 10,000 | 10,000 | 10,000 | 10,000 | 10,000 | 10,000 | 10,000 | 10,000 | 10,000 | 10,000 | 10,000 | 0 | 110,000 |
| Interest Revenue | 152 | 157 | 186 | 220 | 257 | 268 | 279 | 291 | 303 | 315 | 329 | 342 | 3,099 |
| **TOTAL REVENUES** | $24,444 | $36,803 | $38,560 | $40,322 | $27,327 | $27,338 | $27,349 | $27,361 | $27,373 | $28,903 | $28,917 | $18,930 | $353,627 |
| | | | | | | | | | | | | | |
| **EXPENSES:** | | | | | | | | | | | | | |
| Salaries | $12,600 | $12,600 | $12,600 | $12,600 | $12,600 | $12,600 | $12,600 | $12,600 | $12,600 | $12,600 | $12,600 | $12,600 | $151,200 |
| Benefits(@ 30%) | 3,780 | 3,780 | 3,780 | 3,780 | 3,780 | 3,780 | 3,780 | 3,780 | 3,780 | 3,780 | 3,780 | 3,780 | 45,360 |
| | | | | | | | | | | | | | |
| Rent | 1,250 | 1,250 | 1,250 | 1,250 | 1,250 | 1,250 | 1,250 | 1,250 | 1,250 | 1,250 | 1,250 | 1,250 | 15,000 |
| Advertising | 1,000 | 1,000 | 1,000 | 1,000 | 500 | 500 | 500 | 500 | 500 | 1,000 | 1,000 | 1,000 | 9,500 |
| Office Expense | 1,222 | 1,840 | 1,928 | 2,016 | 1,366 | 1,367 | 1,367 | 1,368 | 1,369 | 1,445 | 1,446 | 947 | 17,681 |
| Travel, Meals, & Entertainment | 1,222 | 1,840 | 1,928 | 2,016 | 1,366 | 1,367 | 1,367 | 1,368 | 1,369 | 1,445 | 1,446 | 947 | 17,681 |
| Insurance | 500 | 500 | 500 | 500 | 500 | 500 | 500 | 500 | 500 | 500 | 500 | 500 | 6,000 |
| Utilities | 300 | 300 | 300 | 300 | 300 | 300 | 300 | 300 | 300 | 300 | 300 | 300 | 3,600 |
| Depreciation | 600 | 600 | 600 | 600 | 600 | 600 | 600 | 600 | 600 | 600 | 600 | 600 | 7,200 |
| Bad Debts From Billings | 489 | 736 | 771 | 806 | 547 | 547 | 341 | 341 | 341 | 372 | 372 | 372 | 6,035 |
| Loan Interest | 130 | 130 | 130 | 130 | 130 | 130 | 130 | 130 | 130 | 130 | 130 | 130 | 1,560 |
| Miscellaneous | 100 | 100 | 100 | 100 | 100 | 100 | 100 | 100 | 100 | 100 | 100 | 100 | 1,200 |
| **Total Expenses** | 23,193 | 24,676 | 24,887 | 25,099 | 23,039 | 23,041 | 22,836 | 22,838 | 22,839 | 23,522 | 23,523 | 22,525 | 282,018 |
| **Profit Before Taxes** | 1,251 | 12,127 | 13,673 | 15,223 | 4,288 | 4,297 | 4,513 | 4,524 | 4,534 | 5,381 | 5,394 | (3,595) | 71,609 |
| | | | | | | | | | | | | | |
| Taxes (40%) | | | | | | | | | | | | | 28,644 |
| | | | | | | | | | | | | | |
| **NET INCOME** | $1,251 | $12,127 | $13,673 | $15,223 | $4,288 | $4,297 | $4,513 | $4,524 | $4,534 | $5,381 | $5,394 | ($3,595) | $42,965 |

## Canevari & Canevari, an Accountancy Corporation Pro Forma Cash Flow Statement for Month 1 through Month 12

| | 1 | 2 | 3 | 4 | 5 | 6 | 7 | 8 | 9 | 10 | 11 | 12 |
|---|---|---|---|---|---|---|---|---|---|---|---|---|
| **SOURCES OF CASH:** | | | | | | | | | | | | |
| Beginning Cash | $20,000 | $18,486 | $24,009 | $30,424 | $36,484 | $35,139 | $33,790 | $31,938 | $30,081 | $28,221 | $26,736 | $25,248 |
| Add: Revenue | 9,000 | 17,000 | 18,000 | 19,000 | 10,000 | 10,000 | 10,000 | 10,000 | 10,000 | 11,000 | 11,000 | 11,000 |
| Depreciation | 600 | 600 | 600 | 600 | 600 | 600 | 600 | 600 | 600 | 600 | 600 | 600 |
| Bank Interest Income (3% of beginning cash) | 46 | 43 | 55 | 70 | 84 | 81 | 78 | 74 | 69 | 65 | 62 | 58 |
| **TOTAL SOURCES** | $29,646 | $36,129 | $42,664 | $50,094 | $47,169 | $45,820 | $44,468 | $42,611 | $40,751 | $39,886 | $38,398 | $36,906 |
| **USES OF CASH:** | | | | | | | | | | | | |
| Total Expenses (from Income Statement) | $11,010 | $11,970 | $12,090 | $13,460 | $11,880 | $11,880 | $12,380 | $12,380 | $12,380 | $13,000 | $13,000 | $13,000 |
| Loan Principal Payback | 150 | 150 | 150 | 150 | 150 | 150 | 150 | 150 | 150 | 150 | 150 | 150 |
| Corporate Income Tax | 0 | 0 | 0 | 0 | 0 | 0 | 0 | 0 | 0 | 0 | 0 | (688) |
| **TOTAL USES OF CASH** | 11,160 | 12,120 | 12,240 | 13,610 | 12,030 | 12,030 | 12,530 | 12,530 | 12,530 | 13,150 | 13,150 | 12,462 |
| **ENDING CASH** | $18,486 | $24,009 | $30,424 | $36,484 | $35,139 | $33,790 | $31,938 | $30,081 | $28,221 | $26,736 | $25,248 | $24,444 |

## Canevari & Canevari, an Accountancy Corporation Pro Forma Cash Flow Statement for Month 13 through Month 24

| | 13 | 14 | 15 | 16 | 17 | 18 | 19 | 20 | 21 | 22 | 23 | 24 |
|---|---|---|---|---|---|---|---|---|---|---|---|---|
| **SOURCES OF CASH:** | | | | | | | | | | | | |
| Beginning Cash | $24,444 | $21,236 | $25,853 | $31,537 | $38,290 | $37,110 | $35,928 | $39,843 | $43,767 | $47,700 | $52,110 | $56,530 |
| Add: Revenue | 10,200 | 19,100 | 20,300 | 21,500 | 11,900 | 11,900 | 21,900 | 21,900 | 21,900 | 23,000 | 23,000 | 13,000 |
| Depreciation | 600 | 600 | 600 | 600 | 600 | 600 | 600 | 600 | 600 | 600 | 600 | 600 |
| Bank Interest Income (3% of beginning cash) | 56 | 49 | 60 | 73 | 88 | 86 | 83 | 92 | 101 | 110 | 120 | 130 |
| **TOTAL SOURCES** | $35,300 | $40,985 | $46,813 | $53,710 | $50,878 | $49,696 | $58,511 | $62,435 | $66,368 | $71,410 | $75,830 | $70,260 |
| **USES OF CASH:** | | | | | | | | | | | | |
| Total Expenses (from Income Statement) | $13,914 | $14,982 | $15,126 | $15,270 | $13,618 | $13,618 | $18,518 | $18,518 | $18,518 | $19,150 | $19,150 | $18,150 |
| Loan Principal Payback | 150 | 150 | 150 | 150 | 150 | 150 | 150 | 150 | 150 | 150 | 150 | 150 |
| Corporate Income Tax | 0 | 0 | 0 | 0 | 0 | 0 | 0 | 0 | 0 | 0 | 0 | 9,903 |
| **TOTAL USES OF CASH** | 14,064 | 15,132 | 15,276 | 15,420 | 13,768 | 13,768 | 18,668 | 18,668 | 18,668 | 19,300 | 19,300 | 28,203 |
| **ENDING CASH** | $21,236 | $25,853 | $31,537 | $38,290 | $37,110 | $35,928 | $39,843 | $43,767 | $47,700 | $52,110 | $56,530 | $42,057 |

### Canevari & Canevari, an Accountancy Corporation Pro Forma Cash Flow Statement
### for Month 25 through Month 36

| | 25 | 26 | 27 | 28 | 29 | 30 | 31 | 32 | 33 | 34 | 35 | 36 |
|---|---|---|---|---|---|---|---|---|---|---|---|---|
| **SOURCES OF CASH:** | | | | | | | | | | | | |
| Beginning Cash | $42,057 | $41,395 | $49,791 | $59,474 | $70,446 | $72,387 | $74,332 | $76,481 | $78,636 | $80,795 | $83,573 | $86,357 |
| Add: Revenue | 21,910 | 32,205 | 33,645 | 35,085 | 24,225 | 24,225 | 24,225 | 24,225 | 24,225 | 25,490 | 25,490 | 15,490 |
| Depreciation | 600 | 600 | 600 | 600 | 600 | 600 | 600 | 600 | 600 | 600 | 600 | 600 |
| Bank Interest Income (3% of beginning cash) | 97 | 96 | 115 | 137 | 163 | 167 | 172 | 176 | 181 | 186 | 193 | 199 |
| **TOTAL SOURCES** | $64,664 | $74,296 | $84,151 | $95,296 | $95,434 | $97,379 | $99,328 | $101,483 | $103,642 | $107,072 | $109,856 | $102,646 |
| **USES OF CASH:** | | | | | | | | | | | | |
| Total Expenses (from Income Statement) | $23,119 | $24,355 | $24,527 | $24,700 | $22,897 | $22,897 | $22,697 | $22,697 | $22,697 | $23,349 | $23,349 | $22,349 |
| Loan Principal Payback | 150 | 150 | 150 | 150 | 150 | 150 | 150 | 150 | 150 | 150 | 150 | 150 |
| Corporate Income Tax | 0 | 0 | 0 | 0 | 0 | 0 | 0 | 0 | 0 | 0 | 0 | 14,098 |
| **TOTAL USES OF CASH** | 23,269 | 24,505 | 24,677 | 24,850 | 23,047 | 23,047 | 22,847 | 22,847 | 22,847 | 23,499 | 23,499 | 36,597 |
| **ENDING CASH** | $41,395 | $49,791 | $59,474 | $70,446 | $72,387 | $74,332 | $76,481 | $78,636 | $80,795 | $83,573 | $86,357 | $66,049 |

### Canevari & Canevari, an Accountancy Corporation Pro Forma Cash Flow Statement
### for Month 37 through Month 48

| | 37 | 38 | 39 | 40 | 41 | 42 | 43 | 44 | 45 | 46 | 47 | 48 |
|---|---|---|---|---|---|---|---|---|---|---|---|---|
| **SOURCES OF CASH:** | | | | | | | | | | | | |
| Beginning Cash | $66,049 | $67,824 | $80,401 | $94,523 | $110,194 | $114,930 | $119,674 | $124,634 | $129,604 | $134,584 | $140,410 | $146,249 |
| Add: Revenue | 24,292 | 36,646 | 38,374 | 40,102 | 27,070 | 27,070 | 27,070 | 27,070 | 27,070 | 28,588 | 28,588 | 18,588 |
| Depreciation | 600 | 600 | 600 | 600 | 600 | 600 | 600 | 600 | 600 | 600 | 600 | 600 |
| Bank Interest Income (3% of beginning cash) | 152 | 157 | 186 | 218 | 254 | 265 | 276 | 288 | 299 | 311 | 324 | 337 |
| **TOTAL SOURCES** | $91,093 | $105,227 | $119,560 | $135,443 | $138,119 | $142,865 | $147,620 | $152,592 | $157,573 | $164,082 | $169,922 | $165,775 |
| **USES OF CASH:** | | | | | | | | | | | | |
| Total Expenses (from Income Statement) | $23,119 | $24,676 | $24,887 | $25,099 | $23,039 | $23,041 | $22,836 | $22,838 | $22,839 | $23,522 | $23,523 | $22,525 |
| Loan Principal Payback | 150 | 150 | 150 | 150 | 150 | 150 | 150 | 150 | 150 | 150 | 150 | 150 |
| Corporate Income Tax | 0 | 0 | 0 | 0 | 0 | 0 | 0 | 0 | 0 | 0 | 0 | 28,644 |
| **TOTAL USES OF CASH** | 23,269 | 24,826 | 25,037 | 25,249 | 23,189 | 23,191 | 22,986 | 22,988 | 22,989 | 23,672 | 23,673 | 51,319 |
| **ENDING CASH** | $67,824 | $80,401 | $94,523 | $110,194 | $114,930 | $119,674 | $124,634 | $129,604 | $134,584 | $140,410 | $146,249 | $114,456 |

### Canevari & Canevari, an Accountancy Corporation
### Pro Forma Balance Sheet
### December 31, 19X1

**ASSETS**

CURRENT ASSETS:

| | | |
|---|---:|---:|
| Cash | $24,444 | $24,444 |

LONG TERM ASSETS:

| | | |
|---|---:|---:|
| Automobile | 13,000 | |
| less: accumulated depreciation | (2,600) | 10,400 |
| | | |
| Office Furniture | 10,000 | |
| less: accumulated depreciation | (2,000) | 8,000 |
| | | |
| Computer Equipment | 13,000 | |
| less: accumulated depreciation | (2,600) | 10,400 |

OTHER ASSETS:

| | | |
|---|---:|---:|
| Supplies | 2,925 | |
| Prepaid Advertising | 3,500 | |
| Prepaid Rent | 2,500 | 8,925 |
| | | |
| TOTAL ASSETS | | $62,169 |

**LIABILITIES AND OWNERS' EQUITY**

LONG TERM LIABILITIES:

| | | |
|---|---:|---:|
| Loan Payable ($65,000 loan) | $63,200 | $63,200 |

**OWNERS' EQUITY**

| | | |
|---|---:|---:|
| Owners' Equity | 20,000 | |
| Retained Earnings | (21,031) | |
| | | |
| TOTAL OWNERS' EQUITY | | (1,031) |
| | | |
| TOTAL LIABILITIES AND OWNERS' EQUITY | | $62,169 |

### Canevari & Canevari, an Accountancy Corporation
### Pro Forma Balance Sheet
### December 31, 19X2

**ASSETS**

CURRENT ASSETS:

| | | |
|---|---|---|
| Cash | $42,057 | $42,057 |

LONG TERM ASSETS:

| | | |
|---|---|---|
| Automobile | 13,000 | |
| less: accumulated depreciation | (5,200) | 7,800 |
| | | |
| Office Furniture | 10,000 | |
| less: accumulated depreciation | (4,000) | 6,000 |
| | | |
| Computer Equipment | 13,000 | |
| less: accumulated depreciation | (5,200) | 7,800 |

OTHER ASSETS:

| | | |
|---|---|---|
| Supplies | 2,925 | |
| Prepaid Rent | 2,500 | 5,425 |

| | | |
|---|---|---|
| TOTAL ASSETS | | $69,082 |

**LIABILITIES AND OWNERS' EQUITY**

LONG TERM LIABILITIES:

| | | |
|---|---|---|
| Loan Payable ($65,000 loan) | $61,400 | $61,400 |

**OWNERS' EQUITY**

| | | |
|---|---|---|
| Owners' Equity | 20,000 | |
| Retained Earnings | (12,318) | |

| | | |
|---|---|---|
| TOTAL OWNERS' EQUITY | | 7,682 |

| | | |
|---|---|---|
| TOTAL LIABILITIES AND OWNERS' EQUITY | | $69,082 |

### Canevari & Canevari, an Accountancy Corporation
### Pro Forma Balance Sheet
### December 31, 19X3

**ASSETS**

CURRENT ASSETS:

| | | |
|---|---|---|
| Cash | $66,049 | $66,049 |

LONG TERM ASSETS:

| | | |
|---|---|---|
| Automobile | 13,000 | |
| less: accumulated depreciation | (7,800) | 5,200 |
| | | |
| Office Furniture | 10,000 | |
| less: accumulated depreciation | (6,000) | 4,000 |
| | | |
| Computer Equipment | 13,000 | |
| less: accumulated depreciation | (7,800) | 5,200 |

OTHER ASSETS:

| | | |
|---|---|---|
| Supplies | 2,925 | |
| Prepaid Rent | 2,500 | 5,425 |

| | |
|---|---|
| TOTAL ASSETS | $85,874 |

**LIABILITIES AND OWNERS' EQUITY**

LONG TERM LIABILITIES:

| | | |
|---|---|---|
| Loan Payable ($65,000 loan) | $59,600 | $59,600 |

**OWNERS' EQUITY**

| | |
|---|---|
| Owners' Equity | 20,000 |
| Retained Earnings | 6,274 |

| | |
|---|---|
| TOTAL OWNERS' EQUITY | 26,274 |

| | |
|---|---|
| TOTAL LIABILITIES AND OWNERS' EQUITY | $85,874 |

### Canevari & Canevari, an Accountancy Corporation
### Pro Forma Balance Sheet
### December 31, 19X4

**ASSETS**

**CURRENT ASSETS:**

| | | |
|---|---|---|
| Cash | $114,456 | $114,456 |

**LONG TERM ASSETS:**

| | | |
|---|---|---|
| Automobile | 13,000 | |
| less: accumulated depreciation | (10,400) | 2,600 |
| Office Furniture | 10,000 | |
| less: accumulated depreciation | (8,000) | 2,000 |
| Computer Equipment | 13,000 | |
| less: accumulated depreciation | (10,400) | 2,600 |

**OTHER ASSETS:**

| | | |
|---|---|---|
| Supplies | 2,925 | |
| Prepaid Rent | 2,500 | 5,425 |
| TOTAL ASSETS | | $127,081 |

**LIABILITIES AND OWNERS' EQUITY**

**LONG TERM LIABILITIES:**

| | | |
|---|---|---|
| Loan Payable ($65,000 loan) | $57,800 | $57,800 |

**OWNERS' EQUITY**

| | | |
|---|---|---|
| Owners' Equity | 20,000 | |
| Retained Earnings | 49,281 | |
| TOTAL OWNERS' EQUITY | | 69,281 |
| TOTAL LIABILITIES AND OWNERS' EQUITY | | $127,081 |

small businesses, which will include preparation and maintenance of firms' financial records as well as performing operational reviews designed to reduce cost and increase efficiency. Finally, Canevari & Canevari will provide financial auditing services to selected municipalities located in the San Gabriel Valley that require independent compilations and/or reviews of their financial statements.

Total start-up costs are expected to be $45,340. Clients will be charged on either a hourly basis (individuals and small business clients) or on a contract basis (government contracts). The return on investment is expected to be a negative 46.43% in year one, but then turns positive for years two, three, and four (32.76%; 46.64%; and 94.76%, respectively). A positive monthly cash flow is generated for each month of the first four years of operation; however, there are several months within the first two years in which Canevari & Canevari shows operating expenses exceeding revenues. Overall, the net income for each of years two, three, and four is positive, with breakeven attained during year four. The ending cash balance at the end of year four ($114,456) allows the partners of Canevari & Canevari to assess the feasibility of expanding and targeting new demographic areas.

Canevari & Canevari will be successful due to the following attributes:

- Unmatched level of professional service and equitable fee structure offered to clients. The partners are dedicated to ensuring that each client is completely and thoroughly satisfied with the level of service provided.

- Demographics of individuals who require income tax services in the target areas conclude that there is a real need for quality income tax preparation services.

- Lack of extensive advertising by competitors makes penetration into the market a viable possibility.

- Establishment of effective feedback controls to ensure that needs of clients are met.

## BIBLIOGRAPHY

American Institute of Certified Public Accountants, *Generally Accepted Accounting Principles,* July 1992.

Comptroller General of the United States, *Government Auditing Standards,* Superintendent of Documents, U.S. Government Printing Office, 1988.

Office of General Services, State of California, *Procurement Guidelines,* May 1992.

Office of Management and Budget, "OMB Circular A-128, 'Audits of State and Local Governments,'" Single Audit Act of 1984.

United States Census Bureau, "1990 Population and Housing Census."

United States Census Bureau, "1980 Population and Housing Census."

United States Department of Internal Revenue Services, Internal Revenue Tax Code, as of June 1, 1992.

# APPENDIX

# Promotional Material

**Canevari & Canevari, An Accountancy Corporation**
2038 Via Esperanza, Suite A
San Dimas, CA 91773
(818) 915-4454

Date _____

Dear _____:

The 199X tax year is over. Now it is time to have your tax return prepared. During the past year, Congress has enacted new tax legislation that may affect the allowability of tax deductions you may take. It is most important that your tax return is prepared by a professional.

We are experienced professional CPAs who are current with the latest tax law changes. We will prepare your tax return using all allowable tax deductions to maximize your tax refund or minimize your tax liability.

In addition to preparing your return, we also offer electronic tax filing with direct deposit and fast refund capabilities. If your tax refund is needed quickly, we can file your return electronically and get your refund back within 48 hours.

We also handle problem taxes, back taxes for past tax years, and out-of-state tax filings.

Call us today at (818) 915-4454 to arrange for an appointment to have your taxes prepared by a tax professional. Our office is conveniently located to serve you.

We look forward to hearing from you soon.

Sincerely,

Mark L. Canevari, CPA

## *Canevari & Canevari, An Accountancy Corporation*
**2038 Via Esperanza, Suite A**
**San Dimas, CA 91773**
**(818) 915-4454**

Date _____

Dear _____ :

### A Tax Quiz for You

1. Does your tax professional send you tax planning suggestions throughout the year?
2. Are you getting more than just a tax return from your accountant?
3. Are you paying the lowest taxes possible?
4. Do you know which tax shelters will give you the greatest tax reduction?

If you answered "yes" to all the questions in the quiz, your tax and financial affairs are probably in good order and you feel confident that you're getting your money's worth from your current accountant.

But chances are you answered "no" to one or more of the questions. You may also have the thought that you are not doing all you could to make the most of your financial situation. You are thinking you should be paying fewer taxes, you should be getting assistance with your investment program, and your affairs need to be reviewed to meet your long-term financial goals.

Therefore, it's time we get together and plan your tax strategies.

There are many advantages when you have Canevari & Canevari prepare your 199X income tax return:

- 20 years' experience preparing income tax returns.
- Paying the lowest tax possible for 199X.
- Tax-saving ideas for 1993.
- Year-round financial and business advice.

**Call Us Today for an Appointment!**

## APPENDIX A

# Sources of Additional Market Research

Following are more than 100 sources based on bibliographies but together by Lloyd M. DeBoer, Dean of the School of Business Administration at George Mason University, Fairfax, Virginia, and the Office of Management and Training of the SBA.

## U.S. GOVERNMENT PUBLICATIONS

The publications in this section are books and pamphlets issued by federal agencies and listed under the issuing agency. Where availability of an individual listing is indicated by GPO (Government Printing Office), the publication may be ordered from the Superintendent of Documents, U.S. Government Printing Office, Washington, DC 20402. When ordering a GPO publication, give the title and series number of the publication, and name of agency. You may also order by phone by calling (202) 783-3238. Contact GPO for current prices.

Publications should be requested by the title and any number given from the issuing agency. Most libraries have some listings to identify currently available federal publications. Some keep a number of selected government publications for ready reference through the Federal Depository Library System.

*American Statistics Index: A Comprehensive Guide and Index to the Statistical Publications of the United States Government.* Washington, DC: Congressional Information Service, 1973–. Monthly, with annual cumulations. This is the most comprehensive index to statistical information generated by the federal agencies, committees of Congress, and special programs of the government. Approximately 7,400 titles of 500 government sources are indexed each year. The two main volumes are arranged by issuing breakdown, technical notes, and time period covered by publication. Separate index volume is arranged by subject and title and also includes the SIC code, the Standard Occupation Classification, and a list of SMSAs (standard metropolitan statistical areas).

### Bureau of the Census
Department of Commerce
Washington, DC 20233

Contact the Public Information Office for a more complete listing of publications. The following is a sample:

*Catalog of United States Census Publications.* Published monthly with quarterly and annual cumulations. A guide to census data and reports. This catalog contains descriptive lists of publications, data files, and special tabulations.

*Census of Agriculture.* Performed in years ending in 4 and 9. Volumes include information on statistics of county; size of farm; characteristics of farm operations; farm income; farm sales; farm expenses; and agricultural services.

*Census of Business.* Compiled every five years (in years ending in 2 and 7). Organized in three units: *Census of Construction Industries.* Information from industries based on SIC codes. Included is information about number of construction firms; employees; receipts; payrolls; payments for materials; components; work supplies; payments for machinery and equipment; and depreciable assets.

*Census of Governments.* Done in years ending in 2 and 7. This is the most detailed source for statistics on government finance. *Census of Housing.* Provides information on plumbing facilities whether a unit is owned or rented, value of home, when built, number of bedrooms, telephones, and more.

*Census of Manufacturers.* Compiled every five years (in years ending in 2 and 7). Reports on 450 different classes of manufacturing industries. Data for each industry includes: information on capital expenditures, value added, number of establishments, employment data, material costs, assets, rent, and inventories. Updated yearly by the *Annual Survey of Manufacturers.*

*Census of Mineral Industries.* Covers areas of extraction of minerals. Information on employees; payroll; work hours; cost of materials; capital expenditures; and quantity and value of materials consumed and products shipped.

*Census of Population.* Compiled every ten years (in years ending in 0). Presents detailed data on population characteristics of states, counties, SMSAs, and census tracts. Demographics data reported include: age, sex, race, marital status, family composition, employment income, level of education, and occupation. Updated annually by the *Current Population Report.*

*Census of Retail Trade.* This report presents statistics for over one hundred different types of retail establishments by state, SMSAs, counties, and cities with populations over 2,500. It includes data on the number of outlets, total sales, employment, and payroll. Updated each month by *Monthly Retail Trade.*

*Census of Selected Services.* Provides statistics similar to those reported by the *Census of Retail Trade* for retail service organizations such as auto repair centers and hotels. Does not include information on real estate, insurance, or the professions. Updated monthly by *Monthly Selected Service Receipts.*

*Census of Transportation.* Information on four major phases of U.S. travel. (1) National Travel Survey, (2) Truck Inventory and Use of Survey, (3) Commodity Transportation Survey, and (4) Survey of Motor Carriers and Public Warehousing.

*Census of Wholesale Trade.* Statistics for over 150 types of wholesaler categories. The data detail the number of establishments, payroll, warehouse space, expenses, end-of-year inventories, legal form of organization, and payroll. Updated each month by *Monthly Wholesale Trade.*

*Statistical Abstract of the United States.* Published annually. This is a useful source for finding current and historical statistics about various aspects of American life. Contents include statistics on income, prices, education, population, law enforcement, environmental conditions, local government, labor force, manufacturing, and many other topics.

*State and Metropolitan Area Data Book.* A Statistical Abstract Supplement. Presents a variety of information on states and metropolitan areas in the U.S. on subjects such as area, population, housing, income, manufacturers, retail trade, and wholesale trade.

*County and City Databook.* Published every five years, this supplements the *Statistical Abstract.* Contains 144 statistical items for each county and 148 items for cities with a population of 25,000 or more. Data is organized by region, division, states, and SMSAs. Standard demographics are contained in addition to other harder-to-find data.

*County Business Patterns.* Annual. Contains a summary of data on number and type (by SIC number) of business establishments as well as their employment and taxable payroll. Data are presented by industry and county.

**Bureau of Economic Analysis**
Department of Commerce
Washington, DC 20230

*Business Statistics.* This is the biennial supplement to the *Survey of Current Business* and contains data on 2,500 series arranged annually for early years, quarterly for the last decade, and monthly for the most recent five years.

**Bureau of Industrial Economics**
Department of Commerce
Washington, DC 20230

*United States Industrial Outlook.* Projections of sales trends for major sectors of the United States economy including business services; consumer services; transportation; consumer goods; and distribution.

**Domestic and International Business Administration**
Department of Commerce
Washington, DC 20230

*County and City Data Book.* Published every other year, supplements the *Statistical Abstract.* Using data taken from censuses and other government publications, it provides breakdowns by city and county for income, population, education, employment, housing, banking, manufacturing, capital expenditures, retail and wholesale sales, and other factors.

*Measuring Markets: A Guide to the Use of Federal and State Statistical Data.* GPO. Provides federal and state government data on population, income, employment, sales, and selected taxes. Explains how to interpret the data to measure markets and evaluate opportunities.

*Selected Publications to Aid Business and Industry.* Listing of federal statistical sources useful to business and industry.

*Statistics of Income.* Annual. Published by the Internal Revenue Service of the Treasury Department. This publication consists of data collected from tax returns filed by corporations, sole proprietorships and partnerships, and individuals.

*State Statistical Abstract.* Every state publishes a statistical abstract, almanac, or economic data book covering statistics for the state, its counties and cities. A complete list of these abstracts is in the back of each volume of the *Statistical Abstract* and *Measuring Markets.*

### International Trade Administration
Department of Commerce
Washington, DC 20230

*Country Market Survey.* These reports describe market sectors and the markets for producer goods, consumer goods, and industrial material.

*Global Market Surveys.* Provides market research to verify the existence and vitality of foreign markets for specific goods as well as Department of Commerce assistance to United States business to help in market penetration.

*Foreign Economic Trends.* Prepared by United States embassies abroad. Each volume has a table of "Key Economic Indicators" and other data on the current economic situation and trends for the country under discussion.

*Overseas Business Reports.* Analyses of trade opportunities, marketing conditions, distribution channels, industry trends, trade regulations, and market prospects are provided.

*Trade Opportunity Program (TOP).* On a weekly basis indexes trade opportunities by product as well as type of opportunity.

### U.S. Small Business Administration
Washington, DC 20416

SBA issues a wide range of management and technical publications designed to help owner-managers and prospective owners of small business. For general information about the SBA office, its policies, and assistance programs, contact your nearest SBA office.

A listing of currently available publications can be obtained free from the Small Business Administration, Office of Public Communications, 409 Third St. SW, Washington, DC 20416 or call 1-800-U-ASK—SBA toll free. The SBA offers 51 publications currently. One particular publication, *Basic Library Reference Sources,* contains a section on marketing information and guides to research. Get the latest *Directory of Publications* by writing or calling the 800 number. You can also obtain a free booklet, *Your Business and the SBA* which gives you an overview of all SBA services and programs.

*Management Aids* (3- to 24-page pamphlet). This series of pamphlets is organized by a broad range of management principles. Each pamphlet in this series discusses a specific management practice to help the owner-manager of a small firm with management problems and business operations. A section on marketing covers a wide variety of topics from advertising guidelines to marketing research to pricing.

# PERIODICALS

United States. International Trade Administration. *Business America: The Magazine of International Trade*. Biweekly. Activities relating to private sector of the Department of Commerce are covered including exports and other international business activities.

United States. Department of Commerce. Bureau of Economic Analysis. *Business Conditions Digest*. Washington, DC: U.S. Government Printing Office. Monthly. Title includes estimates on forecasts for recent months. Very useful for data not yet published elsewhere.

United States. Council of Economic Advisors. *Economic Indicators*. Washington, DC: U.S. Government Printing Office. Monthly. Statistical tables for major economics indicators are included. Section on credit is useful for marketers. Statistics quoted annually for about six years and monthly for the past year.

United States. Board of Governors of the Federal Reserve System. *Federal Reserve Bulletin*. Washington, DC: U.S. Government Printing Office. Monthly. Contains official statistics on national banking, international banking, and business.

United States. Bureau of Labor Statistics. *Monthly Labor Review*. Washington, DC: U.S. Government Printing Office. Monthly. This publication covers all aspects of labor including wages, productivity, collective bargaining, new legislation, and consumer prices.

United States. Department of Commerce. Bureau of Economic Analysis. *Survey of Current Business*. Washington, DC: U.S. Government Printing Office. Monthly, with weekly supplements. The most useful source for current business statistics. Each issue is divided into two sections. The first covers general business topics; the second, "Current Business Statistics," gives current data for 2,500 statistical series or topics. Also, indexed in *Business Periodicals Index*.

United States. Department of the Treasury. *Treasury Bulletin*. Washington, DC: U.S. Government Printing Office. Monthly. Statistical tables are provided on all aspects of fiscal operations of government as well as money-related activities of the private sector. Useful for consumer background or from a monetary view.

# DIRECTORIES

The selected national directories are listed under categories of specific business or general marketing areas in an alphabetical subject index.

When the type of directory is not easily found under the alphabetical listing of a general marketing category, such as "jewelry," look for a specific type of industry or outlet, for example, "department stores."

## Apparel

*Hat Life Year Book (Men's)*. Annual. Includes renovators, importers, classified list of manufacturers, and wholesalers of men's headwear. Hat Life Year Book, 551 Summit Ave., Jersey City, NJ 07306.

*Knitting Times—Buyer's Guide Issue*. Annual. Lists manufacturers and suppliers of knitted products, knit goods, materials, supplies, services, etc. National Knitwear and Sportswear Association, 386 Park Ave. South, New York, NY 10016.

*Men's & Boys' Wear Buyers, Nation-Wide Directory of* (exclusive of New York metropolitan area). Annually in August. More than 20,000 buyers and merchandise managers for 6,100 top department, family clothing, and men's and boys' wear specialty stores. Telephone number, buying office, and postal zip code given for each firm. Also available in individual state editions. The Salesman's Guide, Inc., 1140 Broadway, New York, NY 10001. Also publishes *Metropolitan New York Directory of Men's and Boys' Wear Buyers*. Semiannually in May and November. (Lists same information for the metropolitan New York area as the nationwide directory.)

*Women's & Children's Wear & Accessories Buyers, Nationwide Directory of* (exclusive of New York metropolitan area). Annually in October. Lists more than 25,000 buyers and divisional merchandise managers for about 6,100 leading department, family clothing, and specialty stores. Telephone number and mail zip code given for each store. Also available in individual state editions. The Salesman's Guide, Inc., 1140 Broadway, New York, NY 10001.

## Appliances—Household

*Appliance Dealers—Major Household Directory*. Annual. Lists manufacturers and distributors in home electronics, appliances, kitchens. Gives complete addresses and phone. Compiled from Yellow Pages. American Business Directories, Inc., 5711 S. 86th Circle, Omaha, NE 68127.

## Automatic Merchandising (Vending)

*NAMA Directory of Members*. Annually in June. Organized by state and by city, lists vending service companies who are NAMA members. Gives mailing address, telephone number, and products vended. Also includes machine manufacturers and suppliers. National Automatic Merchandising Association, 20 N. Wacker Dr., Chicago, IL 60606.

## Automotive

*Manufacturers' Representatives Division*. Irregular. Alphageographical listing of about 300 representatives including name, address, telephone number, territories covered, and lines carried. Automotive Service Industrial Association, 444 N. Michigan Ave., Chicago, IL 60611.

*Automotive Warehouse Distributors Association Membership Directory*. Annually in April. Includes listing of manufacturers, warehouse distributors, their products, personnel, and territories. Automotive Warehouse Distributors Association, 9140 Ward Parkway, Kansas City, MO 64114.

*Automotive Consultants Directory.* Annually in November. Lists 380 consultants and consulting firms in automotive engineering specialties, including safety, manufacturing, quality control, engine design, marketing, etc. Society of Automotive Engineers, 400 Commonwealth Dr., Warrendale, PA 15096-0001.

## Aviation

*World Aviation Directory.* Published twice a year in March and September. Gives administrative and operating personnel of airlines, aircraft, and engine manufacturers and component manufacturers and distributors, organizations, and schools. Indexed by companies, activities, products, and individuals. McGraw-Hill, Inc. 1156 15th St. NW, Washington, DC 20005.

## Bookstores

*Book Trade Directory, American.* Annually in July. Lists more than 25,000 retail and wholesale booksellers in the United States and Canada. Entries alphabetized by state (or province), and then by city and business name. Each listing gives address, telephone numbers, key personnel, types of books sold, subject specialties carried, sidelines and services offered, and general characteristics. For wholesale entries gives types of accounts, import-export information, and territory limitations. R. R. Bowker Company, 245 W. 17th St., New York, NY 10011.

## Building Supplies

*Building Supply News Buyers Guide.* Annually in May. Classified directory of manufacturers of lumber, building materials, equipment, and supplies. Cahners Publishing Co., 1350 E. Touhy Ave., Des Plaines, IL 60018.

## Business Firms

*Dun & Bradstreet Million Dollar Directory—Top 50,000 Companies.* Annually. Lists about 50,000 top corporations. Arranged alphabetically. Gives business name, state of incorporation, address, telephone number, SIC numbers, function, sales volume, number of employees, and names of officers and directors, principal bank, accounting firm, and legal counsel. Dun's Marketing Services, Dun & Bradstreet, Inc., 3 Sylvan Way, Parsippany, NJ 07054-3896.

*Dun & Bradstreet Million Dollar Directory.* Annually in February. Lists about 160,000 businesses with a net worth of $500,000 or more. Arranged alphabetically. Dun's Marketing Services, Dun & Bradstreet, Inc., 3 Sylvan Way, Parsippany, NJ 07054-3896.

## Buying Offices

*Buying Offices and Accounts, Directory of.* Annually in March. Approximately 220 New York, Chicago, Los Angeles, Dallas, and Miami resident buying offices, corporate offices, and merchandise brokers together with 7,700 accounts listed under its own buying office complete with local address and alphabetically by address and buying office. The Salesman's Guide, Inc., 1140 Broadway, New York, NY 10001.

## China and Glassware

*American Glass Review.* Glass Factory Directory Issue. Annually in March. Issued as part of subscription (13th issue) to *American Glass Review:* Lists companies manufacturing flat glass, tableware glass and fiber glass, giving corporate and plant addresses, executives, type of equipment used. Doctorow Communications, Inc., 1115 Clifton Ave., Clifton, NJ 07013.

*China Glass & Tableware Red Book Directory Issue.* Annually in September. Issued as part of subscription (13th issue) to *China Glass & Tableware.* Lists about 1,000 manufacturers, importers, and national distributors of china, glass, and other table appointments, giving corporate addresses and executives. Doctorow Publications, Inc., 1115 Clifton Ave., Clifton, NJ 07013.

## City Directories Catalog

*Municipal Year Book.* Annual. Contains a review of municipal events of the year, analyses of city operations, and a directory of city officials in all the states. International City Management Association, 777 N. Capitol St. NE, Washington, DC 20002-4201.

## College Stores

*College Stores, Directory of.* Published every two years. Lists about 3,000 college stores, geographically with manager's name, kinds of goods sold, college name, number of students, whether men, women, or both, whether the store is college owned or privately owned. B. Klein Publications, P.O. Box 8503, Coral Springs, FL 33065.

## Confectionery

*Candy Buyers' Directory.* Annually in January. Lists candy manufacturers; importers and United States representatives, and confectionery brokers. The Manufacturing Confectionery Publishing Co., 175 Rock Rd., Glen Rock, NJ 07452

## Construction Equipment

*Construction Equipment Buyer's Guide.* Annually in November. Lists 1,500 construction equipment distributors and manufacturers; includes company names, names of key personnel, addresses, telephone numbers, branch locations, and lines handled or type of equipment produced. Cahners Publishing Co., 1350 E. Touhy Ave., Des Plaines, IL 60018.

## Conventions and Trade Shows

*Directory of Conventions.* Annually in January. Contains over 18,000 cross-indexed listings of annual events, gives dates, locations, names and addresses of executives in charge, scope, expected attendance. Bill Communications, Inc., 633 Third Ave., New York, NY 10017.

*Trade Show and Exhibits Schedule.* Annually in January with supplement in July. Lists over 10,000 exhibits, trade shows, expositions, and fairs held throughout the world with dates given two years in advance. Listings run according to industrial classification covering all industries and professions; full information on dates, city, sponsoring organization, number of exhibits, attendance; gives title and address of executive in charge. Bill Communications, Inc., 633 Third Ave., New York, NY 10017.

## Dental Supply

*Dental Supply Houses, Hayes Directory of.* Annually in August. Lists wholesalers of dental supplies and equipment with addresses, telephone numbers, financial standing and credit rating. Edward N. Hayes, Publisher, 4229 Birch St., Newport Beach, CA 92660.

## Department Stores

*Sheldon's Retail.* Annual. Lists 1,500 large independent department stores, 600 major department store chains, 150 large independent and chain home-furnishing stores, 700 large independent women's specialty stores, and 450 large women's specialty store chains alphabetically by states. Gives all department buyers with lines bought by each buyer, and addresses and telephone numbers of merchandise executives. Also gives all New York, Chicago, Dallas, Atlanta, and Los Angeles buying offices, the number and locations of branch stores, and an index of all store/chain headquarters. Phelon, Sheldon & Marsar, Inc., 15 Industrial Ave., Fairview, NJ 07022.

## Discount Stores

*Discount Department Stores, Directory of.* Annually. Lists headquarters address, telephone number, location, square footage of each store, lines carried, leased operators, names of executives and buyers (includes Canada). Also special section on leased department operators. Chain Store Guide Publications, 425 Park Ave., New York, NY 10022.

## Drug Outlets—Retail and Wholesale

*Chain Drug Stores Guide, Hayes.* Annually in September. Lists headquarters address, telephone numbers, number and location of units, names of executives and buyers, wholesale drug distributors. Edward N. Hayes, 4229 Birch St., Newport Beach, CA 92660.

*Druggist Directory, Hayes.* Annually in March. Lists about 52,900 retail and 700 wholesale druggists in the United States, giving addresses, financial standing, and credit rating. Also publishes regional editions for one or more states. Computerized mailing labels available. Edward N. Hayes, 4229 Birch St., Newport Beach, CA 92660.

*Drug Topics Red Book.* Annually in March. Gives information on wholesale drug companies, chain drug stores headquarters, department stores maintaining toilet goods or drug departments, manufacturers' sales agents, and discount houses operating toilet goods, cosmetic, proprietary medicine or prescription departments. Medical Economics Company, 680 Kinderkamack Rd., Oradell, NJ 07649.

*National Wholesale Druggists' Association Membership and Executive Directory.* Annually in January. Lists 800 American and foreign wholesalers and manufacturers of drugs and allied products. National Wholesale Druggists' Association, Box 238, Alexandria, VA 22313.

### Electrical and Electronics

*Electronic Industry Telephone Directory.* Annually in August. Contains over 22,890 listings of manufacturers, representatives, distributors, government agencies, contracting agencies, and others. Harris Publishing Co., 2057 Aurora Rd., Twinsburg, OH 44087.

*Electrical Wholesale Distributors, Directory of.* Detailed information on 3,400 companies with over 7,630 locations in the United States and Canada, including name, address, telephone number, branch and affiliated houses, products handled, etc. McGraw-Hill, Inc., 1221 Avenue of the Americas, New York, NY 10020.

*Who's Who in Electronics, Regional/National Source Directory.* Annually in January. Detailed information (name, address, telephone number, products handled, territories, etc.) on 12,500 electronics manufacturers, and 4,800 industrial electronic distributors and branch outlets. Purchasing index with 1,600 product breakdowns for buyers and purchasing agents. Harris Publishing Co., 2057 Aurora Rd., Twinsburg, OH 44087.

### Electrical Utilities

*Electrical Utilities, Electrical World, Directory of.* Annually in November. Complete listings of electric utilities (investor-owned, municipal, and government agencies in United States and Canada) giving their addresses and personnel, and selected data on operations. McGraw-Hill, Inc., Directory of Electric Utilities, 1221 Avenue of the Americas, New York, NY 10020.

### Embroidery

*Embroidery Directory.* Annually in November. Alphabetical listing with addresses and telephone numbers of manufacturers, merchandisers, designers, cutters, bleacheries, yarn dealers, machine suppliers, and other suppliers to the Schiffli lace and embroidery industry. Schiffli Lace and Embroidery Manufacturers Association, Inc., 8555 Tonnelle Ave., North Bergen, NJ 07087.

### Export and Import

*American Export Register.* Annually in September. Includes over 30,000 importers and exporters and products handled. Thomas International Publishing Co., Inc., 1 Penn Plaza, 250 West 34th St., New York, NY 10119.

*Canadian Trade Directory, Fraser's.* Annually in May. Contains more than 42,000 Canadian companies. Also lists over 14,000 foreign companies who have Canadian representatives. Fraser's Trade Directories, Maclean Hunter Ltd., 777 Bay St., Toronto, Ontario, Canada, M5W 1A7.

## Flooring

*Flooring Directory and Buying Guide Issue.* Annually in October. Reference to sources of supply, giving their products and brand names, leading distributors, manufacturers' representatives, and associations. Edgell Communications, 7500 Old Oak Ave., Cleveland, OH 44130.

## Food Dealers—Retail and Wholesale

*Food Brokers Association, National Directory of Members.* Annually in April. Arranged by states and cities, lists member food brokers in the United States and Europe, giving names and addresses, products they handle and services they perform. National Food Brokers Association, 1010 Massachusetts Ave., Washington, DC 20001.

*National Frozen Food Association Directory.* Annually in January. Lists packers, distributors, supplies, refrigerated warehouses, wholesalers, and brokers; includes names and addresses of each firm and their key officials. Contains statistical marketing data. National Frozen Food Association, 604 W. Derry Rd., Hershey, PA 17033.

*Food Industry Register, Thomas'.* Annually in May. Volume 1: Lists supermarket chains, wholesalers, brokers, frozen food brokers, exporters, warehouses. Volume 2: Contains information on products and services, manufacturers, sources of supplies, importers. Volume 3: A-Z index of 48,000 companies. Also, a brand name/trademark index. Thomas Publishing Co., One Penn Plaza, New York, NY 10119.

*Tea and Coffee Buyers' Guide, Ukers' International.* Annual. Includes revised and updated lists of participants in the tea and coffee and allied trades. The Tea and Coffee Trade Journal, Lockwood Trade Journal, Inc., 130 W. 42nd St., 22nd Floor, New York, NY 10036.

## Gas Companies

*Gas Companies, Brown's Directory of North American and International.* Annually in November. Includes information on every known gas utility company and holding company worldwide. Energy Publications Division, Edgell Communications, Inc., 1 East First St., Duluth, MN 55802.

*LP/Gas.* Annually in March. Lists suppliers, supplies, and distributors. Energy Publications Division, Edgell Communications, Inc., 1 East First St., Duluth, MN 55802.

## Gift and Art

*Gift and Decorative Accessory Buyers Directory.* Annually in September. Included in subscription price of monthly magazine, *Gifts and Decorative Accessories.* Alphabetical listing of manufacturers, importers, jobbers, and representatives in the gift field.

Listing of trade names, trademarks, brand names, and trade associations. Geyer-McAllister Publications, 51 Madison Ave., New York, NY 10010

*Gift, Housewares and Home Textile Buyers, Nationwide Directory of.* Annually with semiannual supplement. For 7,000 types of retail firms lists store name, address, type of store, number of stores, names of president, merchandise managers, and buyers, etc., for giftwares and housewares. State editions also available. The Salesman's Guide, Inc., 1140 Broadway, New York, NY 10001.

*Gift & Stationery Business Directory Issue.* Annually in September. Alphabetical listing by category of each (manufacturer, representative, importer, distributor, or jobber) of about 1,900. Includes identification of trade names and trademarks, and statistics for imports, manufacturing, and retail sales. Gralla Publications, 1515 Broadway, Suite 3201, New York, NY 10036.

*Gift Shops Directory.* 68,490 listings. American Business Directories, Inc., 5711 S. 86th Circle, Omaha, NE 68127.

## Hardware

*Wholesaler Directory (Hardware).* Irregularly issued. Alphabetical listing of hardware wholesalers, and distributors of lumber and building materials. National Retail Hardware Association, 5822 W. 74th St., Indianapolis, IN 46278.

## Home Furnishings

*The Antique Dealers Directory.* Annual. Lists 31,000 dealers with name, address, and phone number as well as size of advertisement and first year advertised in Yellow Pages. American Business Directories, Inc. 5711 S. 86th Circle, Omaha, NE 68127.

*Home Fashions—Buyer's Guide Issue.* Annually in December. Lists names and addresses of manufacturers, importers, and regional sales representatives. Fairchild Publications, Capital Cities Media, Inc., 7 E. 12th St., New York, NY 10003.

*Interior Decorator's Handbook.* Semiannually in spring and fall. Published expressly for decorators and designers, interior decorating staff of department and furniture stores. Lists firms handling items used in interior decoration. Columbia Communications, Inc., 370 Lexington Ave., New York, NY 10017.

## Hospitals

*Hospitals, Directory of.* Annually in January. Lists 7,800 hospitals, with selected data. SMG Marketing Group, Inc., 1342 N. LaSalle Dr., Chicago, IL 60610.

## Hotels and Motels

*Hotels and Motels Directory.* Annually. Lists more than 61,040 hotels and motels. American Business Directories, Inc. 5711 S. 86th Circle, Omaha, NE 68127.

*OAG Travel Planner and Hotel Red Book.* Quarterly. Lists over 26,000 hotels in the United States. Also lists 14,500 destination cities, etc. Official Airline Guide Inc., 2000 Clearwater Dr., Oak Brook, IL 60521.

*Hotel Systems, Directory of.* Annually in March. Lists over 800 hotel systems in the Western hemisphere. American Hotel Association Directory Corporation, 1201 New York Ave. NW, Washington, DC 20005.

## Housewares

*NHMA Membership Directory and Buyer's Desk Top Guide to Houseware Manufacturers.* Annually in March. Compilation of resources of the housewares trade, includes listing of their products, trade names, and a registry of manufacturers' representatives. National Housewares Manufacturers Association, 1324 Merchandise Mart, Chicago, IL 60654.

## Jewelry

*Jewelers' Circular/Keystone-Jewelers' Directory Issue.* Annual in June. Lists manufacturers, importers, distributors, and retailers of jewelry; diamonds; precious, semiprecious, and imitation stones; watches, silverware; and kindred articles. Includes credit ratings. Chilton Co., Chilton Way, Radnor, PA 19098.

## Liquor

*Wine and Spirits Wholesalers of America—Member Roster and Industry Directory.* Annually in January. Lists names of 700 member companies; includes parent house and branches, addresses, and names of managers. Also, has register of 1,900 suppliers and gives state liquor control administrators, national associations, and trade press directory. Wine and Spirits Wholesalers of America, Inc., 1023 15th St. NW, Fourth Fl., Washington, DC 20005.

## Mailing List Houses

*Mailing List Houses, Directory of.* Lists 1,800 list firms, brokers, compilers, and firms offering their own lists for rent; includes the specialties of each firm. Arranged geographically. Todd Publications, 18 N. Greenbush Rd., West Nyack, NY 10994.

## Mail Order Businesses

*Mail Order Business Directory.* Lists 10,000 names or mail order firms with buyers' names, and lines carried. Arranged geographically. B. Klein Publications, P.O. Box 8503, Coral Springs, FL 33065.

## Manufacturers

*MacRae's Blue Book.* Annually in March. In three volumes: Volume 1—Corporate Index lists company names and addresses alphabetically, with 40,000 branch and/or sales office telephone numbers. Volumes 2 and 3—companies listed by product classifications. MacRae's Blue Book, Business Research Publications, 817 Broadway, New York, NY 10003.

*Manufacturers, Thomas' Register of American.* Annual. Volume 1–14—products and services; suppliers of each product category grouped by state and city. Vols. 15–16 contain company profiles. Vols. 17–23—manufacturers' catalogs. More than 150,000 firms are listed under 50,000 product headings. Thomas Publishing Co., One Penn Plaza, New York, NY 10119.

## Manufacturers' Sales Representatives

*Manufacturers & Agents National Association Directory of Members.* Annually in May/June. Contains individual listings of manufacturers' agents throughout the United States, Canada, and several foreign countries. Listings cross-referenced by alphabetical, geographical, and product classification. Manufacturers' Agents National Association, Box 3467, Laguna Hills, CA 92654.

## Mass Merchandisers

*Major Mass Market Merchandisers, Nationwide Directory of* (exclusive of New York, metropolitan area). Annual. Lists men's, women's, and children's wear buyers who buy for about 257,000 units—top discount, variety, supermarket and drug chains; factory outlet stores; leased department operators. The Salesman's Guide, Inc., 1140 Broadway, New York, NY 10001.

## Metalworking

*Metalworking Directory, Dun & Bradstreet.* Annually in June. Lists about 65,000 metalworking and metal producing plants with 20 or more production employees. Arranged geographically. Dun's Marketing Services Division, Dun & Bradstreet Corporation, 3 Sylvan Way, Parsippany, NJ 07054-3896.

## Military Market

*Military Market Magazine—Buyers' Guide Issue.* Annually in January. Lists manufacturers and suppliers of products sold in military commissaries. Also lists manufacturers' representatives and distributors. Army Times Publishing Co., Times Journal Co., 6883 Commercial Dr., Springfield, VA 22159.

## Paper Products

*Sources of Supply Buyers' Guide.* Lists 1,700 mills and converters of paper, film, foil, and allied products, and paper merchants in the United States alphabetically with addresses, principal personnel, and products manufactured. Also lists trade associations, brand names, and manufacturers' representatives. Advertisers and Publishers Service, Inc., 300 N. Prospect Ave., Park Ridge, IL 60068.

## Physicians and Medical Supply Houses

*Medical Directory, American.* Volumes 1–4 give complete information about 633,000 physicians in the United States and possessions—alphabetical and geographical listings. American Medical Association, 535 North Dearborn St., Chicago, IL 60610.

*Physician and Hospital Supply Houses, Hayes' Directory of.* Annually in August. Listings of 1,850 U.S. wholesalers doing business in physician, hospital and surgical supplies and equipment; includes addresses, telephone numbers, financial standing, and credit ratings. Edward N. Hayes, Publisher, 4229 Birch St., Newport Beach, CA 92660.

## Plumbing

*Manufacturers' Representatives, Directory of.* Annually in February. Lists 2,000 representatives of manufacturers selling plumbing, heating and cooling equipment, components, tools and related products to this industry through wholesaler channels, with detailed information on each. Delta Communications, 400 N. Michigan Ave., Chicago, IL 60611.

## Premium Sources

*Premium Suppliers and Services, Directory of.* Annually in February. Lists about 1,800 suppliers with title, telephone number, address. Gralla Publications, 1515 Broadway, Suite 3201, New York, NY 10036.

*Incentive Resource Guide Issue.* Annually in February. Contains classified directory of suppliers, and list of manufacturers' representatives serving the premium field. Also, lists associations and clubs, and trade shows. Bill Communications, 633 Third Ave., New York, NY 10017.

## Purchasing—Government

*U.S. Government Purchasing and Sales Directory.* Irregularly issued. Booklet designed to help small business receive an equitable share of government contracts. Lists types of purchases for both military and civilian needs, catalogs procurement offices by state. Lists SBA regional and branch offices. Order from Superintendent of Documents, U.S. Government Printing Office, Washington, DC 20402.

## Refrigeration and Air Conditioning

*Air Conditioning, Heating & Refrigeration News—Directory Issue.* Annually in January. Lists 1,900 manufacturers and 3,000 wholesalers and factory outlets in refrigeration, heating, and air-conditioning. Business News Publishing Co., 755 W. Big Beaver Rd., 10th Fl., Troy, MI 48084.

## Restaurants

*Chain Restaurant Operators, Directory of.* Annually in May. Lists headquarters address, telephone number, number and location of units, trade names used, whether unit is company operated or franchised, executives and buyers, annual sales volume for chains of restaurants, cafeterias, drive-ins, hotel and motel food operators, industrial caterers, etc. Chain Store Information Services, 425 Park Ave., New York, NY 10022.

## Roofing and Siding

*RSI Trade Directory Issue.* Annually in April. Has listing guide to products and equipment manufacturers, jobbers and distributors, and associations in the roofing, siding, and home improvement industries. RSI Directory, Edgell Communications, Inc., 7500 Old Oak Blvd., Cleveland, OH 44130.

## Selling Direct

*Direct Selling Companies, World Directory.* Annually in April. About 30 direct selling associations and 750 associated member companies. Includes names of contact persons, company product line, method of distribution, etc. World Federation of Direct Selling Associations, 1776 K St. NW, Suite 600, Washington, DC 20006.

## Shoes

*National Directory of Footwear Companies/Footwear Buyers' Guide.* Biennial. Lists about 400 New York and 300 out-of-town and foreign manufacturers. New York City Footwear Buyers' Guide, 47 W. 34th St., Suite 601, New York, NY 10001

## Shopping Centers

*Shopping Center Directory.* Annual. Alphabetical listing of 30,000 shopping centers, location, owner/developer, manager, physical plant (number of stores, square feet), and leasing agent. National Research Bureau, Division of Information, Product Group, Automated Marketing Systems, Inc., 310 S. Michigan Ave., Chicago, IL 60604.

## Specialty Stores

*Women's Apparel Stores, Phelon's.* Lists over 7,000 women's apparel and accessory shops with store headquarters name and address, number of shops operated, New York City buying headquarters or representatives, lines of merchandise bought and sold, name of principal officers and buyers, store size, and price range. Phelon, Sheldon, & Marsar, Inc., 15 Industrial Ave., Fairview, NJ 07022.

## Sporting Goods

*Sporting Goods Buyers, Nationwide Directory of.* Including semiannual supplements. Lists over 7,500 top retail stores with names of buyers and executives, for all types of sporting goods, athletic apparel and athletic footwear, hunting and fishing, and outdoor equipment. The Salesman's Guide, Inc., 1140 Broadway, New York, NY 10001.

*Sporting Goods Business—Directory of Products, Services and Suppliers Issue.* Annually in August. 3,000 suppliers of sporting goods merchandise and equipment. Gralla Publications, 1515 Broadway, Suite 3201, New York, NY 10036.

## Stationers

*Giftware and Stationery Business—Directory Issue.* Annually in September. Alphabetical listing by company of over 1,900 manufacturers, importers, distributors, and representatives. Gralla Publications, 1515 Broadway, Suite 3201, New York, NY 10036.

## Textiles

*Textile Blue Book, Davison's.* Annually in February. Contains over 8,400 separate company listings (name, address, etc.) for the United States and Canada. Firms included are cotton, wool, synthetic mills, knitting mills, cordage, twine, and duck manufacturers, dry goods commission merchants, converters, yarn dealers, cordage manufacturers' agents, wool dealers and merchants, cotton merchants, exporters, brokers, and others. Davison Publishing Co., Box 477, Ridgewood, NJ 07451.

## Toys and Novelties

*Playthings—Who Makes It Issue.* Annually in June. Lists manufacturers, products, trade names, suppliers to manufacturers, supplier products, licensors, manufacturers' representatives, toy trade associations, and trade show managements. Geyer-McAllister Publications, Inc., 51 Madison Ave., New York, NY 10010.

*Small World—Directory Issue.* Annually in December. Lists 200 wholesalers, manufacturers, manufacturers' representatives of toys, games, and hobbies for children and infants. Earnshaw Publications Inc., 225 West 34th St., Suite 1212, New York, NY 10122.

## Trailer Parks

*Campground Directory, Woodall's.* Annual. Lists and star-rates public and private campgrounds in North American continent alphabetically by town with location and description of facilities. Also lists more than 800 RV service locations. Regional editions available. Woodall Publishing Company, 28167 North Keith Dr., Lake Forest, IL 60045

## Trucking

*Trucksource: Sources of Trucking Industry Information.* Annually in November. Includes over 700 sources of information on the trucking industry, classified by subject. American Trucking Association, 2200 Mill Road, Alexandria, VA 22314-4677.

## Variety Stores

*General Merchandise, Variety and Specialty Stores, Directory of.* Annually in March. Lists headquarters address, telephone number, number of units and locations, executives and buyers. Chain Store Guide Information Services, 425 Park Ave., New York, NY 10022.

## Warehouses

*Public Warehousing, Guide to.* Annually in July. Lists leading public warehouses in the United States and Canada, as well as major truck lines, airlines, steamship lines, liquid and dry bulk terminals, material handling equipment suppliers, ports of the world and railroad piggyback services and routes. Chilton Co., Chilton Way, Radnor, PA 19089.

*Members Associated Warehouses, Directory of.* Irregularly. Listing of 90 members. Associated Warehouses, Inc., Box 471, Cedar Knolls, NJ 07927.

## OTHER IMPORTANT DIRECTORIES

The following business directories are helpful to those persons doing marketing research. Most of these directories are available for reference at the larger libraries. For additional listings, consult the *Guide to American Directories* at local libraries.

*AUBER Bibliography of Publications of University Bureaus of Business and Economic Research.* Lists studies published by Bureaus of Business and Economic Research affiliated with American colleges and universities. Done for the Association for University Bureaus of Business and Economic Research. Issued annually. Previous volumes available. Association for University Business and Economic Research, c/o Indiana Business Research Center, 801 W. Michigan St., BS 4015, Indianapolis, IN 46223.

*Bradford's Directory of Marketing Research Agencies and Management Consultants in the United States and the World.* Gives names and addresses of over 1,600 marketing research agencies in the United States, Canada, and abroad. Lists service offered by agency, along with other pertinent data, such as date established, names of principal officers, and size of staff. Bradford's Directory of Marketing Research Agencies, P.O. Box 276, Fairfax, VA 22030.

*Consultants and Consulting Organizations Directory.* Contains 16,000 entries. Guides reader to appropriate organization for a given consulting assignment. Entries include names, addresses, phone numbers, and data on services performed. Gale Research Company, 835 Penobscot Bldg., Detroit, MI 48226-4094.

*Research Centers Directory.* Lists more than 11,000 nonprofit research organizations. Descriptive information provided for each center, including address, telephone number, name of director, data on staff, funds, publications, and a statement concerning its principal fields of research. Has special indexes. Gale Research Company, 835 Penobscot Bldg., Detroit, MI 48226-4094.

*MacRae's Blue Book—Manufacturers.* Annual. In three volumes: Vol. 1 is an index by corporations; Vols. 2–3 are a classification by products showing under each classification manufacturers of that item. Business Research Publications, Inc., 817 Broadway, New York, NY 10003.

*Thomas' Food Industry Register.* Annually in May. Lists wholesale grocers, chain store organizations, voluntary buying groups, food brokers, exporters and importers of food products, frozen food brokers, distributors and related products distributed through grocery chains in two volumes. Thomas Publishing Company, One Penn Plaza, New York, NY 10019.

*Thomas' Register of American Manufacturers.* Annually in February. In 23 volumes. Vols. 1–14 contain manufacturers arranged geographically under each product, and capitalization or size rating for each manufacturer, under 50,000 product headings.

Vols. 15 and 16 contain company profiles and a brand or trade name section with more than 112,000 listings. Vols. 17–23 are catalogs from more than 1,500 firms. Thomas Publishing Co., One Penn Plaza, New York, NY 10019.

# SOURCES OF ADDITIONAL INFORMATION

*Business Competition Intelligence,* by William L. Sammon, Mark A. Kurland, and Robert Spitalnic, published by John Wiley & Sons, Inc., 605 Third Avenue, New York, NY 10158.

*Business Research: Concept and Practice,* by Robert G. Murdick, published by Richard D. Irwin, Inc., 1818 Ridge Road, Homewood, IL 60430.

*Competitor Intelligence,* by Leonard M. Fuld, published by John Wiley & Sons, Inc., 605 Third Avenue, New York, NY 10158.

*Do-It-Yourself Marketing Research,* by George E. Breen, published by McGraw-Hill Book Co., 1221 Avenue of the Americas, New York, NY 10020.

*Honomichl on Marketing Research,* by Jack J. Honomichl, published by NTC Business Books, 4255 West Touhy Avenue, Lindenwood, IL 60646-1975.

*A Manager's Guide to Marketing Research,* by Paul E. Green and Donald E. Frank, published by John Wiley & Sons, Inc., 605 Third Avenue, New York, NY 10158.

*Market and Sales Forecasting,* by F. Keay, published by John Wiley & Sons, Inc., 605 Third Avenue, New York, NY 10158.

*Marketing Research: A Management Overview,* by Evelyn Konrad and Rod Erickson, published by AMACOM, a division of the American Management Association, 135 West 50th Street, New York, NY 10020.

*Research for Marketing Decisions,* by Paul E. Green and Donald S. Tull, published by Prentice-Hall, Inc., Englewood Cliffs, NJ 07632.

# Forms to Help You Develop the Business Plan

**Objectives, Goals, Differential Advantage Statement**

| *Objectives* | *Time to Achieve* |
|---|---|
| 1. _____ | _____ |
| 2. _____ | _____ |
| 3. _____ | _____ |
| 4. _____ | _____ |
| 5. _____ | _____ |

| *Goals* | *Time to Achieve* |
|---|---|
| 1. _____ | _____ |
| 2. _____ | _____ |
| 3. _____ | _____ |
| 4. _____ | _____ |
| 5. _____ | _____ |

*Statement of Differential Advantage:*

_____

_____

_____

_____

_____

_____

_____

_____

_____

_____

_____

_____

_____

_____

_____

_____

_____

_____

_____

**Situational Analysis: Environmental Questions for the Marketing Plan**

*Target Market*

Geographic location _____

Special climate or topography _____

_____

*Consumer Buyers*

Cultural, ethnic, religious, or racial groups _____

_____

_____

Social class(es) _____

Reference group(s) _____

Basic demographics:   Sex _____        Age range _____

Education _____        Income _____

Household size and description _____

_____

Stage of family life cycle _____

Family work status:   Husband _____        Wife _____

Occupation (husband and wife) _____

Decision maker _____        Purchase agent _____

Risk perception:   Functional _____        Psychological _____

Physical _____        Social _____        Financial _____

Income for each family member _____

Disposable income _____

Additional descriptions, classifications, and traits of target market _____

_____

_____

_____

_____

_____

Target market wants and needs  1. _____

2. _____        3. _____

4. _____        5. _____

Product general description _____

_____

Frequency of usage _____        Traits _____

_____

**Situational Analysis: Environmental Questions for the Marketing Plan**    (*Continued*)

Marketing factor sensitivity _____

_____

_____

Size of target market _____

Growth trends _____

*Media Habits*

|  | Hours/Week | Category |
|---|---|---|
| Television | _____ | _____ |
| Radio | _____ | _____ |
| Magazines | _____ | _____ |
| Newspapers | _____ | _____ |

*Industrial Buyers*

Decision makers _____

_____

_____

_____

Primary motivation of each decision maker _____

_____

_____

_____

_____

_____

Amount of money budgeted for purchase _____

_____

_____

Purchase history _____

_____

_____

_____

_____

Additional descriptions, classifications, and traits of target market _____

_____

_____

**Situational Analysis: Environmental Questions for the Marketing Plan**   (*Continued*)

Target market wants and needs  1. _____

2. _____      3. _____

4. _____      5. _____

Product general description _____

_____

Frequency of usage _____      Traits _____

Marketing factor sensitivity _____

_____

_____

Size of target market _____

Growth trends _____

*Media Habits*

|  | Hours/Week | Category |
|---|---|---|
| Television | _____ | _____ |
| Radio | _____ | _____ |
| Magazines | _____ | _____ |
| Newspapers | _____ | _____ |

|  | Number/Year | Category |
|---|---|---|
| Trade shows | _____ | _____ |
| Conferences | _____ | _____ |

*Competition*

| Competitor | Products | Market Share | Strategy |
|---|---|---|---|
|  |  |  |  |
|  |  |  |  |
|  |  |  |  |
|  |  |  |  |
|  |  |  |  |
|  |  |  |  |
|  |  |  |  |
|  |  |  |  |
|  |  |  |  |
|  |  |  |  |
|  |  |  |  |

**Situational Analysis: Environmental Questions for the Marketing Plan** (*Continued*)

*Competition* (*Continued*)

| Competitor | Products | Market Share | Strategy |
|---|---|---|---|
| | | | |
| | | | |
| | | | |

*Resources of the Firm*

Strengths:

1. _____
2. _____
3. _____
4. _____
5. _____

Weaknesses:

1. _____
2. _____
3. _____
4. _____
5. _____

*Technological Environment*

_____
_____
_____

*Economic Environment*

_____
_____
_____

*Political Environment*

_____
_____
_____
_____

*Legal and Regulatory Environment*

_____
_____
_____
_____

**Situational Analysis: Environmental Questions for the Marketing Plan**   (*Continued*)

*Social and Cultural Environment*

_____

_____

_____

*Other Important Environmental Aspects*

_____

_____

_____

_____

_____

*Problems/Threats*

1. _____

2. _____

3. _____

4. _____

5. _____

*Opportunities*

1. _____

2. _____

3. _____

4. _____

5. _____

## Competitive Profiles

| Date _____ | Attributes/Performance Characteristics | | | | | | |
|---|---|---|---|---|---|---|---|
| **Products** | | | | | | | |
| | | | | | | | |
| | | | | | | | |
| | | | | | | | |
| | | | | | | | |
| | | | | | | | |
| | | | | | | | |
| | | | | | | | |
| | | | | | | | |
| | | | | | | | |
| | | | | | | | |

### Percentages of Sales in Your Business Area

Product _____  Date _____

|  |  | Introduction | Growth | Maturity | Decline |
|---|---|---|---|---|---|
| Current | Sales % |  |  |  |  |
|  | Profits |  |  |  |  |
| Target | Sales % |  |  |  |  |
|  | Profits |  |  |  |  |

Copyright © 1983 by Dr. William A. Cohen.

### Recent Trends of Competitor's Products, Share, and Strength

Your Product _____    Date _____

Strength code: VW = very weak    W = weak    M = medium    S = strong    VS = very strong

| Competitor | Market Share | Strength | Products |
|---|---|---|---|
|  |  |  |  |
|  |  |  |  |
|  |  |  |  |
|  |  |  |  |
|  |  |  |  |
|  |  |  |  |
|  |  |  |  |
|  |  |  |  |
|  |  |  |  |

### Historical Trend Analysis Matrix

Product _____    Date _____

|  | Period 1 | Period 2 | Period 3 | Period 4 | Trend |
|---|---|---|---|---|---|
| Sales |  |  |  |  |  |
| Profits |  |  |  |  |  |
| Margins |  |  |  |  |  |
| Market share |  |  |  |  |  |
| Prices |  |  |  |  |  |

Complete matrix with following information:     Characterize trends as:

| | |
|---|---|
| Very low or very small | Declining steeply    ↓ |
| Low or small | Declining    ↘ |
| Average | Plateau    → |
| High or large | Ascending    ↗ |
| Very high or very large | Ascending steeply    ↑ |

# Cash-Flow Projections

| | Start-Up or Prior to Loan | Month 1 | Month 2 | Month 3 | Month 4 | Month 5 | Month 6 | Month 7 | Month 8 | Month 9 | Month 10 | Month 11 | Month 12 | Total |
|---|---|---|---|---|---|---|---|---|---|---|---|---|---|---|
| Cash (beginning of month) | | | | | | | | | | | | | | |
| Cash on hand | | | | | | | | | | | | | | |
| Cash in bank | | | | | | | | | | | | | | |
| Cash in investments | | | | | | | | | | | | | | |
| Total Cash | | | | | | | | | | | | | | |
| Income (during month) | | | | | | | | | | | | | | |
| Cash sales | | | | | | | | | | | | | | |
| Credit sales payments | | | | | | | | | | | | | | |
| Investment income | | | | | | | | | | | | | | |
| Loans | | | | | | | | | | | | | | |
| Other cash income | | | | | | | | | | | | | | |
| Total Income | | | | | | | | | | | | | | |
| Total Cash and Income | | | | | | | | | | | | | | |
| Expenses (during month) | | | | | | | | | | | | | | |
| Inventory or new material | | | | | | | | | | | | | | |
| Wages (including owner's) | | | | | | | | | | | | | | |
| Taxes | | | | | | | | | | | | | | |
| Equipment expense | | | | | | | | | | | | | | |
| Overhead | | | | | | | | | | | | | | |
| Selling expense | | | | | | | | | | | | | | |
| Transportation | | | | | | | | | | | | | | |
| Loan repayment | | | | | | | | | | | | | | |
| Other cash expenses | | | | | | | | | | | | | | |
| Total Expenses | | | | | | | | | | | | | | |
| Cash Flow Excess (end of month) | | | | | | | | | | | | | | |
| Cash Flow Cumulative (monthly) | | | | | | | | | | | | | | |

Product/Project Development Schedule

| Task | 1 | 2 | 3 | 4 | 5 | 6 | 7 | 8 | 9 | 10 | 11 | 12 |
|------|---|---|---|---|---|---|---|---|---|----|----|----|
|      |   |   |   |   |   |   |   |   |   |    |    |    |
|      |   |   |   |   |   |   |   |   |   |    |    |    |
|      |   |   |   |   |   |   |   |   |   |    |    |    |
|      |   |   |   |   |   |   |   |   |   |    |    |    |
|      |   |   |   |   |   |   |   |   |   |    |    |    |
|      |   |   |   |   |   |   |   |   |   |    |    |    |
|      |   |   |   |   |   |   |   |   |   |    |    |    |
|      |   |   |   |   |   |   |   |   |   |    |    |    |

Strategy Development Actions

| List of Strategic Actions | Months after Strategy Initiation/$ Allocated | | | | | | | | | | | Total $ |
|---|---|---|---|---|---|---|---|---|---|---|---|---|
| | 1 | 2 | 3 | 4 | 5 | 6 | 7 | 8 | 9 | 10 | 11 | |
| | | | | | | | | | | | | |
| | | | | | | | | | | | | |
| | | | | | | | | | | | | |
| | | | | | | | | | | | | |
| | | | | | | | | | | | | |
| | | | | | | | | | | | | |
| | | | | | | | | | | | | |
| | | | | | | | | | | | | |
| | | | | | | | | | | | | |
| | | | | | | | | | | | | |
| | | | | | | | | | | | | |
| | | | | | | | | | | | | |
| | | | | | | | | | | | | |
| | | | | | | | | | | | | |
| | | | | | | | | | | | | |
| | | | | | | | | | | | | |
| | | | | | | | | | | | | |
| Total $ Allocated | | | | | | | | | | | | |

SPU # _____

**Balance Sheet**

| | Year 1 | Year 2 |
|---|---|---|
| **Current Assets** | | |
| Cash | | |
| Accounts receivable | | |
| Inventory | | |
| **Fixed Assets** | | |
| Real estate | | |
| Fixtures and equipment | | |
| Vehicles | | |
| **Other Assets** | | |
| Licenses | | |
| Goodwill | | |
| **Total Assets** | | |
| **Current Liabilities** | | |
| Notes payable (due within 1 year) | | |
| Accounts payable | | |
| Accrued expenses | | |
| Taxes owed | | |
| **Long-Term Liabilities** | | |
| Notes payable (due after 1 year) | | |
| Other | | |
| **Total Liabilities** | | |
| **Net Worth** (assets minus liabilities) | | |

*Note:* Total liabilities plus net worth should equal assets.

**SWOTS Analysis Sheet**

Product _____    Date _____

Strengths _____

_____

_____

_____

_____

Weaknesses _____

_____

_____

_____

_____

Opportunities _____

_____

_____

_____

_____

Threats _____

_____

_____

_____

_____

Sales _____

_____

_____

_____

_____

## Analysis of Competitor Short-Term Tactics

| Your Product _____ Date _____ | | | |
|---|---|---|---|
| Competitor | Actions | Probable Meaning of Action | Check Most Likely |
| | | | |
| | | | |
| | | | |
| | | | |
| | | | |
| | | | |
| | | | |
| | | | |
| | | | |
| | | | |
| | | | |
| | | | |
| | | | |
| | | | |
| | | | |
| | | | |
| | | | |

Recent Trends in Competitive Products

| Your Product _____ Date _____ | | | | |
|---|---|---|---|---|
| Company | Product | Quality and Performance Characteristics | Shifts in Distribution Channels | Relative Advantage of Each Competitive Product |
| | | | | |
| | | | | |
| | | | | |
| | | | | |
| | | | | |
| | | | | |
| | | | | |
| | | | | |
| | | | | |
| | | | | |
| | | | | |

Products versus Potential Market Segments

| Date _____ | | | | | | | | | | | | | | | |
|---|---|---|---|---|---|---|---|---|---|---|---|---|---|---|---|
| **Potential Market Segments** | | | | | | | | | | | | | | | |
| **Products** | | | | | | | | | | | | | | | |
| | | | | | | | | | | | | | | | |
| | | | | | | | | | | | | | | | |
| | | | | | | | | | | | | | | | |
| | | | | | | | | | | | | | | | |
| | | | | | | | | | | | | | | | |
| | | | | | | | | | | | | | | | |
| | | | | | | | | | | | | | | | |
| | | | | | | | | | | | | | | | |
| | | | | | | | | | | | | | | | |
| | | | | | | | | | | | | | | | |
| | | | | | | | | | | | | | | | |
| | | | | | | | | | | | | | | | |
| | | | | | | | | | | | | | | | |
| | | | | | | | | | | | | | | | |
| | | | | | | | | | | | | | | | |
| | | | | | | | | | | | | | | | |

Numerical code:

1 = Currently meets needs fully.
2 = Minor changes in product needed.
3 = Significant changes in product needed.

4 = Major changes in product needed.
5 = Totally new product required.

# Index